Lectures on
Linear Sequential Machines

Lectures on Linear Sequential Machines

Michael A. Harrison
University of California
Berkeley

ACADEMIC PRESS New York and London 1969

ACADEMIC PRESS, INC.
111 Fifth Avenue, New York, New York 10003

United Kingdom Edition published by
ACADEMIC PRESS, INC. (LONDON) LTD.
Berkeley Square House, London W1X 6BA

LIBRARY OF CONGRESS CATALOG CARD NUMBER: 76-84154

PRINTED IN THE UNITED STATES OF AMERICA

To My Doctoral Students

Oscar, Don, Hervé, Mario, and Jim

and

To My Most Promising Student

Craig

Preface

This book was developed from a course on linear sequential circuits taught at Berkeley. During my reading of the literature, I felt that a different point of view was needed. In my view, discrete linear systems should be studied over arbitrary fields and not be restricted to finite fields. In the finite case, linearity is often a hindrance, not an asset.

There is no book devoted wholly or in part to discrete linear systems except for Gill's [13], which is exclusively concerned with the finite case. It also deals extensively with the case of autonomous machines (e.g., shift registers) and with the "zero submachines" (alias quiescent systems). This present book does not treat these special topics and is devoted to the general case over arbitrary fields. In this way, I hope to expose the basic theory of infinite linear automata and to relate it to the theory of sequential machines. In the discrete setting, the role of linearity can be clearly seen and the modern analysis needed to do continuous systems does not obscure the basic simplicity of these devices. After reading this book, the continuous case will seem natural.

In reading the literature, I was surprised to find that many simple and basic questions about linear systems are not yet known. I have listed many of these questions as open problems. Most of all, I hope that the general approach given here will stimulate further research into these topics.

This book could serve as a senior or graduate text for a one quarter or one semester course on discrete linear systems. It is also suitable as an additional reference in a basic course in systems or automata theory.

I assume that the reader has had a good course in linear algebra. In Chapter 0, I have sketched the theory of the decomposition of a single linear transformation (in terms of matrices). Hopefully, the reader can start the book at Chapter 1 and only refer to Chapter 0 for an occasional result or definition. Chapter 0 does give some interesting algorithms for computing canonical forms of matrices which are not well known. An instructor can incorporate some of this material on linear algebra into the course. A two lecture review of the main theorems of linear algebra might be helpful.

In the words of the Beatles, "I get by with a little help from my friends." I would particularly like to thank J. A. Brzozowski, C. A. Desoer, H. Gallaire, A. Gill, J. N. Gray, G. T. Herman, J. P. Jacob, and P. P. Varaiya for many valuable technical discussions. I also wish to thank the Air Force Office of Scientific Research and the National Science Foundation for their generous support over the past several years.

These notes were typed rapidly and accurately by Bonnie Bullivant and Icole Brown and their cooperation is deeply appreciated.

I owe a special debt to B. N. Parlett. If it were not for his especially fine work, this book could not have been written.

August 26, 1969

MICHAEL A. HARRISON
Berkeley, California

Contents

Preface vii

CHAPTER 0. Special Topics in Linear Algebra . . . **3**

1. The Smith Canonical Form 3
2. Similar Matrices and Some Important Polynomials. 8
3. Companion Matrices, Cyclic Spaces and Direct Sums. 13
4. The Rational Canonical Form 20
5. The Classical Canonical Form 28

CHAPTER 1. Basic Notions of Sequential Machine Theory **31**

1. Basic Definitions. 31
2. Minimization of Sequential Machines. 36
3. Structure of Sequential Machines 41
4. The Monoid of a Machine 49
5. Some Finiteness Conditions 53

CHAPTER 2. Basic Properties of Linear Sequential Machines **59**

1. Definitions 59
2. Similar and Minimal LSM's. 65
3. Finiteness Conditions for LSM's. 75
4. Controllability and LSM's with Initial States . 80

CHAPTER 3. Relations and Decision Problems for LSM's 91
1. Input-Output Relations of LSM's 91
2. Relational Equivalence Implies Functional Equivalence for LSM's 94
3. Decidability and Computable Fields 97
4. The Equivalence Problem for LSM's is Decidable 99
5. Other Decision Questions 101
6. Accessibility 106

CHAPTER 4. Realizations and Their Properties . . . 115
1. Definitions and Basic Facts about Realizations 115
2. A Nonlinear Machine 120
3. An Algorithm for Obtaining Finite Realizations 121
4. Proof That the Realization Algorithm Works . 128
5. Change of Ground Fields 133

CHAPTER 5. Decompositions of LSM's 139
1. Preliminaries of Linear Realizations 139
2. Parallel Decompositions I 143
3. Parallel Decompositions II ($\mathbf{B} = \mathbf{0}$). 147
4. Parallel Decomposition (Case 5) 156
5. The Main Theorem on Parallel Decompositions 192
6. Serial Realizations 193
7. The Main Theorem on Serial Decompositions 196
8. Epilogue on Linear Decompositions 197
   Appendix 199

REFERENCES 203

Index 205

To the Reader:

Since some basic knowledge of linear algebra is assumed, most readers can begin at Chapter 1. Chapter 0 contains some material on the rational canonical form and is not needed until the middle of Chapter 2. The notational conventions are to write matrices in bold face, like **A**. We shall use the following special symbols:

$\mathbb{N} = \{0, 1, 2, \ldots\}$, the natural numbers,

$\mathbb{Z} = \{\cdots, -2, -1, 0, 1, 2, \cdots\}$, the integers,

$\mathbb{Q}$ = the field of rational numbers,

$\mathbb{R}$ = the field of real numbers,

$\mathbb{C}$ = the field of complex numbers,

$\mathbb{Z}_p$ = the field of integers modulo a prime p.

Most of the problems are straightforward. Problems which are starred are more difficult.

Chapter 0

Special Topics in Linear Algebra

It is assumed that the reader has had previous exposure to a basic course in linear algebra. All the standard properties of fields, vector spaces, and matrices are assumed to be known. In a few cases, we will need some results in linear algebra which would appear in a second course. The purpose of the present chapter is to expose most of these topics. In this chapter, the development is particularly concise and some important theorems are given as problems. It is hoped that all readers will start at Chapter 1 and refer to this chapter only for special topics with which they are unfamiliar.

In no case is this chapter to be taken as a substitute for the serious study of linear algebra. Cf [15, 25, 36].

1. The Smith Canonical Form

We shall now begin to expose the theory of the rational canonical form. In order to accomplish this, we must take a detour and first consider the Smith canonical form. Let F be the field and x be an indeterminate over F. Let $\mathbf{A}$ be an $m \times n$ matrix over the ring of F-polynomials, written $F[x]$.

We shall show that any such matrix is equivalent* to a matrix in a special form.

THEOREM 0.1. Let F be a field, x an indeterminate over F and $\mathbf{A}$ an $m \times n$ matrix over $F[x]$ whose rank is r. Then $\mathbf{A}$ is equivalent to a matrix $\mathbf{B} = \begin{bmatrix} \mathbf{B}' & \mathbf{0} \\ \mathbf{0} & \mathbf{0} \end{bmatrix}$ where

$$\mathbf{B}' = \begin{bmatrix} m_1 & & & & \mathbf{0} \\ & m_2 & & & \\ & & \cdot & & \\ & & & \cdot & \\ & & & & \cdot \\ & \mathbf{0} & & & m_r \end{bmatrix}$$

The m_i are in $F[x]$ and† $m_i \mid m_{i+1}$ for $1 \leq i < r$. The m_i are called the *invariant factors* of $\mathbf{A}$.

Proof. Successive operations will be performed on $\mathbf{A}$. To simplify the proof, at each stage, we call the matrix $\mathbf{A}$.

If $\mathbf{A} = \mathbf{0}$, we are done. Otherwise some nonzero element exists. Take this element as a_{11} by interchanging rows and columns if necessary. The strategy is to choose a_{11} to be of least degree.

If there is an element in the first column, say a_{i1} not divisible by a_{11}, then use the division algorithm for polynomials and write $a_{i1} = qa_{11} + r$ where $r \neq 0$ and $\deg r < \deg a_{11}$. Then multiply the first row by q and subtract it from the ith row. This makes $a_{i1} = r$. Now take $a_{11} = r$ by interchanging rows 1 and i. Repetition leads to the case where all elements in the first

* We say $\mathbf{B}$ is *equivalent* to $\mathbf{A}$ if there exist unimodular matrices $\mathbf{P}$ and $\mathbf{Q}$ so that $\mathbf{B} = \mathbf{PAQ}$. A matrix is *unimodular* if it has an inverse.

† $m_i(x) \mid m_{i+1}(x)$ if $m_{i+1}(x) = m_i(x)q(x)$ for some polynomial $q(x)$.

column (similarly row) are divisible by a_{11}. This only takes a finite number of steps.

It is now easy to make every element in the first column (and row) equal to 0 except a_{11}.

It may not be the case that a_{11} divides every other element of **A**. Suppose $a_{11} \nmid a_{ij}$. Then add the ith row to the first row. This makes $a_{1j} = a_{ij}$. Since $a_{11} \nmid a_{1j}$, we now lower the degree of a_{11} by the previous method. By dividing by a constant, we may assume that a_{11} is monic.*

By working on the last $m - 1$ rows and $n - 1$ columns, we obtain a_{22}, a monic polynomial and we have all other elements of the second row (and column) equal to 0. Such computations will not affect the first row (and column). Finally $a_{11} \mid a_{22}$. One merely repeats the entire operation. ∎

REMARK. **B** is called the *Smith Canonical Form* of **A**.

EXAMPLE. Given $\mathbf{A} = \begin{pmatrix} x(x-1) & x-1 & x^2-1 \\ x(x-2) & 1 & x \end{pmatrix}$

we will find **B** and also unimodular matrices **P** and **Q** so that **PAQ** = **B**. The key to finding **P** and **Q** is to adjoin a 2 × 2 identity matrix to the right of **A** and a 3 × 3 identity matrix below **A**. All row and column operations are also done on these matrices.

Adjoining row and column matrices, we get

$$\begin{array}{ccc|cc} x(x-1) & x-1 & x^2-1 & 1 & 0 \\ x(x-2) & 1 & x & 0 & 1 \\ \hline 1 & 0 & 0 & & \\ 0 & 1 & 0 & & \\ 0 & 0 & 1 & & \end{array}$$

* A polynomial $p(x) = \sum_{i=0}^{n} a_i x^i$ is *monic* if $a_n = 1$.

Interchanging columns 1 and 2 yields

$$\begin{array}{ccc:cc} x-1 & x(x-1) & x^2-1 & 1 & 0 \\ 1 & x(x-2) & x & 0 & 1 \\ \hdashline 0 & 1 & 0 & & \\ 1 & 0 & 0 & & \\ 0 & 0 & 1 & & \end{array}$$

Interchanging rows 1 and 2 produces

$$\begin{array}{ccc:cc} 1 & x(x-2) & x & 0 & 1 \\ x-1 & x(x-1) & x^2-1 & 1 & 0 \\ \hdashline 0 & 1 & 0 & & \\ 1 & 0 & 0 & & \\ 0 & 0 & 1 & & \end{array}$$

We multiply column 1 by $x(x-2)$ and subtract it from column 2

$$\begin{array}{ccc:cc} 1 & 0 & x & 0 & 1 \\ x-1 & -(x-1)(x^2-3x) & x^2-1 & 1 & 0 \\ \hdashline 0 & 1 & 0 & & \\ 1 & -x(x-2) & 0 & & \\ 0 & 0 & 1 & & \end{array}$$

We multiply column 1 by x and subtract it from column 3

$$\begin{array}{ccc:cc} 1 & 0 & 0 & 0 & 1 \\ x-1 & -(x-1)(x^2-3x) & x-1 & 1 & 0 \\ \hdashline 0 & 1 & 0 & & \\ 1 & -x(x-2) & -x & & \\ 0 & 0 & 1 & & \end{array}$$

Multiplying row 1 by $x - 1$ and subtracting it from row 2 yields

$$\begin{array}{ccc|cc} 1 & 0 & 0 & 0 & 1 \\ 0 & -(x-1)(x^2-3x) & x-1 & 1 & 1-x \\ \hline 0 & 1 & 0 & & \\ 1 & -x(x-2) & -x & & \\ 0 & 0 & 1 & & \end{array}$$

Interchanging columns 2 and 3 yields

$$\begin{array}{ccc|cc} 1 & 0 & 0 & 0 & 1 \\ 0 & x-1 & -(x-1)(x^2-3x) & 1 & 1-x \\ \hline 0 & 0 & 1 & & \\ 1 & -x & -x(x-2) & & \\ 0 & 1 & 0 & & \end{array}$$

Multiplying column 2 by $x^2 - 3x$ and adding it to the 3rd column produces

$$\begin{array}{ccc|cc} 1 & 0 & 0 & 0 & 1 \\ 0 & x-1 & 0 & 1 & 1-x \\ \hline 0 & 0 & 1 & & \\ 1 & -x & -x^3+2x^2+2x & & \\ 0 & 1 & x^2-3x & & \end{array}$$

Therefore $\mathbf{B} = \begin{bmatrix} 1 & 0 & 0 \\ 0 & x-1 & 0 \end{bmatrix}$ with $\mathbf{P} = \begin{bmatrix} 0 & 1 \\ 1 & 1-x \end{bmatrix}$ and

$$\mathbf{Q} = \begin{bmatrix} 0 & 0 & 1 \\ 1 & -x & (-x^3+2x^2+2x) \\ 0 & 1 & x^2-3x \end{bmatrix}$$

As a computational check, note that

$$\mathbf{PAQ} = \mathbf{B}$$

PROBLEMS

1. Prove that the technique shown in the example for computing **P** and **Q** such that **PAQ** = **B** actually works.

2. Are **P** and **Q** unique as computed by the method of the example? If not, how badly are they not unique? That is, could there be infinitely many such **P** and **Q**?

2. Similar Matrices and Some Important Polynomials

We recall that two matrices **A** and **B** are *similar* just in case $\mathbf{B} = \mathbf{PAP}^{-1}$ for some nonsingular matrix **P**. This is, of course, an equivalence relation. The importance of similarity is that two matrices are similar if and only if they represent the same linear transformation.

It is convenient at this time to introduce matrix polynomials. Let F be our underlying field and M_n be the set of $n \times n$ matrices (over F). Then $M_n[x]$ is the set of polynomials in x whose coefficients are $n \times n$ matrices. Any such polynomial is said to have *order n*. A matrix polynomial $\mathbf{G}(x) = \sum_{i=0}^{m} \mathbf{G}_i x^i$ is said to be *regular* if $\det \mathbf{G}_m \neq 0$.

If we let $\mathbf{G}(x) = \sum_{i=0}^{m} \mathbf{G}_i x^i$ and $\mathbf{H}(x) = \sum_{i=0}^{p} \mathbf{H}_i x^i$ where $\mathbf{G}_i, \mathbf{H}_j \in M_n$ and $\mathbf{G}_m \neq \mathbf{0}$, $\mathbf{H}_p \neq \mathbf{0}$. Then define

$$\mathbf{G}(x) + \mathbf{H}(x) = \sum_{i=0}^{\max(m,p)} (\mathbf{G}_i + \mathbf{H}_i)x^i$$

where $\mathbf{G}_i = \mathbf{0}_m$ for $i > m$ and $\mathbf{H}_i = \mathbf{0}_m$ for $i > p$. Also

$$\mathbf{GH}(x) = \sum_{i=0}^{m+p} \mathbf{J}_i x^i$$

where $\mathbf{J}_i = \sum_{j=0}^{i} \mathbf{G}_j \mathbf{H}_{i-j}$. Of course $\deg(\mathbf{G} + \mathbf{H}) \leq \max(\deg \mathbf{G}, \deg \mathbf{H})$. $\deg(\mathbf{GH}) = \deg(\mathbf{G}) + \deg(\mathbf{H})$ if and only if **G** or **H** is regular.

Division of such polynomials requires care since M_n is not commutative.

DEFINITION. Let $\mathbf{G}(x) = \sum_{i=0}^{m} \mathbf{G}_i x^i$ where $\mathbf{G}_m \neq \mathbf{0}$. Let $\mathbf{H}(x) = \sum_{i=0}^{p} \mathbf{H}_i x^i$ be regular. We say that $\mathbf{Q}(x)$ is a *right quotient* and $\mathbf{R}(x)$ a *right remainder* of $\mathbf{G}$ by $\mathbf{H}$ if

$$\mathbf{G}(x) = \mathbf{Q}(x)\mathbf{H}(x) + \mathbf{R}(x)$$

and (*i*) $\mathbf{R}(x) = \mathbf{0}$
or

(*ii*) $\deg \mathbf{R}(x) < \deg \mathbf{H}(x)$

Left quotients and remainders are defined analogously. We write $\mathbf{G}(x) = \mathbf{H}(x)\mathbf{Q}_l(x) + \mathbf{R}_l(x)$ for left division. In general, $(\mathbf{Q}_l, \mathbf{R}_l) \neq (\mathbf{Q}, \mathbf{R})$ as the following example shows.

EXAMPLE. Let $F = \mathbb{Z}_2$ and define

$$\mathbf{G}(x) = \begin{bmatrix} x & 0 \\ 0 & 0 \end{bmatrix} \qquad \mathbf{H}(x) = \begin{bmatrix} 0 & 1 + x \\ 1 + x & 0 \end{bmatrix}$$

Clearly $\det \mathbf{H} \neq 0$. For right division,

$$\mathbf{G}(x) = \mathbf{Q}(x)\mathbf{H}(x) + \mathbf{R}(x)$$

Thus $\mathbf{Q}(x) = \begin{bmatrix} 0 & 1 \\ 0 & 0 \end{bmatrix}$ and $\mathbf{R}(x) = \begin{bmatrix} 1 & 0 \\ 0 & 0 \end{bmatrix}$. For left division,

$$\mathbf{G}(x) = \mathbf{H}(x)\mathbf{Q}_l(x) + \mathbf{R}_l(x)$$

and $\mathbf{Q}_l(x) = \begin{bmatrix} 0 & 0 \\ 1 & 0 \end{bmatrix} \neq \mathbf{Q}(x)$, while $\mathbf{R}_l(x) = \mathbf{R}(x)$.

The following proposition says that division on each side is unique.

THEOREM 0.2. Let $\mathbf{G}, \mathbf{H} \in M_n[x]$ with $\mathbf{H}$ regular. There exists a unique right (left) quotient and a unique right (left) remainder of $\mathbf{G}$ by $\mathbf{H}$.

Proof. The proof is essentially the same as the case of scalar polynomials. ▮

Let $\mathbf{G}(x) = \mathbf{G}_0 + \cdots + \mathbf{G}_m x^n$ where $\mathbf{G}_m \neq \mathbf{0}$ and each $\mathbf{G}_i \in M_n$. It makes no difference if one writes

$$\mathbf{G}(x) = \sum_{i=0}^{m} \mathbf{G}_i x^i \tag{1}$$

or

$$\mathbf{G}(x) = \sum_{i=0}^{m} x^i \mathbf{G}_i \tag{2}$$

However when one replaces x by some matrix $\mathbf{A}$, the values of (1) and (2) can change. We call (1) the *right value*, written $\mathbf{G}(\mathbf{A})$, and (2) the *left value*, $\mathbf{G}_l(\mathbf{A})$. The following result is immediate.

THEOREM 0.3. When a matrix polynomial $\mathbf{G}(x)$ is divided on the right (left) by $(x\mathbf{I} - \mathbf{A})$, the remainder is $\mathbf{G}(\mathbf{A})$ (respectively $\mathbf{G}_l(\mathbf{A})$).

The following result will prove to be of practical importance in a later section.

THEOREM 0.4. Let $\mathbf{A}_0$, $\mathbf{A}_1$, $\mathbf{B}_0$, $\mathbf{B}_1$ be constant matrices over some field F where $\det \mathbf{A}_0 \neq 0$ and $\det \mathbf{B}_0 \neq 0$. If $\mathbf{B}_0 x + \mathbf{B}_1 = \mathbf{P}(x)(\mathbf{A}_0 x + \mathbf{A}_1)\mathbf{Q}(x)$ where $\mathbf{P}(x)$ and $\mathbf{Q}(x)$ are unimodular matrices over $F[x]$, then there exist nonsingular matrices $\mathbf{P}$ and $\mathbf{Q}$ over F such that

$$\mathbf{B}_0 x + \mathbf{B}_1 = \mathbf{P}(\mathbf{A}_0 x + \mathbf{A}_1)\mathbf{Q}.$$

Proof. Since $\mathbf{P}(x)$ is unimodular, $(\mathbf{P}(x))^{-1}$ exists and we have

$$(\mathbf{P}(x))^{-1}(\mathbf{B}_0 x + \mathbf{B}_1) = (\mathbf{A}_0 x + \mathbf{A}_1)\mathbf{Q}(x) \tag{1}$$

We divide $(\mathbf{P}(x))^{-1}$ on the left by $(\mathbf{A}_0 x + \mathbf{A}_1)$ and similarly $\mathbf{Q}(x)$ on the right by $\mathbf{B}_0 x + \mathbf{B}_1$, i.e.,

$$(\mathbf{P}(x))^{-1} = (\mathbf{A}_0 x + \mathbf{A}_1)\mathbf{S}(x) + \mathbf{M}$$
$$\mathbf{Q}(x) = \mathbf{T}(x)(\mathbf{B}_0 x + \mathbf{B}_1) + \mathbf{Q}$$

where $\mathbf{M}, \mathbf{Q} \in M_n$.

Using these identities in (1) gives

$$((\mathbf{A}_0x + \mathbf{A}_1)\mathbf{S}(x) + \mathbf{M})(\mathbf{B}_0x + \mathbf{B}_1)$$
$$= (\mathbf{A}_0x + \mathbf{A}_1)(\mathbf{T}(x)(\mathbf{B}_0x + \mathbf{B}_1) + \mathbf{Q})$$

or

$$(\mathbf{A}_0x + \mathbf{A}_1)(\mathbf{T}(x) - \mathbf{S}(x))(\mathbf{B}_0x + \mathbf{B}_1)$$
$$= \mathbf{M}(\mathbf{B}_0x + \mathbf{B}_1) - (\mathbf{A}_0x + \mathbf{A}_1)\mathbf{Q} \quad (2)$$

Clearly

$$\mathbf{S}(x) = \mathbf{T}(x)$$

Because if $\mathbf{S}(x) \neq \mathbf{T}(x)$, since det $\mathbf{A}_0 \neq 0$ and det $\mathbf{B}_0 \neq 0$, the degree of the left hand side of two is ≥ 2 [because $\mathbf{A}_0\mathbf{B}_0 \neq \mathbf{0}$]. On the right hand side, the degree is at most 1.

From (2)

$$\mathbf{M}(\mathbf{B}_0x + \mathbf{B}_1) = (\mathbf{A}_0x + \mathbf{A}_1)\mathbf{Q} \quad (3)$$

It clearly suffices to show that $\mathbf{M}$ is nonsingular. [For then, $\mathbf{MP} = I$ for some $\mathbf{P}$. Hence $\mathbf{M} = \mathbf{P}^{-1}$. Applying this to (3) yields the desired result.]

To show this, we divide $\mathbf{P}(x)$ on the left by $\mathbf{B}_0x + \mathbf{B}_1$, i.e.,

$$\mathbf{P}(x) = (\mathbf{B}_0x + \mathbf{B}_1)\mathbf{U}(x) + \mathbf{P}$$

We know that

$$\mathbf{I} = (\mathbf{P}(x))^{-1}\mathbf{P}(x) = (\mathbf{P}(x))^{-1}(\mathbf{B}_0x + \mathbf{B}_1)\mathbf{U}(x) + \mathbf{P}^{-1}(x)\mathbf{P}$$
$$\mathbf{I} = (\mathbf{A}_0x + \mathbf{A}_1)\mathbf{Q}(x)\mathbf{U}(x) + ((\mathbf{A}_0x + \mathbf{A}_1)\mathbf{S}(x) + \mathbf{M})\mathbf{P}$$
$$\mathbf{I} = (\mathbf{A}_0x + \mathbf{A}_1)(\mathbf{Q}(x)\mathbf{U}(x) + \mathbf{S}(x)\mathbf{P}) + \mathbf{MP}$$

Equating constant terms gives

$$\mathbf{MP} = \mathbf{I}$$

Thus $\mathbf{P}$ is nonsingular and $\mathbf{Q}$ is nonsingular since $\mathbf{B}_0 = \mathbf{PA}_0\mathbf{Q}$. ▮

COROLLARY. $\mathbf{P}$ is the left remainder of $\mathbf{P}(x)$ when divided on the left by $\mathbf{B}_0x + \mathbf{B}_1$. $\mathbf{Q}$ is the right remainder of $\mathbf{Q}(x)$ when divided on the right by $\mathbf{B}_0x + \mathbf{B}_1$.

Next we turn our attention to some polynomials associated with any matrix. Let an $n \times n$ matrix $\mathbf{A}$ over F be given. The set $M_{\mathbf{A}} = \{f(x) \in F[x] \mid f(\mathbf{A}) = \mathbf{0}\}$ is an ideal* in $F[x]$. Since $F[x]$ is a principal ideal domain,† there is a monic polynomial $m_{\mathbf{A}}(x)$ which divides every $f(x) \in M_{\mathbf{A}}$. $m_{\mathbf{A}}(x)$ is the *minimum polynomial* of $\mathbf{A}$. Of course $m_{\mathbf{A}}(\mathbf{A}) = \mathbf{0}$.

There is another polynomial to be associated with any matrix $\mathbf{A}$. For each $\mathbf{A}$, define the *characteristic polynomial* of $\mathbf{A}$ as

$$\varphi_{\mathbf{A}}(x) = \det (x\mathbf{I} - \mathbf{A})$$

Of course if $\mathbf{B}$ is similar to $\mathbf{A}$, then $\varphi_{\mathbf{B}} = \varphi_{\mathbf{A}}$ because

$$\begin{aligned}\varphi_{\mathbf{B}} &= \det (x\mathbf{I} - \mathbf{PAP}^{-1}) = \det (\mathbf{P}(x\mathbf{I} - \mathbf{A})\mathbf{P}^{-1}) \\ &= \det \mathbf{P} \det (x\mathbf{I} - \mathbf{A}) \det \mathbf{P}^{-1} = \varphi_{\mathbf{A}}\end{aligned}$$

The converse is false; it is easy to produce nonsimilar matrices with the same characteristic polynomials.

We now relate the characteristic and minimum polynomials.

THEOREM 0.5. (Cayley–Hamilton). Let $\mathbf{A}$ be in M_n, then $m_{\mathbf{A}}(x) \mid \varphi_{\mathbf{A}}(x)$ and $\varphi_{\mathbf{A}}(\mathbf{A}) = \mathbf{0}$.

Proof. Let $\mathbf{B}(x) = \operatorname{adj} (x\mathbf{I} - \mathbf{A})$.‡ Using an elementary fact about the adjoint,§ we have

$$(x\mathbf{I} - \mathbf{A})\mathbf{B}(x) = \varphi_{\mathbf{A}}(x)\mathbf{I}$$
$$\mathbf{B}(x)(x\mathbf{I} - \mathbf{A}) = \varphi_{\mathbf{A}}(x)\mathbf{I}$$

---

* An *ideal* I of any commutative ring R is a nonempty subset I such that $a, b \in I$ implies $a - b \in I$ and for each $a \in I$, $b \in R$, we have that $ab \in I$.

† A *principal ideal domain* has the property that all ideals I have a single element d such that $I = \{kd \mid k \in R\}$.

‡ Let $\mathbf{C} = (c_{ij})$ be any matrix. The matrix $\mathbf{D} = (d_{ij})$ where $d_{ij} = (-1)^{i+j} \det \mathbf{D}'_{ij}$ where $\mathbf{D}'_{ij}$ is obtained from $\mathbf{D}$ by deleting row j and column i. $\mathbf{D}$ is said to be the *adjoint* of $\mathbf{C}$ and we write $\mathbf{D} = \operatorname{adj} \mathbf{C}$.

§ For any $\mathbf{C} \in M_n$,

$$\mathbf{C}(\operatorname{adj} \mathbf{C}) = (\operatorname{adj} \mathbf{C})\mathbf{C} = (\det \mathbf{C})\mathbf{I}.$$

Therefore $\varphi_{\mathbf{A}}(x)\mathbf{I}$ is divisible on left and on the right by $x\mathbf{I} - \mathbf{A}$. By Theorem 0.3, this is only possible if the remainder is the $\mathbf{0}$ matrix. Thus $\varphi_{\mathbf{A}}(\mathbf{A})\mathbf{I} = \varphi_{\mathbf{A}}(\mathbf{A}) = \mathbf{0}$. Since $\varphi_{\mathbf{A}}(\mathbf{A}) = \mathbf{0}$, $m_{\mathbf{A}}(x) \mid \varphi_{\mathbf{A}}(x)$. ∎

We note the following simple result for future use.

THEOREM 0.6. Let $\mathbf{A} \in M_n$. There is a number $p \leq n$ and $d_0, \ldots, d_{p-1} \in F$ so that

$$\mathbf{A}^p = \sum_{0 \leq j < p} d_j \mathbf{A}^j$$

and for each $i \geq 0$

$$\mathbf{A}^{p+i} = \sum_{0 \leq j < p} d_j(i) \mathbf{A}^j$$

for some $d_j(i) \in F$.

Proof. The second equation follows from the first by induction on i. To show the first, let $m_{\mathbf{A}}(x) = x^p + \sum_{0 \leq j < p} (-d_j)x^j$. Then $m_{\mathbf{A}}(\mathbf{A}) = \mathbf{0}$ implies the first equation. $p \leq n$ since $\varphi_{\mathbf{A}}(\mathbf{A}) = \mathbf{0}$ and $\varphi_{\mathbf{A}}(x)$ has degree n. ∎

PROBLEMS

1. Show that $F[x]$ is isomorphic to $M_1[x]$.

2. Give a counterexample to Theorem 0.4 if the assumption $\det \mathbf{A}_0 \neq 0$ or $\det \mathbf{B}_0 \neq 0$ is violated.

3. Show that if $\mathbf{B}$ is similar to $\mathbf{A}$, then $m_{\mathbf{B}}(x) = m_{\mathbf{A}}(x)$.

4. A matrix $\mathbf{A}$ is called *nilpotent* if $\mathbf{A}^m = \mathbf{0}$ for some m. Show that $m_{\mathbf{A}}(x)$ where $\mathbf{A}$ is nilpotent is x^h where h is the least integer so that $\mathbf{A}^h = \mathbf{0}$. [The least h such that $\mathbf{A}^h = \mathbf{0}$ is called the *degree* of a nilpotent matrix.]

3. Companion Matrices, Cyclic Spaces and Direct Sums

Let $f(x)$ be a monic polynomial of degree n, say $f(x) = x^n + \sum_{i=0}^{n-1} c_i x^i$. An $n \times n$ matrix is associated with f in the following manner. The *companion matrix* of f is

$$\mathbf{C}_f = \begin{bmatrix} 0 & 1 & 0 & \cdot & \cdot & \cdot & \cdot & 0 \\ 0 & 0 & 1 & 0 & \cdot & \cdot & \cdot & 0 \\ & & \cdot & & & & & \\ & & \cdot & & & & & \\ & & \cdot & & & & & \\ 0 & 0 & \cdot & \cdot & \cdot & \cdot & 0 & 1 \\ -c_0 & -c_1 & & & & & & -c_{n-1} \end{bmatrix}$$

EXAMPLES. If $f(x) = x^3 - 3x + 2$, then

$$\mathbf{C}_f = \begin{bmatrix} 0 & 1 & 0 \\ 0 & 0 & 1 \\ -2 & 3 & 0 \end{bmatrix}$$

If $f(x) = 1$, then $\mathbf{C}_f$ is null. If $f(x) = x$ then $\mathbf{C}_f = (0)$.

The following result involves a routine calculation.

THEOREM 0.7. Let f be a monic polynomial of degree n. The minimum polynomial of $\mathbf{C}_f$ is $f(x)$. The characteristic polynomial of $\mathbf{C}_f$ is $f(x)$.

Next we decompose a vector space as a direct sum.*

THEOREM 0.8. Let $\mathbf{A}$ be a matrix (with minimum polynomial $m(x)$) of a linear transformation $\alpha: V \to V$. If $m(x) = f(x)g(x)$ where $f(x)$, $g(x)$ are monic relatively prime polynomials,

---

* Let X and Y be subspaces of a vector space V. V is said to be a *direct sum* of vector spaces X and Y, written $V = X \oplus Y$, if each $v \in V$ may be uniquely written $v = x + y$ for some $x \in X$ and $y \in Y$. If $V = X \oplus Y$, then the union of a basis of X with a basis of Y is a basis of V. It follows that if $V = X \oplus Y$, $\dim V = \dim X + \dim Y$.

then $V = X \oplus Y$ where X is the null space* of $f(\alpha)$ and Y the null space of $g(\alpha)$.

Proof. Since $f(x)$ is relatively prime to $g(x)$, there exist $r(x)$, $s(x)$ so that

$$1 = r(x)f(x) + s(x)g(x)$$

or

$$1 = r(\alpha)f(\alpha) + s(\alpha)g(\alpha)$$

or

$$v = x + y = vr(\alpha)f(\alpha) + vs(\alpha)g(\alpha)$$

where $x = vs(\alpha)g(\alpha)$ and $y = vr(\alpha)f(\alpha)$.

$$xf(\alpha) = vs(\alpha)g(\alpha)f(\alpha) = vs(\alpha)m(\alpha) = \mathbf{0}$$

Similarly $yg(\alpha) = \mathbf{0}$.

To show uniqueness, suppose

$$v = x_1 + y_1 = x_2 + y_2$$

Then $w = x_1 - x_2 = y_2 - y_2$ has the property that $wf(\alpha) = \mathbf{0}$ and $wg(\alpha) = \mathbf{0}$. Then $w = w \cdot 1 = wr(\alpha)f(\alpha) + ws(\alpha)g(\alpha) = \mathbf{0}$. Therefore $x_1 = x_2$ any $y_1 = y_2$. ∎

The following definition is important in many applications.

DEFINITION. Let U be a subspace of vector space V and $\alpha: V \to V$ a linear transformation. U is said to be an α-*invariant subspace* if $u \in U$ implies $u\alpha \in U$.

By repeated use of the previous theorem, we have the following result.

THEOREM 0.9. Let V be a finite dimensional vector space over a field F and $\alpha: V \to V$ be a linear transformation on

---

* Let $f(x)$ be a polynomial. The *null space* of $f(\alpha)$ is $\{v \mid vf(\alpha) = 0\}$ which is a vector space.

V with minimum polynomial $m(x)$. Suppose that $m(x) = \prod_{i=1}^{h} p_i^{e_i}(x)$ where $e_i > 0$, and each $p_i(x)$ is irreducible over F. Then

$$V = Z_1 \oplus \cdots \oplus Z_k$$

where each Z_i is the null space of $(p_i(\alpha))^{e_i}$. If α_i is the restriction of α to Z_i, then α_i has minimum polynomial $(p(x))^{e_i}$.

Note that this decomposition is unique up to order because the prime factorization of $m(x)$ is unique.

DEFINITION. Let $\mathbf{A}$ be an $m \times m$ matrix and $\mathbf{B}$ an $n \times n$ matrix. The $(m + n) \times (m + n)$ matrix defined below is the *direct sum* of $\mathbf{A}$ and $\mathbf{B}$, written $\mathbf{A} \oplus \mathbf{B}$ and $\mathbf{A} \oplus \mathbf{B} = \begin{bmatrix} \mathbf{A} & \mathbf{0} \\ \mathbf{0} & \mathbf{B} \end{bmatrix}$.

By refining previous techniques, we obtain the following result.

THEOREM 0.10. Let V be a finite dimensional vector space and $\alpha: V \to V$ be a linear transformation. If $V = X_1 \oplus \cdots \oplus X_n$ where each subspace X_i is α-invariant and α restricted to X_i can be represented by $\mathbf{A}_i$, then α can be represented as $\mathbf{A} = \mathbf{A}_1 \oplus \cdots \oplus \mathbf{A}_n$, i.e., a matrix of α is similar to $\mathbf{A}$.

Proof. Let X_{i0} be a basis of X_i. Since $X_0 = \bigcup_{i=1}^{n} X_{i0}$ is a basis of V, it suffices to represent α with respect to X_0. For each $v \in V$ $(v \neq \mathbf{0})$, there is a unique X_i such that $v \in X_i$. Since $v\alpha \in X_i$, all rows of $\mathbf{A}$ are zero if they do not refer to the basis of X_i, i.e., only $\mathbf{A}_i$ is not zero. Clearly $\mathbf{A} = \mathbf{A}_1 \oplus \cdots \oplus \mathbf{A}_n$. ∎

We have described the manner in which V decomposes as a direct sum. We shall now decompose the direct summands even further.

Suppose $v \in V$ and $\alpha: V \to V$ is a linear transformation. One can consider $\{g(x) \mid vg(\alpha) = \mathbf{0}\}$. This set is an ideal with generator $m_v(x)$. Note that $m_v(\alpha) = \mathbf{0}$ (similarly $m_v(\mathbf{A}) = \mathbf{0}$ where $\mathbf{A}$ is a matrix of α). The following lemma is used in the sequel.

LEMMA 0.1. Let V be a vector space and $\alpha: V \to V$ be a linear transformation on V. There exists a vector $v \in V$ so that $m_v(x) = m(x)$ where $m(x)$ is the minimum function of α.

Proof. The argument is left as Problem 2. ∎

Let $\alpha: V \to V$ be a linear transformation and let $v \in V$ be fixed. Let $Z(v, \alpha)$ be the vector space spanned by $\{v, v\alpha, v\alpha^2, \ldots\}$. Now we list some properties of $Z(v, \alpha)$, the *cyclic space* generated by v and α.

THEOREM 0.11. Let α be a linear transformation on a finite dimensional space V and let $v \in V$.

(1) $Z(v, \alpha)$ is α-invariant.

(2) The minimum polynomial of α on $Z(v, \alpha)$, say

$$m_{Z(v,\alpha)}(x) = m_v(x).$$

(3) $\dim Z(v, \alpha) = \deg m_v(x)$.

(4) $Z(v, \alpha)$ is contained in any α-invariant subspace which contains v.

Proof. (1) and (4) are straightforward. To prove (3), we show that $S = \{v\alpha^i \mid 0 \le i < s = \deg m_v(x)\}$ is a basis of $Z(v, \alpha)$. Let $u \in Z(v, \alpha)$ so $u = \sum_{i=0}^{n-1} c_i(v\alpha^i)$ where $n = \dim V$. Let $h(x) = \sum_{i=0}^{n-1} c_i x^i$ so that $u = vh(\alpha)$. Write

$$h(x) = m_v(x)q(x) + r(x)$$

where $\deg r(x) < s$. Then $u = vh(\alpha) = v(m_v(\alpha)q(\alpha) + r(\alpha)) = vr(\alpha)$. This shows S spans $Z(v, \alpha)$. To show that S is linearly independent, suppose $\sum_{i=0}^{s-1} c_i v\alpha^i = \mathbf{0}$ with some $c_i \neq 0$. Then $vh(\alpha) = \mathbf{0}$ for some polynomial $h(x)$ of degree t where $0 < t < s$. This contradicts that $m_v(x)$ is the minimal such polynomial.

To show (2), if $u \in Z(v, \alpha)$, $u = vg(\alpha)$ for some polynomial $g(x)$. Then

$$um_v(\alpha) = vg(\alpha)m_v(\alpha) = \mathbf{0}$$

So

$$m_{Z(v,\alpha)}(x) \mid m_v(x)$$

If there is a polynomial $h(x)$ such that $Z(v, \alpha)h(\alpha) = \mathbf{0}$, then $uh(\alpha) = \mathbf{0}$ for each $u \in Z(v, \alpha)$. In particular, let $u = v$. Then $m_v(x) \mid h(x)$, and now choose $h(x) = m_{Z(v,\alpha)}(x)$. So

$$m_v(x) \mid m_{Z(v,\alpha)}(x)$$

Since they are monic, $m_{Z(v,\alpha)}(x) = m_v(x)$. ▮

We call a linear transformation $\alpha: V \to V$ *cyclic* if there is a vector v such that $V = Z(v, \alpha)$. Similar nomenclature is used for matrices. It is clear that the restriction of α to a cyclic subspace is a cyclic transformation. The identity transformation on V is not cyclic if $\dim V > 1$.

THEOREM 0.12. Let α be a cyclic linear transformation on V and let $m(x)$ be the minimum polynomial of α. There exists a basis of V such that α can be represented by the companion matrix $\mathbf{C}_{m(x)}$.

Proof. Let $m(x) = c_0 + \cdots + c_{n-1}x^{n-1} + x^n$. There is a vector v so that $V = Z(v, \alpha)$. As a basis, choose $\{v\alpha^i \mid 0 \leq i < n\}$. With respect to this basis α has matrix $\mathbf{C}_{m(x)}$. ▮

Now that cyclic spaces have been introduced, we can state the following result.

THEOREM 0.13. Let V be a finite dimensional vector space and let α be a linear transformation on V whose minimal polynomial is some power of an irreducible polynomial. Then there exist vectors $v_1, \ldots, v_r$ such that $V = Z(v_1, \alpha) \oplus \cdots \oplus Z(v_r, \alpha)$.

Proof. The (nontrivial) proof is left as Problem 4. ▮

COROLLARY. There is a basis so that a matrix $\mathbf{A}$ of α is $\mathbf{A} = \mathbf{C}_{p^{e_1}(x)} \oplus \cdots \oplus \mathbf{C}_{p^{e_r}(x)}$, where the definition of the e_i is in Problem 4.

If $\mathbf{A}$ is any matrix, we say that the *invariant factors* of A are the invariant factors of $x\mathbf{I} - \mathbf{A}$.

One can compute the e_i from the invariant factors of $\mathbf{A}$. We shall say more on this point in the next section.

PROBLEMS

1. Let $\mathbf{A}$ be an $m \times m$ matrix and $\mathbf{B}$ be an $n \times n$ matrix. The $(m+n) \times (m+n)$ matrix defined below is called the *direct sum of* $\mathbf{A}$ *and* $\mathbf{B}$, written $\mathbf{A} \oplus \mathbf{B}$.

$$\mathbf{A} \oplus \mathbf{B} = \begin{bmatrix} \mathbf{A} & \mathbf{0} \\ \mathbf{0} & \mathbf{B} \end{bmatrix}$$

Prove the following. For square matrices $\mathbf{A}$, $\mathbf{B}$, $\mathbf{C}$, $\mathbf{A}_i$, $\mathbf{B}_i$ over a field F and with $\mathbf{A}_1$ and $\mathbf{A}_2$, $\mathbf{B}_1$ and $\mathbf{B}_2$ of the same size,

(a) $\mathbf{A} \oplus (\mathbf{B} \oplus \mathbf{C}) = (\mathbf{A} \oplus \mathbf{B}) \oplus \mathbf{C}$
(b) For each $c \in F$, $c(\mathbf{A} \oplus \mathbf{B}) = c\mathbf{A} \oplus c\mathbf{B}$
(c) $(\mathbf{A}_1 + \mathbf{A}_2) \oplus (\mathbf{B}_1 + \mathbf{B}_2) = (\mathbf{A}_1 \oplus \mathbf{B}_1) + (\mathbf{A}_2 \oplus \mathbf{B}_2)$
(d) $(\mathbf{A}_1 \oplus \mathbf{B}_1)(\mathbf{A}_2 \oplus \mathbf{B}_2) = \mathbf{A}_1\mathbf{A}_2 \oplus \mathbf{B}_1\mathbf{B}_2$
(e) $(\mathbf{A} \oplus \mathbf{B})^T = \mathbf{A}^T \oplus \mathbf{B}^T$
(f) If $\mathbf{A}$ and $\mathbf{B}$ are nonsingular, then

$$(\mathbf{A} \oplus \mathbf{B})^{-1} = \mathbf{A}^{-1} \oplus \mathbf{B}^{-1}$$

(g) rank $(\mathbf{A} \oplus \mathbf{B}) =$ rank $\mathbf{A}$ + rank $\mathbf{B}$
(h) $\mathbf{A} \oplus \mathbf{B}$ is similar to $\mathbf{B} \oplus \mathbf{A}$
(i) If $\mathbf{A}'$ is similar to $\mathbf{A}$ and $\mathbf{B}'$ is similar to $\mathbf{B}$, then, $\mathbf{A}' \oplus \mathbf{B}'$ is similar to $\mathbf{B}' \oplus \mathbf{A}'$.
(j) If $f(x) = \sum_{i=0}^{r} c_i x^i$ is in $F[x]$ and $\mathbf{A} = \mathbf{A}_1 \oplus \cdots \oplus \mathbf{A}_k$, then $f(\mathbf{A}) = f(\mathbf{A}_1) \oplus \cdots \oplus f(\mathbf{A}_k)$.

2. Prove Lemma 0.1.

3. Show that a linear transformation (or matrix) is cyclic if and only if its minimum function is equal to its characteristic function.

*4. Prove Theorem 0.13. Hint: Let $W = Z(v_1, \alpha) \oplus \cdots \oplus Z(v_r, \alpha)$ where $m(x)$ is a power of an irreducible polynomial. Show that $m_{v_i}(x) = p^{e_i}(x)$. Put a total order $\prec$ on the exponent sequence which occurs in the decomposition of a subspace. Show that if $W_0 \prec W_1 \prec \cdots \prec W_s$ where each W_i is a direct sum of cyclic subspaces of V, then $s \leq (n + 1)^n$. Finally, show that if $W = Z(v_1, \alpha) \oplus \cdots \oplus Z(v_r, \alpha)$ is a proper subspace of V, then there exists a direct sum $W' = Z(v_1', \alpha) \oplus \cdots \oplus Z(v_r', \alpha)$ such that $W \prec W'$.

4. The Rational Canonical Form

In our development, we have seen how to take a linear transformation $\alpha: V \to V$ and decompose V into a direct sum of subspaces each of which has a minimum polynomial which is a power of an irreducible polynomial. For spaces of this type, we have seen how to decompose them into direct sums of cyclic spaces. Combining these results leads to the following.

THEOREM 0.14. Let V be a finite dimensional vector space and $\alpha: V \to V$ a linear transformation on V. V is the direct sum of cyclic primary subspaces.*

Proof. By Theorem 0.9, $V = V_1 \oplus \cdots \oplus V_r$ where V_i is the null space of some power of an irreducible polynomial. By Theorem 0.14, each V_i is a direct sum of cyclic subspaces. ∎

COROLLARY. (Rational Canonical Form). Any square matrix $\mathbf{B}$ is similar to $\mathbf{A} = \mathbf{A}_1 \oplus \cdots \oplus \mathbf{A}_s$ where each $\mathbf{A}_i = \mathbf{C}_{p_i^{e_{i1}}(x)} \oplus \cdots \oplus \mathbf{C}_{p_i^{e_{ir_i}}(x)}$.

Using similar techniques leads to the following result.

---

* A *primary subspace* is one in which the minimum polynomial is a power of an irreducible polynomial.

THEOREM 0.15. Let V be a finite dimensional vector space and $\alpha: V \to V$ a linear transformation with matrix $\mathbf{A}$. Let $m_1(x), \ldots, m_k(x)$ be the invariant factors of $\mathbf{A}$ and $m_i \mid m_{i+1}$ for $1 \leq i < k$. If $m_{k-r}(x) = 1$ but $m_{k-r+1}(x) \neq 1$ then there exist $v_1, \ldots, v_r$ so that $V = Z(v_1, \alpha) \oplus \cdots \oplus Z(v_r, \alpha)$. (Moreover, $m_{v_j}(x) = m_{k+1-j}(x)$ for $1 \leq j \leq r$.)

Translating to a matrix theoretic statement gives the following result.

THEOREM 0.16. (Rational Canonical Form). Any square matrix $\mathbf{A}$ is similar to

$$\mathbf{D} = \mathbf{C}_{m_k(x)} \oplus \cdots \oplus \mathbf{C}_{m_1(x)}$$

where $x\mathbf{I} - \mathbf{A}$ has Smith form $\mathbf{B} \oplus \mathbf{0}$, $\mathbf{B}$ is $r \times r$ and

$$\mathbf{B} = \begin{bmatrix} 1 & & & & & & & \\ & \cdot & & & & & & \\ & & \cdot & & & & & \\ & & & \cdot & & & & \\ & & & & 1 & & & \\ & & & & & m_1 & & \\ & & & & & & \ddots & \\ & & & & & & & m_k \end{bmatrix}$$

Proof. Theorem 0.15. Also cf. [15, 36]. ▮

It then follows that two matrices are similar if and only if they have the same invariant factors, or the same rational canonical form.

We now give methods for finding the rational canonical form of a given matrix. This allows us to test for similarity of a given pair of matrices. We also wish to determine an algorithm for computing a matrix which carries one similar matrix into another.

Algorithm 0.1. Given an $n \times n$ matrix $\mathbf{A}$, do the following:

(1) Form $x\mathbf{I} - \mathbf{A}$.

(2) Place $x\mathbf{I} - \mathbf{A}$ into Smith canonical form which is of the form

$$\mathbf{B} \oplus \mathbf{0} \qquad \text{where} \qquad \mathbf{B} \text{ is } r \times r$$

and $r = \text{rank } \mathbf{A}$

$$\mathbf{B} = \begin{bmatrix} 1 & & & & & & \\ & \ddots & & & & & \\ & & 1 & & & & \\ & & & m_1 & & & \\ & & & & \ddots & & \\ & & & & & & m_k \end{bmatrix}$$

where each $m_i > 1$ and each $m_i \mid m_{i+1}$ for $1 \le i < k$.

(3) Form $\mathbf{A}' = \mathbf{C}_{m_k} \oplus \cdots \oplus \mathbf{C}_{m_1}$ where $\mathbf{C}_m$ is the companion matrix of m. $\mathbf{A}'$ is the rational canonical form of $\mathbf{A}$.

This algorithm provides a method for determining the rational canonical form of a given matrix. We now show that the algorithm gives a test for similarity of matrices.

Algorithm 0.2. To decide if two $n \times n$ matrices $\mathbf{A}$ and $\mathbf{B}$ are similar,

(1) Compute $\mathbf{A}'$, the rational canonical form of $\mathbf{A}$.
(2) Compute $\mathbf{B}'$, the rational canonical form of $\mathbf{B}$.
(3) $\mathbf{A}' = \mathbf{B}'$ if and only if $\mathbf{A}$ is similar to $\mathbf{B}$.

We now improve our algorithm in the following sense. Given two similar matrices, we give a constructive procedure for finding the similarity mapping which carries one into the other.

We now present a method for placing $\mathbf{A}$ into rational canonical form and finding the transforming matrix.

Algorithm 0.3. Given a matrix $\mathbf{A}$ over *any* field F:

(1) Form $x\mathbf{I} - \mathbf{A}$.
(2) Place $x\mathbf{I} - \mathbf{A}$ into Smith canonical form. In doing so adjoin an $n \times n$ identity matrix to the right of $x\mathbf{I} - \mathbf{A}$.
(3) Using the invariant factors obtained in (2), write down $\mathbf{A}'$. Call the modified identity matrix $\mathbf{P}_1(x)$.
(4) Form $x\mathbf{I} - \mathbf{A}'$ and repeat step (2). Call the modified identity matrix $\mathbf{P}_2(x)$.
(5) Compute $\mathbf{P}_2^{-1}(x)$.
(6) Define $\mathbf{T}(x) = \mathbf{P}_2^{-1}(x)\mathbf{P}_1(x) = \sum_i x^i\mathbf{T}_i$ where the $\mathbf{T}_i$ are constant matrices.
(7) Define $\mathbf{T} = \mathbf{T}_l(\mathbf{A}') = \sum_i (\mathbf{A}')^i\mathbf{T}_i$.

THEOREM 0.17. The matrix $\mathbf{T}$ defined in the preceding algorithm has the property that $\mathbf{TAT}^{-1} = \mathbf{A}'$.

Proof. If $\mathbf{A}$ and $\mathbf{B}$ have the same invariant factors, then, using the Smith form, $x\mathbf{I} - \mathbf{A}$ is equivalent to $x\mathbf{I} - \mathbf{B}$. There exist unimodular matrices $\mathbf{P}(x)$ and $\mathbf{Q}(x)$ such that

$$x\mathbf{I} - \mathbf{B} = \mathbf{P}(x)(x\mathbf{I} - \mathbf{A})\mathbf{Q}(x)$$

By Theorem 0.4, there exist nonsingular matrices $\mathbf{P}$, $\mathbf{Q}$, such that

$$x\mathbf{I} - \mathbf{B} = \mathbf{P}(x\mathbf{I} - \mathbf{A})\mathbf{Q} \tag{1}$$

with $\mathbf{P} = \mathbf{P}_l(\mathbf{B})$ the left remainder of $\mathbf{P}(x)$ by $x\mathbf{I} - \mathbf{B}$. From (1)

$$\mathbf{PQ} = \mathbf{I} \qquad \text{so} \qquad \mathbf{T} = \mathbf{P} = \mathbf{Q}^{-1}$$

(1) implies $\mathbf{B} = \mathbf{TAT}^{-1}$.

To complete the proof, we return to the algorithm. Since $\mathbf{A}$ is similar to $\mathbf{A}'$. $x\mathbf{I} - \mathbf{A}$ is equivalent to $x\mathbf{I} - \mathbf{A}'$. There exist

$\mathbf{P}_1(x)$, $\mathbf{P}_2(x)$, $\mathbf{Q}_1(x)$, and $\mathbf{Q}_2(x)$ such that

$$\mathbf{P}_1(x)(x\mathbf{I} - \mathbf{A})\mathbf{Q}_1(x) = \text{Smith form}$$
$$= \mathbf{P}_2(x)(x\mathbf{I} - \mathbf{A}')\mathbf{Q}_2(x) = \text{Smith form}$$

or

$$\mathbf{P}_1(x)(x\mathbf{I} - \mathbf{A})\mathbf{Q}_1(x) = \mathbf{P}_2(x)(x\mathbf{I} - \mathbf{A}')\mathbf{Q}_2(x)$$
$$\mathbf{P}_2^{-1}(x)\mathbf{P}_1(x)(x\mathbf{I} - \mathbf{A})\mathbf{Q}_1(x)\mathbf{Q}_2^{-1}(x) = x\mathbf{I} - \mathbf{A}'$$

Defining $\mathbf{T}(x) = \mathbf{P}_2^{-1}(x)\mathbf{P}_1(x)$ and taking $\mathbf{T} = \mathbf{T}_l(\mathbf{A}')$ gives the result. ▌

The previous algorithm gives a way of deciding if two $n \times n$ matrices $\mathbf{A}$ and $\mathbf{B}$ are similar and finding a nonsingular matrix $\mathbf{P}$ so that $\mathbf{B} = \mathbf{PAP}^{-1}$. The algorithm first produces $\mathbf{T}_1$ so that $\mathbf{A}' = \mathbf{T}_1\mathbf{A}\mathbf{T}_1^{-1}$ where $\mathbf{A}'$ is the rational canonical form of $\mathbf{A}$. Then one finds $\mathbf{T}_2$ so that $\mathbf{B}' = \mathbf{T}_2\mathbf{B}\mathbf{T}_2^{-1}$ where $\mathbf{B}' = \mathbf{A}'$. Then $\mathbf{P} = \mathbf{T}_2^{-1}\mathbf{T}_1$ has the property that $\mathbf{B} = \mathbf{PAP}^{-1}$.

EXAMPLE. Let $F = \mathbb{Q}$ the rational numbers and

$$\mathbf{A} = \begin{pmatrix} 1 & 1 & 1 \\ 1 & 1 & 1 \\ 1 & 1 & 1 \end{pmatrix}$$

We start with $x\mathbf{I} - \mathbf{A}$ and adjoin a 3×3 identity matrix

$$\left(\begin{array}{ccc|ccc} x-1 & -1 & -1 & 1 & 0 & 0 \\ -1 & x-1 & -1 & 0 & 1 & 0 \\ -1 & -1 & x-1 & 0 & 0 & 1 \end{array}\right)$$

Interchange columns 1 and 2 and multiply column one by -1

$$\left(\begin{array}{ccc|ccc} 1 & x-1 & -1 & 1 & 0 & 0 \\ 1-x & -1 & -1 & 0 & 1 & 0 \\ 1 & -1 & x-1 & 0 & 0 & 1 \end{array}\right)$$

Subtract the 1st row from the 3rd row

$$\begin{array}{ccc|ccc} 1 & x-1 & -1 & 1 & 0 & 0 \\ 1-x & -1 & -1 & 0 & 1 & 0 \\ 0 & -x & x & -1 & 0 & 1 \end{array}$$

Multiply row 1 by $x - 1$ and add it to row 2

$$\begin{array}{ccc|ccc} 1 & x-1 & -1 & 1 & 0 & 0 \\ 0 & x^2-2x & -x & x-1 & 1 & 0 \\ 0 & -x & x & -1 & 0 & 1 \end{array}$$

Multiply column 1 by $1 - x$ and add to column 2. Then add column 1 to column 3.

$$\begin{array}{ccc|ccc} 1 & 0 & 0 & 1 & 0 & 0 \\ 0 & x^2-2x & -x & x-1 & 1 & 0 \\ 0 & -x & x & -1 & 0 & 1 \end{array}$$

Add row 2 to row 3.

$$\begin{array}{ccc|ccc} 1 & 0 & 0 & 1 & 0 & 0 \\ 0 & x^2-2x & -x & x-1 & 1 & 0 \\ 0 & x^2-3x & 0 & x-2 & 1 & 1 \end{array}$$

Interchange columns 2 and 3. Multiply column 2 by -1.

$$\begin{array}{ccc|ccc} 1 & 0 & 0 & 1 & 0 & 0 \\ 0 & x & x^2-2x & x-1 & 1 & 0 \\ 0 & 0 & x^2-3x & x-2 & 1 & 1 \end{array}$$

Multiply column 2 by $x - 2$ and subtract it from column 3.

$$\begin{array}{ccc|ccc} 1 & 0 & 0 & 1 & 0 & 0 \\ 0 & x & 0 & x-1 & 1 & 0 \\ 0 & 0 & x^2-3x & x-2 & 1 & 1 \end{array}$$

The rational canonical form of **A** is

$$\mathbf{A}' = \begin{bmatrix} 0 & 1 & 0 \\ 0 & 3 & 0 \\ 0 & 0 & 0 \end{bmatrix}$$

and

$$\mathbf{P}_1(x) = \begin{bmatrix} 1 & 0 & 0 \\ x-1 & 1 & 0 \\ x-2 & 1 & 1 \end{bmatrix}$$

The computation is repeated using $\mathbf{A}'$. We start with

$$\left.\begin{matrix} x & -1 & 0 \\ 0 & x-3 & 0 \\ 0 & 0 & x \end{matrix}\;\right|\;\begin{matrix} 1 & 0 & 0 \\ 0 & 1 & 0 \\ 0 & 0 & 1 \end{matrix}$$

Interchange column 1 and column 2 and multiply the new column 1 by -1.

$$\left.\begin{matrix} 1 & x & 0 \\ 3-x & 0 & 0 \\ 0 & 0 & x \end{matrix}\;\right|\;\begin{matrix} 1 & 0 & 0 \\ 0 & 1 & 0 \\ 0 & 0 & 1 \end{matrix}$$

Multiply row 1 by $x - 3$ and add it to row 2.

$$\left.\begin{matrix} 1 & x & 0 \\ 0 & x^2-3x & 0 \\ 0 & 0 & x \end{matrix}\;\right|\;\begin{matrix} 1 & 0 & 0 \\ x-3 & 1 & 0 \\ 0 & 0 & 1 \end{matrix}$$

Multiplying column 1 by x and subtracting it from column 2 yields

$$\left.\begin{matrix} 1 & 0 & 0 \\ 0 & x^2-3x & 0 \\ 0 & 0 & x \end{matrix}\;\right|\;\begin{matrix} 1 & 0 & 0 \\ x-3 & 1 & 0 \\ 0 & 0 & 1 \end{matrix}$$

Interchange columns 2 and 3, then rows 2 and 3

$$\begin{array}{ccc|ccc} 1 & 0 & 0 & 1 & 0 & 0 \\ 0 & x & 0 & 0 & 0 & 1 \\ 0 & 0 & x^2 - 3x & x - 3 & 1 & 0 \end{array}$$

Thus

$$\mathbf{P}_2(x) = \begin{bmatrix} 1 & 0 & 0 \\ 0 & 0 & 1 \\ x - 3 & 1 & 0 \end{bmatrix}$$

Using standard techniques

$$\mathbf{P}_2^{-1}(x) = \begin{bmatrix} 1 & 0 & 0 \\ 3 - x & 0 & 1 \\ 0 & 1 & 0 \end{bmatrix}$$

Then

$$\mathbf{P}(x) = \mathbf{P}_2^{-1}(x)\mathbf{P}_1(x) = \begin{bmatrix} 1 & 0 & 0 \\ 1 & 1 & 1 \\ x - 1 & 1 & 0 \end{bmatrix}$$

$$\mathbf{T} = \mathbf{T}_l(\mathbf{A}') = \begin{bmatrix} 1 & 0 & 0 \\ 1 & 1 & 1 \\ -1 & 1 & 0 \end{bmatrix}$$

To check our computations, we compare

$$\mathbf{TA} = \begin{bmatrix} 1 & 0 & 0 \\ 1 & 1 & 1 \\ -1 & 1 & 0 \end{bmatrix} \begin{bmatrix} 1 & 1 & 1 \\ 1 & 1 & 1 \\ 1 & 1 & 1 \end{bmatrix} = \begin{bmatrix} 1 & 1 & 1 \\ 3 & 3 & 3 \\ 0 & 0 & 0 \end{bmatrix}$$

and

$$\mathbf{A'T} = \begin{bmatrix} 0 & 1 & 0 \\ 0 & 3 & 0 \\ 0 & 0 & 0 \end{bmatrix} \begin{bmatrix} 1 & 0 & 0 \\ 1 & 1 & 1 \\ -1 & 1 & 0 \end{bmatrix} = \begin{bmatrix} 1 & 1 & 1 \\ 3 & 3 & 3 \\ 0 & 0 & 0 \end{bmatrix}$$

PROBLEMS

*1. Justify the use of the Smith form by showing that the invariant factors determine the rational canonical form.

2. Let $\mathbf{A}_n$ be the $n \times n$ matrix of all 1's.

$$\text{Let } \mathbf{B}_n = \begin{bmatrix} n & 0 & \cdots & 0 \\ 0 & 0 & & \\ \cdot & & & \\ \cdot & & & \\ \cdot & & & \\ 0 & \cdot & \cdots & 0 \end{bmatrix}$$

Show that for each $n \geq 1$, $\mathbf{A}_n$ is similar to $\mathbf{B}_n$.

5. The Classical Canonical Form

We shall indicate another canonical form which is useful. It will be a simple matter to extend our earlier results to this new case. We begin with an analog to companion matrices.

DEFINITION. Let $p(x)$ be a monic irreducible polynomial of degree h. Let $\mathbf{R} = \mathbf{C}_p$, the companion matrix of $p(x)$ and $\mathbf{J}$ the $h \times h$ matrix which is all zero except the lower left entry which is 1. Then the *hypercompanion* matrix of $[p(x)]^e$, written $\mathbf{C}^*_{[p(x)]^e}$, is the $he \times he$ matrix

$$\mathbf{C}^*_{[p(x)]^e} = \begin{bmatrix} \mathbf{R} & \mathbf{J} & \mathbf{0} & \cdots\cdots & \mathbf{0} \\ \mathbf{0} & \mathbf{R} & \mathbf{J} & \mathbf{0} \cdots\cdots & \mathbf{0} \\ \cdot & & & & \cdot \\ \cdot & & & & \cdot \\ \cdot & & & & \cdot \\ \mathbf{0} & \cdots\cdots & \mathbf{0} & \mathbf{R} & \mathbf{J} \\ \mathbf{0} & \cdots\cdots & \cdots & \mathbf{0} & \mathbf{R} \end{bmatrix}$$

THEOREM 0.18. Let $p(x)$ be a monic irreducible polynomial of degree h, then $\mathbf{C}_{[p(x)]^e}$ is similar to $\mathbf{C}^*_{[p(x)]^e}$.

Proof. Let $m_v(x) = [p(x)]^e$ and consider $Z(v, \alpha)$ where α is the linear transformation induced by $\mathbf{C}_{[p(x)]^e}$. Consider the set

$$X = \{v, v\alpha, \ldots, v\alpha^{h-1}, vp(\alpha), v\alpha p(\alpha), \ldots, v\alpha^{h-1}p(\alpha),$$
$$v(p(\alpha))^2, \ldots, v\alpha^{h-1}(p(\alpha))^2, v(p(\alpha))^{e-1}, \ldots, v\alpha^{h-1}(p(\alpha))^{e-1}\}$$

It is easy to verify that X is a basis of $Z(v, \alpha)$. Let $p(x) = x^h + \sum_{i=0}^{h-1} c_i x^i$.

We must show that the representation of α with respect to X is $\mathbf{C}^*_{[p(x)]^e}$. This is clear except perhaps when the index of the row is a multiple of h. Suppose $i = rh$ and $v_i = v\alpha^{h-1}[p(\alpha)]^{r-1}$. Compute that

$$v_i\alpha = v\alpha^h[p(\alpha)]^{r-1} = v\left(p(\alpha) - \sum_{i=0}^{h-1} c_i\alpha^i\right)[p(\alpha)]^{r-1}$$
$$= -\left(\sum_{i=0}^{h-1} c_i v\alpha^i(p(\alpha))^{r-1}\right) + v(p(\alpha))^r$$

This formula establishes the form. ∎

It is now possible to give the classical canonical form of a matrix.

THEOREM 0.19. (Classical Canonical Form). Any square matrix is similar to $\mathbf{A} = \mathbf{A}_1 \oplus \cdots \oplus \mathbf{A}_s$ where each $\mathbf{A}_i = \mathbf{C}^*_{p_i^{e_{i1}}(x)} \oplus \cdots \oplus \mathbf{C}^*_{p_i^{e_{ir_i}}(x)}$.

Proof. Use Theorem 0.18 in the Corollary to Theorem 0.14. ∎

One can prove that the polynomials occurring in the decomposition of $\mathbf{A}_i$ above are the elementary divisors of $\mathbf{A}_i$ as given in the following definition.

DEFINITION. Let $\mathbf{A}$ be a matrix with invariant factors $m_1(x), \ldots, m_k(x)$ where $m_i \mid m_{i+1}$ for $1 \leq i < k$. Then write the prime decomposition of the invariant factors as

$$m_k(x) = [p_1(x)]^{e_{k1}} \cdots [p_r(x)]^{e_{kr}}$$

$$\vdots$$

$$m_1(x) = [p_1(x)]^{e_{11}} \cdots [p_r(x)]^{e_{1r}}$$

where $e_{kj} \geq e_{(k-1)j} \geq \cdots e_{1j} \geq 0$. All the polynomials $[p_i(x)]^{e_{ij}}$ with $e_{ij} > 0$ constitute the *elementary divisors* of **A**.

Thus, the elementary divisors can be uniquely defined by the invariant factors.

Note that the rational canonical form depends exclusively on the invariant factors while the classical form depends on the elementary divisors. Since the invariant factors do not depend on the field structure and the elementary divisors do, we have the following fact.

PROPOSITION 0.1. Let F and F' be fields with $F \subseteq F'$. The rational canonical form for an F matrix is the same whether F or F' is regarded as the field.

PROBLEMS

1. A field F is *algebraically closed* if each polynomial in $F[x]$ has a root in F. If F is algebraically closed, does the classical canonical form simplify for F-matrices?

2. Prove Proposition 0.1 and then give an example which shows that a similar proposition is not true for the classical form.

3. Give a detailed algorithm for placing a given matrix in its classical canonical form.

Chapter 1

Basic Notions of Sequential Machine Theory

In this chapter, some of the basic properties of sequential machines are given. Unlike most references on this topic, our interest is with general properties of arbitrary, not just finite, machines. Many of the algorithms for the finite case will be given in the problems. The reader interested in further details of the finite case should see [17, 20, 22, 24].

1. Basic Definitions

A sequential machine is a device with a number of internal states, an input set, and an output set. The device is constrained to act in the following way. The device is in some state, receives an input and then moves to some other state and produces an output. The action is repeated until the input sequence is exhausted.

We now begin to describe this intuitive model more carefully. First, the notation for sequences is given.

Let Σ be any nonempty set. A *word* is a finite length Σ-sequence. If x and y are words, so is their *concatenation* xy. For example, if $x = 010$, $y = 1$ then $xy = 0101$ and $yx = 1010$.

Note that concatenation is not commutative. Let Λ denote the null sequence which has the property that $x\Lambda = \Lambda x$ for each word x. The *length* of any word x, written $lg(x)$ is the number of symbols in x. Thus $lg(010) = 3$ and $lg(\Lambda) = 0$.

Let X and Y be sets of words. The *product* of X and Y is $XY = \{xy \mid x \in X, y \in Y\}$. Exponent notation is also convenient. Take $X^0 = \{\Lambda\}$, $X^{i+1} = X^iX$ for $i \geq 0$. The *star operation* (or *Kleene Closure*) of a set of words X is $X^* = \bigcup_{i\geq 0} X^i$. Also define $X^+ = \bigcup_{i\geq 1} X^i$. Note that $\Lambda \in X^*$ for any set X (even $X = \emptyset$, the empty set). $\Lambda \in X^+$ if and only if $\Lambda \in X$.

We remark in passing that Σ^* is a free monoid under concatenation. If Σ is finite, then Σ^* is finitely generated.

We now introduce sequential machines.

DEFINITION. A *sequential machine* is a 5-tuple $M = \langle Q, \Sigma, \Delta, \delta, \lambda\rangle$ where

(i) Q is a nonempty set of *states.*
(ii) Σ is a nonempty set of *input symbols.*
(iii) Δ is a nonempty set of *output symbols.*
(iv) δ is a map from $Q \times \Sigma$ into Q called the *direct transition function.*
(v) λ is a map from $Q \times \Sigma$ into Δ called the *output function.*

We shall say that a sequential machine is finite when Q, Σ, and Δ are finite. Conventional [17, 22, 24] sequential machine theory deals with finite machines and calls our definition a Mealy machine as opposed to a Moore (or state output) machine in which λ maps Q into Δ.

The formalism introduced so far gives a sequential machine and allows it to operate on input sequences of length one. We must extend these mappings to $Q \times \Sigma^*$.

DEFINITION. Let $M = \langle Q, \Sigma, \Delta, \delta, \lambda\rangle$ be a sequential machine. For each $q \in Q$, $x \in \Sigma^*$, and $a \in \Sigma$,

$$\delta(q, \Lambda) = q$$
$$\delta(q, xa) = \delta(\delta(q, x), a)$$

There are two different ways to extend the output function λ. It will be necessary for us to use both of them.

DEFINITION. Let $M = \langle Q, \Sigma, \Delta, \delta, \lambda\rangle$ be a sequential machine. For each $q \in Q$, $x \in \Sigma^*$, and $a \in \Sigma$,

$$\lambda(q, \Lambda) = \Lambda$$
$$\lambda(q, xa) = \lambda(q, x)\lambda(\delta(q, x), a)$$

and

$$\hat{\lambda}(q, xa) = \lambda(\delta(q, x), a)$$

From this definition we see that $\lambda_q(x) = \lambda(q, x)$ is a length preserving† function from Σ^* into Δ^* which is the concatenation of the output symbols produced by the individual input symbols.

$\hat{\lambda}_q(x) = \hat{\lambda}(q, x)$ is a map from Σ^+ into Δ which gives the last output symbol produced by M when started in state q and reading input x.

EXAMPLE. Let $M = \langle Q, \Sigma, \Delta, \delta, \lambda\rangle$ where $Q = \{q_0, q_1, q_2\}$ and $\Sigma = \Delta = \{0, 1\}$. δ and λ are given by tables.

	0	1
q_0	q_0	q_0
q_1	q_1	q_1
q_2	q_1	q_0

δ - function

	0	1
q_0	0	1
q_1	0	0
q_2	0	1

λ - function

† A function φ from Σ^* to Δ^* is said to be *length preserving* if $lg(\varphi x) = lg(x)$.

It is sometimes helpful to draw a state diagram for a sequential machine. We illustrate this by giving the state diagram of the previous example.

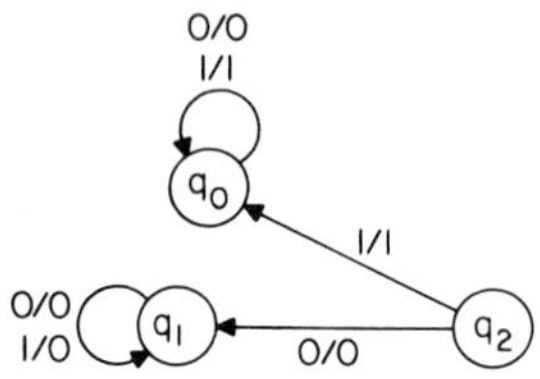

A State Diagram

Continuing the example, note that

$$\delta(q_2, 101) = q_0$$
$$\lambda(q_2, 101) = 101$$

and

$$\hat{\lambda}(q_2, 101) = 1$$

It is a straightforward matter to check these computations by formal manipulations.

We now turn to viewing sequential machines by their input-output characteristics. There are two ways to do this. One can view the device as the totality of input-output pairs of the system. Alternately, the device can be viewed as a set of functions from Σ^* to Δ^*, one function for each internal state. We now formalize these notions.

DEFINITION. Let $M = \langle Q, \Sigma, \Delta, \delta, \lambda \rangle$ be a sequential machine. Define $F(M) = \{\lambda_q \mid q \in Q\}$ and $R(M) = \{(x, \lambda(q, x)) \mid x \in \Sigma^*, q \in Q\}$. $F(M)$ is the *set of functions of M* while $R(M)$ is *input-output relation of M.*

Two sequential machines M_1 and M_2 over the same input and output alphabets are said to be *equivalent* (*relationally equivalent*) if $F(M_1) = F(M_2)(R(M_1) = R(M_2))$. Note that if M_1 is equivalent to M_2 (written $M_1 \equiv M_2$) then $R(M_1) = R(M_2)$. It is important to note that the converse is not true. To see this, consider the following example.

Example. Let M_1 be the sequential machine of the preceding example. Let M_2 be shown below.

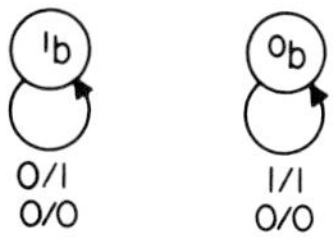

$R(M_1) = R(M_2) = \{(0, 0), (1, 0)\}^* \cup \{(0, 0), (1, 1)\}^*$. However $M_1 \not\equiv M_2$ since there is no function in M_2 which corresponds to λ_{q_2}. [More explicitly $\lambda_1(q_2, 01) = 00 \neq 01 = \lambda_2(q_0, 01)$ and $\lambda_1(q_2, 1) = 1 \neq 0 = \lambda_2(q_1, 1)$.]

PROBLEMS

1. Let $M = \langle Q, \Sigma, \Delta, \delta, \lambda\rangle$ be a *finite* sequential machine and call $R(M)$ a *sequential relation* and λ_q a *finite sequential function*. Prove the following results. A relation $R \subseteq (\Sigma \times \Delta)^*$ is a sequential relation if and only if there exists a finite number of finite sequential functions $\lambda_1, \ldots, \lambda_n$ such that

   (a) $R = \bigcup_{i=1}^{n} \lambda_i$

   (b) For each $a \in \Sigma$ and each finite sequential function λ_i, there exists a finite sequential function λ_j such that for all $x \in \Sigma^*$, $\lambda_i(ax) = \lambda_i(a)\lambda_j(x)$.

2. Let $M = \langle Q, \Sigma, \Delta, \delta, \lambda\rangle$ be a sequential machine. M is *strongly connected* if for each $q, q' \in Q$ there exists $x \in \Sigma^*$ such that $\delta(q, x) = q'$. Consider the following proposition. If true, prove it. If not, give a counterexample.

   Statement. Let M_1 and M_2 be finite strongly connected sequential machines. If $R(M_1) = R(M_2)$ then $M_1 \equiv M_2$.

3. A *finite automaton* is a 5-tuple $A = \langle Q, \Sigma, \delta, q_0, F\rangle$ where Q, Σ, δ are as in a finite sequential machine. $q_0 \in Q$ is the *initial state* while $F \subseteq Q$ is the set of *final states*. The set of

tapes *accepted* by A, written $T(A)$, is defined as $T(A) = \{x \in \Sigma^* \mid \delta(q_0, x) \in F\}$. A set $X \subseteq \Sigma^*$ is *regular* if there exists a finite automaton A such that $X = T(A)$. Let $M_1 = \langle Q_1, \Sigma, \Delta, \delta_1, \lambda_1 \rangle$ be a finite sequential machine. Show that for each $q \in Q$ and each $b \in \Delta$, $X_{q,b} = \{x \in \Sigma^* \mid \hat{\lambda}(q, x) = b\}$ is regular. Is every regular set representable as some $X_{q,b}$?

*4. Let Σ be finite and fixed. Show that the family of Σ-regular sets is the least family of sets containing the finite subsets of Σ^* and closed under finite applications of union, product, and *.

5. Let $a, b, c, d \in \Sigma^*$. Show that $ab = cd$ implies there is $e \in \Sigma^*$ such that either $a = ce$ and $d = eb$ or else $c = ae$ and $b = ed$.

6. Let $a, b \in \Sigma^*$. Show that $ab = ba$ implies there is some $c \in \Sigma^*$ so that $a = c^m$ and $b = c^n$ for some $m, n \geq 0$.

*7. Let $a, b, c \in \Sigma^*$. Show that if $a^2b^2 = c^2$ then $ab = ba$.

2. Minimization of Sequential Machines

The important notion of equivalent states will be introduced and then we will show how minimal machines play a central role in the theory.

DEFINITION. Let $M_i = \langle Q_i, \Sigma, \Delta, \delta_i, \lambda_i \rangle$, $i = 1, 2$, be sequential machines. States $q_i \in Q_i$, $i = 1, 2$, are said to be *equivalent* if

$$\lambda_1(q_1, x) = \lambda_2(q_2, x)$$

for each $x \in \Sigma^*$. We write $q_1 \equiv q_2$.

The definition is phrased to allow $M_1 = M_2$ and we can discuss equivalent states in the same machine.

Note that $\equiv$ is an equivalence relation on $Q_1 \cup Q_2$. Moreover it is a "right congruence relation" as the following lemma shows. See [22] for a detailed discussion of such relations. Also note that $q_1 \equiv q_2$ if and only if $\hat{\lambda}(q_1, x) = \hat{\lambda}(q_2, x)$ for each $x \in \Sigma^+$.

LEMMA 1.1. Let $M_i = \langle Q_i, \Sigma, \Delta, \delta_i, \lambda_i \rangle$ for $i = 1, 2$, be sequential machines. If $q_i \in Q_i$, $i = 1, 2$, and $q_1 \equiv q_2$ then $\delta_1(q_1, a) \equiv \delta_2(q_2, a)$ for each $a \in \Sigma$.

Proof. Let $x \in \Sigma^+$.

$$\hat{\lambda}_1(\delta(q_1, a), x) = \hat{\lambda}_1(q_1, ax) = \hat{\lambda}_2(q_2, ax) = \hat{\lambda}_2(\delta(q_2, a), x)$$

Therefore $\delta_1(q_1, a) \equiv \delta_2(q_2, a)$. ▮

COROLLARY. $q_1 \equiv q_2$ implies $\delta_1(q_1, x) \equiv \delta_2(q_2, x)$ for each $x \in \Sigma^*$.

The following definition is important.

DEFINITION. Let $M = \langle Q, \Sigma, \Delta, \delta, \lambda \rangle$ be a sequential machine. M is said to be *minimal*† if $q_1 \equiv q_2$ implies $q_1 = q_2$ for each $q_1, q_2 \in Q$.

Before proceeding to the main results, we need the important ideas of homomorphisms and isomorphisms.

DEFINITION. Let $M_i = \langle Q_i, \Sigma, \Delta, \delta_i, \lambda_i \rangle$, $i = 1, 2$, be sequential machines. φ is said to be a *homomorphism* from M_1 into (onto) M_2 if φ is a map from Q_1 into (onto) Q_2 such that

$$\varphi\delta_1(q, a) = \delta_2(\varphi q, a)$$

and

$$\lambda_1(q, a) = \lambda_2(\varphi q, a)$$

for each $(q, a) \in Q_1 \times \Sigma$.

If a homomorphism is one-to-one, it is called an *isomorphism.* M_2 is a *homomorphic image* of M_1 if there is a homomorphism from M_1 *onto* M_2. M_1 is *isomorphic* to M_2 if there is an

† In the literature, the word *reduced* is also used.

isomorphism of M_1 *onto* M_2. Of course, isomorphic sequential machines are equivalent but not conversely.

Now we prove the main results of this section.

THEOREM 1.1. For each sequential machine $M_1 = \langle Q_1, \Sigma, \Delta, \delta_1, \lambda_1 \rangle$, there is a minimal machine M such that $M_1 \equiv M$. If M_2 is any machine equivalent to M_1, then M is a homomorphic image of M_2.

Proof. Let $M = \langle Q, \Sigma, \Delta, \delta, \lambda \rangle$ where M is constructed from M_1 by taking $Q = \{[q] \mid q \in Q_1\}$ where $[q]$ is the equivalence class of the relation $\equiv$ which contains q. $\delta([q], a) = [\delta_1(q, a)]$ and $\lambda([q], a) = \lambda_1(q, a)$. M, which is really $M_1/\equiv$, is well defined. [For $q_1 \equiv q_2$ implies $\delta_1(q_1, a) \equiv \delta_1(q_2, a)$ so that $\delta([q_1], a) = \delta([q_2], a)$ using Lemma 1.1. Moreover $q_1 \equiv q_2$ implies $\lambda_1(q_1, a) = \lambda_1(q_2, a)$ so $\lambda([q_1], a) = \lambda([q_2], a)$.]. Clearly M is minimal [for if $[q] \equiv [q']$, then $\lambda([q], x) = \lambda([q'], x)$ implies $\lambda_1(q, x) = \lambda_1(q', x)$ so $q \equiv q'$ or $[q] = [q']$.] Since M is clearly equivalent to M_1, the first sentence of the theorem is proven. Let $M_2 = \langle Q_2, \Sigma, \Delta, \delta_2, \lambda_2 \rangle$ be a sequential machine such that $M_2 \equiv M_1$. Define a mapping φ from Q_2 into Q as follows. For each $q' \in Q_2$ there is a state $q \in Q_1$ such that $q \equiv q'$. Define

$$\varphi(q') = [q]$$

First we argue that φ is a map, i.e., single valued. There may be two states q_1 and $q_2 \in Q_1$ such that $q' \equiv q_1$ and $q' \equiv q_2$. But then $q_1 \equiv q_2$ and $\varphi(q') = [q_1] = [q_2]$. We claim that φ is onto since given $[q]$, q in Q_1 has the property $q \equiv [q]$ and there is some $q' \in Q_2$ such that $[q] \equiv q'$. Thus $\varphi(q') = [q]$. Lastly we verify that φ is a homomorphism. Let $a \in \Sigma$ and $q' \in Q_2$ be arbitrary. There is $q \in Q_1$, depending on q', such that $q' \equiv q \equiv [q]$. By Lemma 1.1, $\delta_2(q', a) \equiv \delta_1(q, a) \equiv \delta([q], a) = [\delta_1(q, a)]$. Now

$$\begin{aligned} \varphi\delta_2(q', a) &= [\delta_1(q, a)] \\ &= \delta([q], a) \\ &= \delta(\varphi q', a) \end{aligned}$$

Therefore φ is a homomorphism onto M. Since $q' \equiv [q]$, we have for each $a \in \Sigma$

$$\lambda_2(q', a) = \lambda([q], a)$$

or

$$\lambda_2(q', a) = \lambda(\varphi q', a) \ \blacksquare$$

We now obtain an important corollary of the previous construction.

THEOREM 1.2. If M_1 and M_2 are minimal sequential machines and $M_1 \equiv M_2$ then M_1 and M_2 are isomorphic.

Proof. First note, that if M_1 if minimal, then machine M constructed from M_1 is isomorphic to M_1. If M_1 and M_2 are minimal and equivalent, Theorem 1.1 gives that M_1 is a homomorphic image of M_2 and M_2 is a homomorphic image of M_1. Thus they are isomorphic. ▮

PROBLEMS

1. There are 10 nonisomorphic machines with two states, two inputs and two outputs. List all 10 machines.

2. Let $M = \langle Q, \Sigma, \Delta, \delta, \lambda \rangle$ be a sequential machine. Define a relation E_k on Q as follows for each positive integer k. $(q_1, q_2) \in E_k$ if and only if $\lambda(q_1, x) = \lambda(q_2, x)$ for all $x \in \bigcup_{i \leq k} \Sigma^i$. Show that E_k is an equivalence relation. Define F_k for $k > 0$ as follows: $(q_1, q_2) \in F_k$ if and only if $\lambda(q_1, x) = \lambda(q_2, x)$ for each $x \in \Sigma^k$. Prove that $F_k = E_k$ for all k.

3. Let M and E_k be defined as in problem 2. Show that $(q_1, q_2) \in E_{k+1}$ if and only if $(q_1, q_2) \in E_k$ and for each $a \in \Sigma$, $(\delta(q_1, a), \delta(q_2, a)) \in E_k$. Note that $E_{k+1} \subseteq E_k$ for all k.

4. Let E_k and M be as in problems 2–3. Show that $E_{k+1} = E_k$ implies $E_{k+j} = E_k$ for each $j \geq 0$.

5. Let M and E_k be as in problems 2–4. Show that if there exists k such that $E_k = E_{k+1}$ then $E_k = \equiv$, i.e., E_k is the state equivalence relation $\equiv$.

6. Let $M = \langle Q, \Sigma, \Delta, \delta, \lambda \rangle$ be a *finite* sequential machine. Show that there is a number k so that $E_k = E_{k+1}$. If n is the number of states of M, find the best such k.

7. Given the following sequential machines, minimize each such machine.

M_1

	0		1	
q_0	q_1	1	q_2	1
q_1	q_1	1	q_3	1
q_2	q_3	0	q_3	0
q_3	q_3	0	q_1	0

M_2

	0		1	
q_0	q_1	1	q_2	1
q_1	q_1	0	q_3	0
q_2	q_3	1	q_3	1
q_3	q_3	0	q_1	0

M_3

	0		1	
q_0	q_1	0	q_2	1
q_1	q_3	0	q_3	0
q_2	q_4	1	q_4	1
q_3	q_3	0	q_3	0
q_4	q_4	1	q_4	1

*8. [A knowledge of the Pólya and DeBruijn theorems in combinatorial analysis is necessary for this problem. Even then, it is nontrivial.] Show that the number of nonisomorphic sequential machines with $|Q| = n$, $|\Sigma| = k$, and $|\Delta| = p$ is

$$\frac{1}{n!}\sum_{(j)} \frac{n!}{\left(\prod_{i=1}^{n} j_i!\, i^{j_i}\right)} \prod_{i=1}^{n}\left(p \sum_{d|i} dj_d\right)^{kj_i}$$

where the sum is over all partitions of n, i.e., all nonnegative integers j_i such that

$$\sum_{i=1}^{n} ij_i = n$$

For any set X, $|X|$ denotes its cardinality.

3. Structure of Sequential Machines

In this section, we introduce some of the basic properties of machine decompositions and realizations. This subject has been extensively studied and is well summarized in [19, 24].

Our discussion is limited to results to be used later.

We begin by describing when one machine can realize another.

DEFINITION. Let $M_i = \langle Q_i, \Sigma, \Delta, \delta_i, \lambda_i \rangle$, $i = 1, 2$. be sequential machines. M_2 is a *state realization* of M_1 if there is a one-to-one map φ from Q_1 into Q_2 such that $\varphi\delta_1(q, a) = \delta_2(\varphi q, a)$ for each $(q, a) \in Q_1 \times \Sigma$. φ is called an *assignment*.

The idea is that some part of M_2 simulates the state transitions of M_1. φ is not necessarily an isomorphism of M_1 into M_2 since no requirement that φ preserve λ is made.

EXAMPLE. Let M_1 and M_2 be defined below. M_2 is a state realization M_1 by the map φ which is given

	0		1	
q_0	q_2	0	q_1	0
q_1	q_0	1	q_1	1
q_2	q_2	1	q_0	1

M_1

	0		1	
(0, 0)	(0, 1)	0	(1, 1)	0
(1, 0)	(0, 1)	0	(1, 1)	0
(1, 1)	(0, 0)	1	(1, 1)	1
(0, 1)	(0, 1)	1	(0, 0)	0

M_2

q	φq
q_0	(0, 0)
q_1	(1, 1)
q_2	(0, 1)

φ

Note that φ is not a homomorphism.

We are now ready to prove two important decomposition results. First recall the following definition.

DEFINITION. Let $M = \langle Q, \Sigma, \Delta, \delta_i, \lambda_i \rangle$ be a sequential machine. An equivalence relation $R \subseteq Q \times Q$ is said to have the *substitution property* or to be a *right congruence relation* on M if for each $a \in \Sigma$, $(q_1, q_2) \in R$ implies $(\delta(q_1, a), \delta(q_2, a)) \in R$.

If R_1 and R_2 are right congruence relations on M, so are $R_1 \cap R_2$ and $R_1 \sqcup R_2 = \{(q, q') \mid \text{there are } r \geq 0, q_0, \ldots, q_r, q_0 = q, q_r = q', (q_i, q_{i+1}) \in R_1 \cup R_2 \text{ for } 0 \leq i < r\}$. $R_1 \sqcup R_2$ is read the "join" of R_1 and R_2. Among these right congruence relations are $0 = \{(q, q) \mid q \in Q\}$ and $1 = \{(q, q') \mid q, q' \in Q\}$. It is easy to verify that the set of all right congruence relations on M form a lattice with 0 and 1. A right congruence on M different from 0 and 1 is said to be nontrivial.

With each right congruence relation is associated a "quotient machine."

DEFINITION. Let $M = \langle Q, \Sigma, \Delta, \delta, \lambda \rangle$ be a sequential machine and let R be a right congruence relation on Q. The *quotient machine without output* $M/R = \langle Q', \Sigma, \Delta, \delta' \rangle$ is defined as $Q' = \{[q] \mid q \in Q\}$ and $\delta'([q], a) = [\delta(q, a)]$. If R *preserves output* (that is, $(q, q') \in R$ implies $\lambda(q, a) = \lambda(q', a)$ for all $a \in \Sigma$) then the *quotient machine* is defined as $M/R = \langle Q', \Sigma, \Delta, \delta', \lambda' \rangle$ where $\lambda'([q], a) = \lambda(q, a)$ and the rest is as above.

EXAMPLE. For any sequential machine M, $\equiv$ is a right congruence relation on Q which preserves the output. Moreover $M/\equiv$ is the minimal machine equivalent to M.

EXAMPLE. Let M be shown below. R is a right congruence relation which preserves the output

		0		1	
	q_0	q_1	1	q_2	1
M	q_1	q_1	0	q_3	0
	q_2	q_3	1	q_3	1
	q_3	q_3	0	q_1	0

$R = \{(q_1, q_3)\} \cup 0$

		0		1	
	p_0	p_1	1	p_2	1
M/R	p_1	p_1	0	p_1	0
	p_2	p_1	1	p_1	1

$p_0 = [q_0]$
$p_1 = [q_1, q_3]$
$p_2 = [q_2]$

Using these methods, we give a necessary and sufficient condition for a sequential machine to admit a "parallel decomposition."

DEFINITION. Let $M_i = \langle Q_i, \Sigma, \Delta_i, \delta_i, \lambda_i \rangle$, $i = 1, 2$, be sequential machines. The *parallel connection* of M_1 and M_2, written $M_1 \textcircled{\|} M_2$, is defined to be $M_1 \textcircled{\|} M_2 = \langle Q_1 \times Q_2, \Sigma, \Delta_1 \times \Delta_2, \delta, \lambda \rangle$ where $\delta((q_1, q_2), a) = (\delta_1(q_1, a), \delta_2(q_2, a))$ and $\lambda((q_1, q_2), a) = (\lambda_1(q_1, a), \lambda_2(q_2, a))$ for each $(q_1, q_2, a) \in Q_1 \times Q_2 \times \Sigma$.

The intuitive picture of $M_1 \textcircled{\|} M_2$ is shown below.

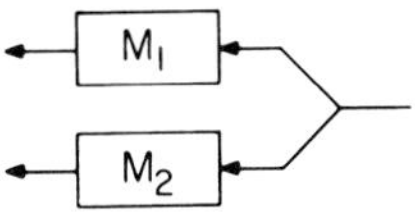

DEFINITION. M has a *parallel decomposition* if M has a state realization by $M_1 \textcircled{\|} M_2$ where M_1 and M_2 are sequential

machines. Such a decomposition is *nontrivial* if the state sets of M_1 and M_2 are in one-to-one correspondence with a proper subset of the state set of M.

This last condition is to insure nontriviality. Note that if Q is finite, then the condition is that the Q_i are strictly smaller than Q. If Q is infinite, the condition gives that $Q - Q_i \neq \emptyset$. For instance, a nontrivial decomposition would allow $Q = \mathbb{N} = \{0, 1, 2, \ldots\}$, $Q_1 = \{0, 2, 4, \ldots\}$, and $Q_2 = \{1, 3, 5, \ldots\}$, but we would call $Q = Q_1 = Q_2 = \mathbb{N}$ a trivial decomposition.

We now give a necessary and sufficient condition for such a decomposition to exist.

THEOREM 1.3. $M = \langle Q, \Sigma, \Delta, \delta, \lambda\rangle$ has a (nontrivial) parallel decomposition if and only if there exist two (nontrivial) right congruence relations R_1, R_2 on M such that $R_1 \cap R_2 = 0$.

Proof. Suppose $M_1 \textcircled{\parallel} M_2$ is a state realization M under map φ, $M_i = \langle Q_i, \Sigma, \Delta_i, \delta_i, \lambda_i\rangle$, $i = 1, 2$, and $\varphi\colon Q \to Q_1 \times Q_2$ is one-to-one. Define $(q, q') \in R_i$ if and only if $\varphi q = (q_1, q_2)$, $\varphi q' = (q_1', q_2')$, and $q_i = q_i'$ for $i = 1, 2$. It is a straightforward task to verify that the R_i are right congruence relations. It only remains to show that $R_1 \cap R_2 = 0$. Suppose $(q, q') \in R_1 \cap R_2$. Then $(q, q') \in R_1$ and $(q, q') \in R_2$. If $q \neq q'$, then $\varphi q \neq \varphi q'$ since φ is one-to-one. Thus $(q_1, q_2) \neq (q_1', q_2')$ which implies $(q, q') \notin R_1$ or $(q, q') \notin R_2$. This is a contradiction of $(q, q') \in R_1 \cap R_2$. Since the decomposition is nontrivial, (i.e., each of M_1 and M_2 has the property that $Q - Q_i \neq \emptyset$, the R_i are nontrivial.

Conversely, let $M = \langle Q, \Sigma, \Delta, \delta, \lambda\rangle$ and let R_i, $i = 1, 2$, be right congruence relations on Q such that $R_1 \cap R_2 = 0$. Then take $M_i = M/R_i$ for $i = 1, 2$. Thus $M_i = \langle\{[q]_i \mid q \in Q\}, \Sigma, \Delta, \delta_i, e\rangle$ where e is the identity map. We must show that $M_1 \textcircled{\parallel} M_2$ is a state realization of M. Define $\varphi q = ([q]_1, [q]_2)$. Since $R_1 \cap R_2 = 0$,

$$[q]_1 \cap [q']_2 = \begin{cases} q & \text{if } q = q' \\ \emptyset & \text{otherwise} \end{cases}$$

Thus we can define an output λ' on $M_1 \circledcirc M_2$ such that

$$\lambda'(([q]_1, [q']_2), a) = \lambda(q, a)$$

if $q = q'$. It is a straightforward matter to verify that $M_1 \circledcirc M_2$ realizes M. ∎

Because of the definition of state realizations, it is not necessary to specify the output as we have done. This is included only to show how the theorem can be applied.

EXAMPLE. Let M be the sequential machine shown below

	0		1	
q_0	q_5	0	q_3	1
q_1	q_4	1	q_2	0
q_2	q_1	0	q_5	0
q_3	q_0	0	q_4	0
q_4	q_3	0	q_1	1
q_5	q_2	1	q_0	1

Let* $R_1 = \{[q_0, q_2, q_4], [q_1, q_3, q_5]\}$, $R_2 = \{[q_0, q_1], [q_2, q_3], [q_4, q_5]\}$. It is easily checked that R_1 and R_2 are right congruence relations. Furthermore $R_1 \cap R_2 = 0$. Now we form M/R_1 and M/R_2

	0	1
p_0	p_1	p_1
p_1	p_0	p_0

	0	1
r_0	r_2	r_1
r_1	r_0	r_2
r_2	r_1	r_0

$p_0 = [q_0, q_2, q_4]$

$p_1 = [q_1, q_3, q_5]$

$M_1 = M/R_1$

$r_0 = [q_0, q_1]$, $r_1 = [q_2, q_3]$

$r_2 = [q_4, q_5]$

$M_2 = M/R_2$

---

* We are using the same symbol for the equivalence relation and the partition.

It is easily verified that $M_1 \textcircled{\scriptsize ||} M_2$ is a state realization of M. We leave it to the reader to supply appropriate outputs so that the state realization φ' becomes an isomorphism of M into $M_1 \textcircled{\scriptsize ||} M_2$.

Next, it is necessary to discuss serial decompositions.

Definition. Let $M_i = \langle Q_i, \Sigma_i, \Delta_i, \delta_i, \lambda_i \rangle$, $i = 1, 2$, be sequential machines such that $\Delta_1 = \Sigma_2$. The *serial connection* is $M = M_2 \ominus M_1 = \langle Q_2 \times Q_1, \Sigma_1, \Delta_2, \delta, \lambda \rangle$ where $\delta((q', q), a) = (\delta_2(q', \lambda_1(q, a)), \delta_1(q, a))$ and $\lambda((q', q), a) = \lambda_2(q', \lambda_1(q, a))$.

The intuitive picture of a serial connection is given below.

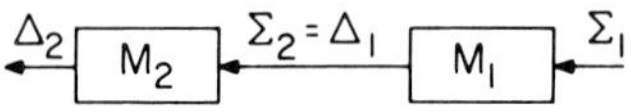

Definition. M has a *serial decomposition* if M has a state realization by $M_2 \ominus M_1$ where M_1, M_2 are sequential machines. Such a decomposition is *nontrivial* if the state sets of the M_i are in one-to-one correspondence with a proper subset of the state set of M.

It is now a straightforward matter to characterize such serial decompositions.

Theorem 1.4. A countable sequential machine* $M = \langle Q, \Sigma, \Delta, \delta, \lambda \rangle$ has a nontrivial series decomposition if and only if there is a nontrivial right congruence relation on Q.

Proof. Let $M_i = \langle Q_i, \Sigma_i, \Delta_i, \delta_i, \lambda_i \rangle$, $i = 1, 2$, $\Delta_1 = \Sigma_2$ and M be state realized by $M_1 \ominus M_2$. Let $\varphi\colon Q \to Q_2 \times Q_1$ be one-to-one. Define $(q, q') \in R$ if and only if $\varphi q = (q_2, q_1)$, $\varphi q' = (q_2', q_1')$, and $q_1 = q_1'$. We omit the (obvious) verification that R is a nontrivial right congruence relation.

* Q is countable.

Conversely, let R be a nontrivial right congruence relation on Q. Assume* $rk(R) = l$ and let the largest class of R have k states. If† $|Q| = n$, then $n \geq k$ and $n \geq l$. Let R' be any equivalence relation on Q such that $R \cap R' = 0$. Of course $R' = 0$ is a trivial solution which shows that R' always exists, but we require a nontrivial one. To see that a nontrivial R' exists, label the elements in the ith block by $1, 2, \ldots, n_i$ where $n_i \leq k$ for $1 \leq i \leq l$. The relation R' identifies states with the same label. Clearly R is an equivalence relation, $rk(R') = k$, and $R \cap R' = 0$. Note that R' is nontrivial since R is. Now define $M_1 = M/R = \langle \{[q]_R \mid q \in Q\}, \Sigma, \{[q]_R \mid q \in Q\} \times \Sigma, \delta_1, e \rangle$ and $M_2 = \langle \{[q']_{R'} \mid q \in Q\}, \{[q]_R \mid q \in Q\} \times \Sigma, \Delta, \delta_2, \lambda_2 \rangle$ with $\delta_2([q']_{R'}, ([q]_R, a)) = [q'']_{R'}$ where $\delta([q]_R \cap [q']_{R'}, a) \in [q'']_{R'}$. Also $\lambda_2([q']_{R'}, ([q]_R, a)) = \lambda([q]_R \cap [q']_{R'}, a)$. Since $|[q]_R \cap [q']_{R'}| \leq 1$, the values are uniquely defined if the sets are not disjoint. If $[q]_R \cap [q']_{R'} = \emptyset$ then, it is a don't care situation and any assignment of values will work. It is a routine matter to verify that $M_1 \ominus M_2$ is a state realization of M under the mapping $\varphi q = ([q]_{R'}, [q]_R)$. ∎

EXAMPLE. Consider the sequential machine M

	0		1	
q_0	q_4	0	q_2	0
q_1	q_3	0	q_1	1
q_2	q_3	1	q_0	1
q_3	q_0	1	q_3	0
q_4	q_1	1	q_4	0

M

Clearly $R = \{[q_0, q_1, q_2], [q_3, q_4]\}$ is a nontrivial right congruence relation on M. The relation $R' = \{[q_0, q_3], [q_1, q_4], [q_2]\}$ and

* For any equivalence relation R, let $rk(R)$ denote the number of equivalence classes of R.

† We use $|Q|$ to be the cardinality of Q.

$R \cap R' = 0$. Then component machines are

	δ 0	δ 1	λ 0	λ 1
p_0	p_1	p_0	$(p_0, 0)$	$(p_0, 1)$
p_1	p_0	p_1	$(p_1, 0)$	$(p_1, 1)$

$$p_0 = [q_0, q_1, q_2] \quad p_1 = [q_3, q_4]$$

$$M_1 = M/R$$

	$(p_0, 0)$	$(p_0, 1)$	$(p_1, 0)$	$(p_1, 1)$
r_0	r_1	r_2	r_0	r_0
r_1	r_0	r_1	r_1	r_1
r_2	r_0	r_0	r_0	r_0

$$r_0 = [q_0, q_3], \quad r_1 = [q_1, q_4], \quad r_2 = [q_2]$$

$$M_2$$

The lower two right-hand entries (both r_0) are "don't cares." They have been set equal to r_0 merely to make M_2 completely specified.

PROBLEMS

1. In these problems we generalize the motion of realizability. Let $M = \langle Q, \Sigma, \Delta, \delta, \lambda \rangle$ and $M' = \langle Q', \Sigma', \Delta', \delta', \lambda' \rangle$ be two sequential machines. M' *realizes* M if there exist three mappings α, β, and φ such that

(i) α maps Σ into Σ'.
(ii) β maps Δ into Δ' and β is one-to-one.
(iii) φ maps Q into non-empty subsets of Q'.
(iv) For each $(q, a) \in Q \times \Sigma$ and $q' \in \varphi q$

$$\delta'(q', \alpha a) \in \varphi\delta(q, a)$$

(v) For each $(q, a) \in Q \times \Sigma$ and $q' \in \varphi q$

$$\lambda'(q', \alpha a) = \beta\lambda(q, a)$$

Furthermore if $|\varphi q| = 1$ for each $q \in Q$, then M' *realizes* M *without state splitting*. Show that if M' realizes M with maps α, β, and φ (with α and β extended to be homomorphisms,† then for all $x \in \Sigma^+$, and $q' \in \varphi q$

$$\lambda'(q', \alpha x) = \beta\lambda(q, x)$$

2. If in the above problem α is onto then show that for each $q \in Q$, $q_1, q_2 \in \varphi q$ implies $q_1 \equiv q_2$.

3. Generalize Theorems 1.3 and 1.4 to the type of realizations given in the previous problems.

4. Complete the examples after Theorems 1.3 and 1.4 by choosing outputs so that the realization map φ becomes an isomorphism into or an injection.

5. In the proof of Theorem 1.4, verify that R is a nontrivial right congruence relation.

4. The Monoid of a Machine

In this section, we briefly introduce the notion of the monoid of a sequential machine. A few basic theorems are derived which will be needed in the sequel.

First we introduce the idea of a submachine.

DEFINITION. Let $M = \langle Q, \Sigma, \Delta, \delta, \lambda\rangle$ be a sequential machine. $M' = \langle Q', \Sigma, \Delta, \delta', \lambda'\rangle$ is a *submachine* of M if

(i) $\emptyset \neq Q' \subseteq Q$
(ii) for each $a \in \Sigma$, $\delta(Q', a) = \{\delta(q', a) \mid q' \in Q'\} \subseteq Q'$
(iii) $\delta' = \delta \cap (Q' \times \Sigma \times Q')$ and $\lambda' = \lambda \cap (Q' \times \Sigma \times \Delta)$

† If $\alpha: \Sigma \to \Sigma'$, α is extended to be a *homomorphism* from Σ^* into $(\Sigma')^*$ by $\alpha(xy) = \alpha x \alpha y$ for each $x, y \in \Sigma^*$.

EXAMPLE. Let M and M' be the sequential machines shown below. M' is a submachine of M.

	0	
q_0	q_0	0
q_1	q_0	1

M

	0	
q_0	q_0	0

M'

Now we deal with the algebraic structure of sequential machines.

DEFINITION. A *monoid* is a triple $\langle S, \cdot, e \rangle$ where S is a nonvoid set and $\cdot$ is a binary operation on S which is associative i.e., $a(bc) = (ab)c$ for all $a, b, c, \in S$. $e \in S$ is the identity so $ae = ea = a$ for all $a \in S$. As usual we have written ab for $a \cdot b$.

Let $M = \langle Q, \Sigma, \Delta, \delta, \lambda \rangle$ be a sequential machine. For each $x \in \Sigma^*$, write x^M as the mapping which takes q into $\delta(q, x)$.

DEFINITION. For each sequential machine M, the *monoid of* M, usually denoted G_M, is $G_M = \{x^M \mid x \in \Sigma^*\}$.

We note that the monoid operation is composition of functions and that Λ^M is the identity mapping on Q. Moreover $(xy)^M = x^M y^M$ for all $x, y \in \Sigma^*$.

EXAMPLE. Consider the sequential machine M shown below.

	0	1
q_0	q_1	q_2
q_1	q_2	q_0
q_2	q_0	q_1

M

	Λ^M	0^M	1^M
q_0	q_0	q_1	q_2
q_1	q_1	q_2	q_0
q_2	q_2	q_0	q_1

G_M

Note that this monoid is a group,* in fact it is the cylic group of order 3.

The following definition plays a key role in our theory of decompositions.

DEFINITION. Let M and M' be sequential machines. M is said to be *state isomorphic* to M' if M' state realizes M via an assignment φ which is also onto.

Note that state isomorphic machines have the same transition structure though nothing is claimed about their outputs.

We begin to relate these concepts.

THEOREM 1.5. If $M_1 = \langle Q_1, \Sigma, \Delta, \delta_1, \lambda_1\rangle$ and $M_2 = \langle Q_2, \Sigma, \Delta, \delta_2, \lambda_2\rangle$ are sequential machines and M_2 is a state realization of M_1, then M_1 is state isomorphic to some submachine M' of M_2.

Proof. Since M_2 is a state realization of M_1, there is a one-to-one map φ from Q_1 into Q_2 such that $\varphi\delta_1(q, a) = \delta_2(\varphi q, a)$. Let $Q' = \varphi Q_1 \subseteq Q_2$. Consider $M' = \langle Q', \Sigma, \Delta, \delta', \lambda'\rangle$ where $\delta' = \delta_2 \cap (Q' \times \Sigma \times Q')$ and similarly for λ' (though it is irrelevant here). Clearly M' is a submachine of M_2.

The map φ restricted to Q' is still one-to-one and is now onto. Hence it is a state isomorphism. ▮

Next we relate the monoids to submachines.

THEOREM 1.6. Let $M = \langle Q, \Sigma, \Delta, \delta, \lambda\rangle$ and $M' = (Q', \Sigma, \Delta, \delta', \lambda'\rangle$ be sequential machines with M' a submachine of M. Then $G_{M'}$ is a homomorphic† image of G_M.

---

* A *group* is a monoid $G = \langle S, \cdot, e\rangle$ such that for each $a \in G$, there is some $b \in G$ so that $ab = e$.

† Let G_1 and G_2 be semigroups. A map φ from G_1 into G_2 is a *homomorphism* if $\varphi ab = \varphi a \varphi b$ for all $a, b \in G_1$.

Proof. The map is φ: $x^M \to x^{M'}$. We leave the trivial details to the reader. ▮

One can note the following easy proposition which follows from the previous result and elementary semigroup theory.

PROPOSITION 1.1. If M' is a submachine of M, then $G_{M'}$ is isomorphic to a submonoid of G_M.

Now we turn to a theorem which relates state isomorphisms with isomorphisms of the monoids.

THEOREM 1.7. Let $M_i = \langle Q_i, \Sigma, \Delta, \delta_i, \lambda_i \rangle$ be sequential machines for $i = 1, 2$ and let $M' = \langle Q', \Sigma, \Delta, \delta', \lambda' \rangle$ be a submachine of M_2. If M_1 is state isomorphic to M', then G_{M_1} is isomorphic to $G_{M'}$.

Proof. The state isomorphism φ maps Q_1 onto Q'. Moreover, φ is one-to-one and for each $(q, x) \in Q_1 \times \Sigma^*$, $\varphi\delta_1(q, x) = \delta_2(\varphi q, x) = \delta'(\varphi q, x)$. In other words $\varphi x^{M_1} = x^{M'}\varphi$. Since φ is one-to-one onto Q', $x^{M'} = \varphi x^{M_1}\varphi^{-1}$. Define the map ψ from G_{M_1} into $G_{M'}$ by $\psi x^{M_1} = \varphi x^{M_1}\varphi^{-1} = x^{M'}$. To show ψ is a homomorphism $\psi(x^{M_1}y^{M_1}) = \psi((xy)^{M_1}) = (xy)^{M'} = x^{M'}y^{M'} = \psi(x^{M_1})\psi(y^{M_1})$. To see that ψ is one-to-one, suppose $\psi(x^{M_1}) = \psi(y^{M_1})$. Then $\varphi x^{M_1}\varphi^{-1} = \varphi y^{M_1}\varphi^{-1}$ which implies $x^{M_1} = y^{M_1}$. ψ is onto since for $x^{M'} \in G_{M'}$, $\varphi^{-1}x^{M'}\varphi \in G_{M_1}$. We have $\psi(\varphi^{-1}x^{M'}\varphi) = x^{M'}$. ▮

Combining the previous theorem and Proposition 1.1 gives the following result.

PROPOSITION 1.2. Let $M_i = \langle Q_i, \Sigma, \Delta, \delta_i, \lambda_i \rangle$, $i = 1, 2$, be sequential machines. If M' is a submachine of M_2 and M_1 is state isomorphic to M', then G_{M_1} is isomorphic to a submonoid of G_{M_2}.

Next, we combine our results into the following final form which will be used later.

THEOREM 1.8. Let M_i, $i = 1, 2$, be sequential machines. If M_2 is a state realization of M_1 then G_{M_1} is isomorphic to a submonoid of G_{M_2}.

Proof. Since M_2 is a state realization of M_1, M_1 is state isomorphic to a submachine M' of M_2 by Theorem 1.5. By the previous proposition, G_{M_1} is isomorphic to a submonoid of G_{M_2}. ▮

PROBLEMS

1. Find a three state sequential machine which is not state isomorphic to the first example of this section, but which has the same monoid.

2. Complete the proof of Theorem 1.6.

3. A sequential machine M is said to be a *group machine* if G_M is a group. Construct a family of finite sequential machines M_n such that $G_{M_n} = S_n$, the symmetric group on n letters. Moreover, the input alphabet for M_n should have two letters.

4. For each monoid G, show that there is some sequential machine M such that $G_M = G$.

5. Let $f\colon \Sigma^+ \to \Delta$. A function f is said to be a finite sequential function if there is some finite sequential machine $M = \langle Q, \Sigma, \Delta, \delta, \lambda\rangle$ so that $f = \hat{\lambda}_q$ for some $q \in Q$. Define a map τ_t as a map from Σ^* to Σ^* by $\tau_t(x) = tx$. Thus τ_t is a left translation mapping. Show that $f\colon \Sigma^+ \to \Delta$ is a finite sequential function if and only if $\{f\tau_t \mid t \in \Sigma^*\}$ is finite.

6. Prove Propositions 1.1 and 1.2.

5. Some Finiteness Conditions

The results presented up to now have not assumed that our sequential machines are finite. There are a number of finiteness conditions which are important in the theory of linear sequential machines and we shall introduce some of these conditions now.

DEFINITIONS. Let $M = \langle Q, \Sigma, \Delta, \delta, \lambda \rangle$ be a sequential machine. With each positive integer p, we associate five conditions which M may or may not satisfy.

(0) (Feedback free condition). For each $x \in \Sigma^p\Sigma^*$; $q_1, q_2 \in Q$;

$$\delta(q_1, x) = \delta(q_2, x)$$

(1) (Definite condition). For each $x \in \Sigma^p\Sigma^*$; $q_1, q_2 \in Q$;

$$\delta(q_1, x) \equiv \delta(q_2, x)$$

(2) For each $x \in \Sigma^p\Sigma^*$; $q \in Q$;†

$$\delta(q, x) \equiv \delta(q, x^{(p)})$$

(3) (Finite memory condition). For each $x \in \Sigma^p\Sigma^*$; $q_1, q_2 \in Q$;

$$\lambda(q_1, x) = \lambda(q_2, x) \quad \text{implies} \quad \delta(q_1, x) \equiv \delta(q_2, x).$$

(4) (p diagnosability condition). For each $x \in \Sigma^p\Sigma^*$; $q_1, q_2 \in Q$;

$$\lambda(q_1, x) = \lambda(q_2, x) \quad \text{implies} \quad q_1 \equiv q_2.$$

Condition (0) is a formal version of the intuitive notion of a feedback free machine because after p units of time, the machine is always in the same state. Condition (1) is known as the definite condition in the literature [14, 16, 22]. Condition (3) is the finite memory condition because knowledge of starting states, input and output determines the final state. Condition (4) is a diagnosability condition in that the output and input determine the initial state (up to equivalence).

We now establish certain relations between these conditions.

† For each $x \in \Sigma^p\Sigma^*$, write $x = yx^{(p)}$ where $x^{(p)}$ denotes the last p symbols of x.

THEOREM 1.9. If M is a sequential machine which satisfies condition (i) $(0 \leq i \leq 4)$ for $p = p_0$ then M satisfies condition (i) for all $p \geq p_0$.

The proof is obvious and is omitted.

We now relate (0) and (1).

THEOREM 1.10. Every feedback free sequential machine M is definite but not conversely unless M is minimal. More precisely (0) implies (1) and if M is minimal, (1) implies (0). There exists a finite sequential machine M' which satisfies (1) for $p = 1$, but does not satisfy (0) for any $p \geq 1$.

The trivial argument is omitted.

It is also easy to relate (1) and (2).

THEOREM 1.11. Condition (1) implies condition (2) but there is a finite minimal machine which satisfies (2) for $p = 1$, but does not satisfy (1) for any $p \geq 1$.

Proof. Let $M = \langle Q, \Sigma, \Delta, \delta, \lambda \rangle$ be a sequential machine. Let $x \in \Sigma^p\Sigma^*$ and write $x = yx^{(p)}$. For any $q_1 \in Q$, $\delta(q_1, x) = \delta(\delta(q_1, y), x^{(p)}) = \delta(q_2, x^{(p)})$ where $q_2 = \delta(q_1, y)$. If M satisfies (1), $\delta(q_1, x^{(p)}) \equiv \delta(q_2, x^{(p)})$ so that $\delta(q_1, x) \equiv \delta(q_1, x^{(p)})$ and so M satisfies (2).

To see that the converse is false, consider M' which is shown below. M' satisfies (2) for $p = 1$ but does not satisfy (1) any for $p \geq 1$. ∎

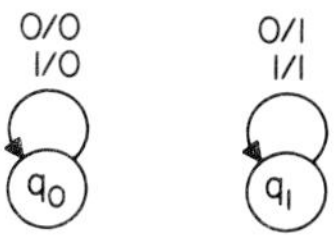

M'

Next, we relate (1) and (3).

THEOREM 1.12. Every definite sequential machine is finite memory but not conversely. More precisely, condition (1) implies (3) but there is a finite minimal machine which satisfies (3) for $p = 1$ but not (1) for any $p \geq 1$.

The argument is immediate and is omitted. The previous counterexample also applies in this case.

Our last result of this type concerns (4) and (3).

THEOREM 1.13. Every diagnosable sequential machine is finite memory but not conversely. More precisely, condition (4) implies (3), but there is a finite minimal machine which satisfies (3) for $p = 1$ but not (4) for any $p \geq 1$.

Proof. To show that (4) implies (3), assume $\lambda(q_1, x) = \lambda(q_2, x)$ for each $x \in \Sigma^p\Sigma^*$; $q_1, q_2 \in Q$. Then $q_1 \equiv q_2$ by (4). By the corollary to Lemma 1.1, $\delta(q_1, x) \equiv \delta(q_2, x)$.

To finish the proof, consider M' shown below. M' satisfies (3) for $p = 1$ but not (4) for any $p \geq 1$. ∎

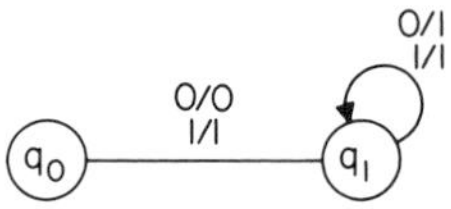

PROBLEMS

1. Consider condition (x) defined below. (x) is equivalent to one of the conditions given. Decide which one and prove it.

(x) For each $x \in \Sigma^p\Sigma^*$, $q \in Q$, $\hat{\lambda}(q, x) = \hat{\lambda}(q, x^{(p)})$.

2. Consider condition (y) defined below. (y) is equivalent to a condition given earlier. Decide which one and prove it.

(y) For each $x \in \Sigma^p\Sigma^*$ and each $q_1, q_2 \in Q$, $\hat{\lambda}(q_1, x) = \hat{\lambda}(q_2, x^{(p)})$.

3. Consider the type of realizability discussed in the problems of Section 3. Suppose M' realizes M and M' is diagnosable (i.e., satisfies condition (4)) then show that for all $q \in Q$, if $q_1, q_2 \in \varphi q$, then $q_1 \equiv q_2$.

4. Exhibit a finite minimal sequential machine which satisfies condition (2) but not condition (3).

5. The following condition is a formal version of the finite memory condition as defined in [17]. Is it equivalent to our condition (3)? Let $M = \langle Q, \Sigma, \Delta, \delta, \lambda \rangle$ be a sequential machine. For $p \geq 1$, the condition is that for each $q_1, q_2 \in Q^*$, each $x \in \Sigma^p\Sigma^*$ and $a \in \Sigma$ we have that $(\lambda(q_1, x))^{(p)} = (\lambda(q_2, x))^{(p)}$ implies $\hat{\lambda}(q_1, xa) = \hat{\lambda}(q_2, xa)$.

Chapter 2

Basic Properties of Linear Sequential Machines

In this chapter the basic definition of a linear sequential machine will be given. The most important properties of such devices are given. The minimal machine of a linear sequential machine is still linear and can be effectively constructed if the field is "effective." Similar machines are introduced and related to minimal machines. Finiteness conditions for LSM's are characterized. Finally controllable LSM's are introduced. It is shown that the notions of controllability and observability imply a decomposition of the state space of a linear system.

1. Definitions

We now introduce our notion of a linear sequential machine. In the language of system theory, these are linear, finite dimensional, time invariant systems. Intuitively, they are sequential machines whose transition and output functions are linear maps.

Let F be a field and m be a nonnegative integer. F_m denotes the vector space of column vectors of dimension m over F. Note that $F_0 = \{\mathbf{0}\}$ is a vector space over F.

DEFINITION. A *linear sequential machine* M (*LSM* for short) is a sequential machine $M = \langle Q, \Sigma, \Delta, \delta, \lambda \rangle$ with the following special properties. There exists a field F and nonnegative integers n, k, and l such that $Q = F_n$, $\Sigma = F_k$, and $\Delta = F_l$. Furthermore there exists an $n \times n$ matrix $\mathbf{A}$ over F, an $n \times k$ matrix $\mathbf{B}$ over F, an $l \times n$ matrix $\mathbf{C}$ over F and an $l \times k$ matrix $\mathbf{D}$ over F such that for each $(q, a) \in Q \times \Sigma$

$$\delta(q, a) = \mathbf{A}q + \mathbf{B}a$$

$$\lambda(q, a) = \mathbf{C}q + \mathbf{D}a$$

Such an LSM M will sometimes be denoted by $\langle F, n, k, l, \mathbf{A}, \mathbf{B}, \mathbf{C}, \mathbf{D} \rangle$, $\langle F, \mathbf{A}, \mathbf{B}, \mathbf{C}, \mathbf{D} \rangle$, or $\langle F, n, k, l, \delta, \lambda \rangle$.

In the preceding definition, we allow $n = 0$. In this case; matrices $\mathbf{A}$, $\mathbf{B}$, and $\mathbf{C}$ are null and the output function $\lambda: a \rightarrow \mathbf{D}a$ describes a combinatorial linear switching circuit. This is the "memoryless" case. [19] Similarly $k = 0$ leads to the *autonomous* networks where $|\Sigma| = 1$.

It is possible to deal with LSM's in terms of linear functions and abstract vector spaces rather than matrices and F_n, etc. This leads to shorter proofs and a more elegant theory, but overlooks certain questions of representability and effectiveness. Since we are concerned with algorithms, we use the matrix representation.

Note that if F is finite, so is any LSM over F. Most of our results will be for arbitrary fields. In order to assure effectivity (i.e., being able to compute) we will often deal with "computable" fields. For the moment, a computable field should be taken to be a field in which we can mechanically compute. Later we shall make this intuitive notion precise.

EXAMPLE. Let $M = \langle \mathbb{Z}_2, \mathbf{A}, \mathbf{B}, \mathbf{C}, \mathbf{D} \rangle$ where $\mathbf{A} = \begin{bmatrix} 10 \\ 11 \end{bmatrix}$, $\mathbf{B} = \begin{bmatrix} 1 \\ 1 \end{bmatrix}$, $\mathbf{C} = (1 \quad 0)$, $\mathbf{D} = (1)$. $\mathbb{Z}_2$ denotes the integers modulo 2. As a sequential machine, M has four states and its state diagram is shown below.

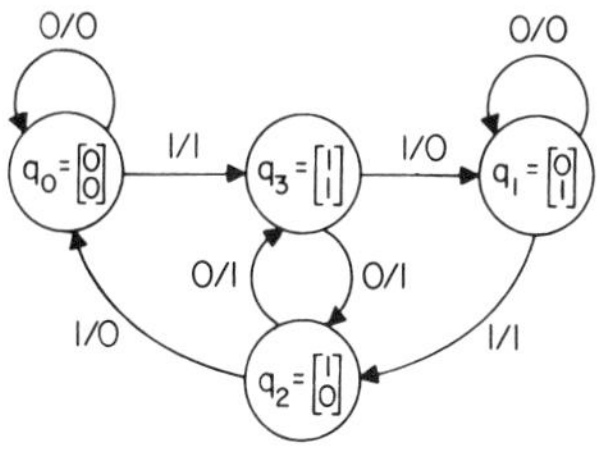

It is easy to associate a circuit description with such a mathematical description. The previous example is a realization of the following circuit.

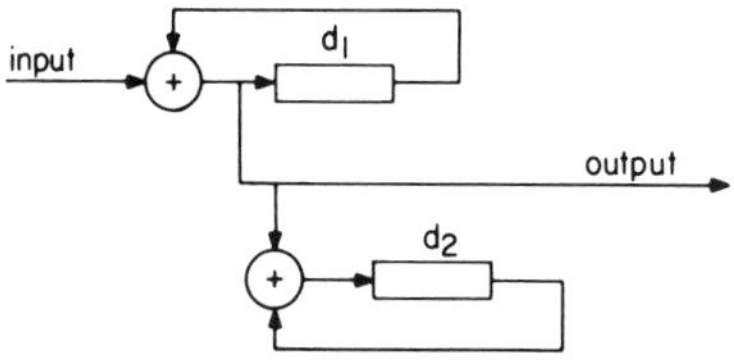

The conversion between these different but equivalent representations is a straightforward process and is relegated to the exercises.

EXAMPLE. Let $M = \langle F, \mathbf{A}, \mathbf{0}_{n\times 1}, \mathbf{0}_{1\times n}, \mathbf{0}_{1\times 1}\rangle$ where $\mathbf{0}_{m\times n}$ is an $m \times n$ all zero matrix and $\mathbf{A}$ is an $n \times n$ companion matrix.

$$\mathbf{A} = \begin{bmatrix} 0 & 1 & 0 & \cdots\cdots & 0 \\ 0 & 0 & 1 & 0 \;\cdots & 0 \\ & \cdot & & & \\ & \cdot & & & \\ & \cdot & & & \\ 0 & 0 & & \cdots \; 0 & 1 \\ -d_0 & -d_1 & & \cdots & -d_{n-1} \end{bmatrix}$$

Thus the minimal polynomial of $\mathbf{A}$ is $m_{\mathbf{A}}(x) = d_0 + d_1 x + \cdots + d_{n-1}x^{n-1} + x^n$. The network associated with M is shown below.

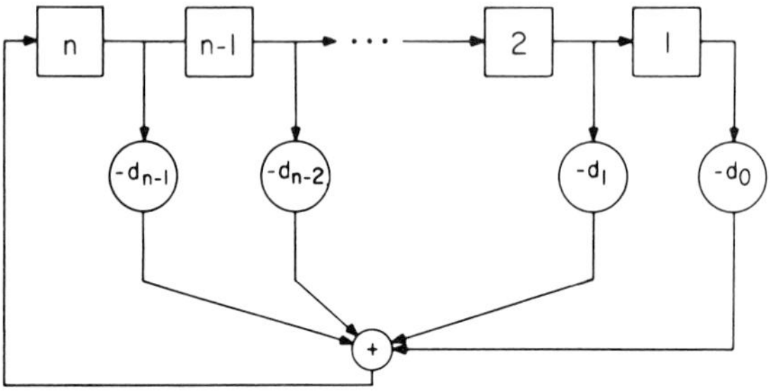

Such a circuit is a *shift register*.

We now prove a straightforward but important result.

THEOREM 2.1. Let $M = \langle F, \mathbf{A}, \mathbf{B}, \mathbf{C}, \mathbf{D} \rangle$ be an LSM. For each $q \in F_n$ and $a_0, \ldots, a_{t-1} \in F_k$, $t > 0$,

(a) $\delta(q, a_0 \cdots a_{t-1}) = \mathbf{A}^t q + \sum_{i=0}^{t-1} \mathbf{A}^{t-i-1}\mathbf{B}a_i$

(b) $\hat{\lambda}(q, a_0 \cdots a_{t-1}) = \mathbf{CA}^{t-1}q + \sum_{i=0}^{t-2} \mathbf{CA}^{t-i-2}\mathbf{B}a_i + \mathbf{D}a_{t-1}$

For each $q, q' \in F_n$, $x \in F_k^+$, $c \in F$

(c) $\delta(q + cq', x) = \delta(q, x) + c\delta(q', \mathbf{0}^{lg(x)})$†

(d) $\hat{\lambda}(q + cq', x) = \hat{\lambda}(q, x) + c\hat{\lambda}(q', \mathbf{0}^{(lgx)})$

(e) $\lambda(q + cq', x) = \lambda(q, x) + c\lambda(q', \mathbf{0}^{lg(x)})$‡

(f) $\hat{\lambda}(q, x) = \hat{\lambda}(q, \mathbf{0}^{lg(x)}) + \hat{\lambda}(\mathbf{0}, x)$

(g) Let $x, y \in F_k^*$ such that $lg(x) = lg(y)$.
$\delta(q, x) = \delta(q, y)$ if and only if $\delta(\mathbf{0}, x) = \delta(\mathbf{0}, y)$

---

† $\mathbf{0}^{lg(x)}$ denotes the zero vector of F_k concatenated with itself $lg(x)$ times.

‡ For any $c \in F$ and $x = a_1 \cdots a_m$, $a_i \in F_l$, $cx = (ca_1) \cdots (ca_m)$. The addition in (e) is componentwise, i.e., $a_1 \cdots a_m + b_1 \cdots b_m = (a_1 + b_1) \cdots (a_m + b_m)$.

(h) Let $q, q' \in F_n$, $x \in F_k^*$.
$\delta(q, x) = \delta(q', x)$ if and only if $\delta(q, \mathbf{0}^{lg(x)}) = \delta(q', \mathbf{0}^{lg(x)})$

(i) Let $q, q' \in F_n$, $x \in F_k^+$.
$\hat{\lambda}(q, x) = \hat{\lambda}(q', x)$ if and only if $\hat{\lambda}(q, \mathbf{0}^{lg(x)}) = \hat{\lambda}(q', \mathbf{0}^{lg(x)})$

Proof. (a) The argument is a straightforward induction on t and is omitted.

(b)

$$\hat{\lambda}(q, a_0 \cdots a_{t-1}) = \lambda(\delta(q, a_0 \cdots a_{t-2}), a_{t-1})$$
$$= \mathbf{C}\left[\mathbf{A}^{t-1}q + \sum_{i=0}^{t-2} \mathbf{A}^{t-i-2}\mathbf{B}a_i\right] + \mathbf{D}a_{t-1}$$

The rest of the statements follow from (a) and (b) or each other. ▌

PROBLEMS

1. Given a sequential machine, $M = \langle F, \mathbf{A}, \mathbf{B}, \mathbf{C}, \mathbf{D}\rangle$, give an algorithm for constructing the network of M.

2. Define *precisely* a linear network and show how to associate an LSM with such a network.

3. Let $M = \langle \mathbb{Z}_2, \mathbf{A}, \mathbf{B}, \mathbf{C}, \mathbf{D}\rangle$ where

$$\mathbf{A} = \begin{bmatrix} 1 & 0 & 1 \\ 0 & 1 & 1 \\ 1 & 0 & 1 \end{bmatrix} \qquad \mathbf{B} = \begin{bmatrix} 0 & 1 \\ 1 & 0 \\ 1 & 0 \end{bmatrix}$$

$$\mathbf{C} = \begin{bmatrix} 1 & 0 & 1 \\ 1 & 1 & 1 \end{bmatrix} \qquad \mathbf{D} = \begin{bmatrix} 0 & 1 \\ 1 & 0 \end{bmatrix}$$

Draw the circuit for M.

4. We can define a time varying LSM by the following methods. A *time-varying LSM* (TVLSM) is an 8-tuple $M = \langle F, n(\ ), \mathbf{A}(\ ), \mathbf{B}(\ ), \mathbf{C}(\ ), \mathbf{D}(\ ), \delta, \lambda\rangle$ where F is a field, n maps

natural numbers into natural numbers. [At time t, $n(t)$ is the dimensionality of M and the state space at time t is $F_{n(t)}$.] Thus $\mathbf{A}(\ )$ is a function from natural numbers (say $\mathbb{N} = \{0, 1 \cdots\}$) into the set of all finite dimensional F-matrices. Moreover $\mathbf{A}(t) = (a_{ij}(t))_{n'(t)\times n(t)}$ where $n'(t) = n(t+1)$. $\mathbf{B}(\ )$ is a function from $\mathbb{N}$ into set of all finite dimensional column vectors over F so that $B(t) = (b_i(t))_{n'(t)\times 1}$. $\mathbf{C}(\ )$ is a function from $\mathbb{N}$ into finite dimensional F row vectors so that $\mathbf{C}(t) = (c_i)_{1\times n(t)}$. $\mathbf{D}(\ )$ is a function from $\mathbb{N}$ into F so $\mathbf{D}(t) = (d(t))$. We have

$$\delta(q(t), a) = \mathbf{A}(t)q(t) + \mathbf{B}(t)a = q(t+1)$$

$$\lambda(q(t), a) = \mathbf{C}(t)q(t) + \mathbf{D}(t)a$$

For each $t \in \mathbb{N}$, $q(t)$, and $x = a_0 \cdots a_{p-1}$, $p \geq 1$, $a_i \in F$, show that

$$\delta(q(t), a_0 \cdots a_{p-1}) = \left[\prod_{i=0}^{p-1} \mathbf{A}(t+i)\right] q(t) + \sum_{i=0}^{p-2} \left[\prod_{j=i+1}^{p-1} \mathbf{A}(t+j)\right] \mathbf{B}(t+i)a_i + \mathbf{B}(t+p-1)a_{p-1}$$

and

$$\lambda(q(t), a_0 \cdots a_{p-1}) = \mathbf{C}(t+p-1)\left[\prod_{i=0}^{p-2} \mathbf{A}(t+i)\right] q(t) + \sum_{i=0}^{p-2} \mathbf{C}(t+p-1)\left[\prod_{j=i+1}^{p-2} \mathbf{A}(t+j)\right] \times \mathbf{B}(t+i)a_i + \mathbf{D}(t+p-1)a_{p-1}$$

Also show that if a TVLSM is an LSM, then these formulas reduce to those given in Theorem 2.1.

5. Let $M = \langle F, \mathbf{A}, \mathbf{B}, \mathbf{C}, \mathbf{D}\rangle$ and fix $a \in F_k$. Define a map $\mu\colon a \to \begin{bmatrix} \mathbf{A} & \mathbf{B}a \\ \mathbf{0}_{1\times n} & \mathbf{I}_1 \end{bmatrix}$ where $\mathbf{0}_{1\times n}$ is a $1 \times n$ zero matrix and $\mathbf{I}_1 = (1)$. Define $\mu(a_0 \cdots a_{t-1})$ with $a_i \in F_k^*$ as $\mu(a_{t-1}) \cdots \mu(a_0)$. Can you say anything about the monoid of an LSM?

2. Similar and Minimal LSM's

In this section, the notion of similarity is introduced for LSM's. This allows a variety of canonical forms of networks to be given. Minimization of LSM's is accomplished and it is shown that if M is an LSM, so is the reduced form of M.

We now define the important concept of similarity.

DEFINITION. Let $M_i = \langle F, \mathbf{A}_i, \mathbf{B}_i, \mathbf{C}_i, \mathbf{D}_i \rangle, i = 1, 2$, be LSM's. M_1 is said to be *similar* to M_2 if there exists a nonsingular matrix $\mathbf{P}$ such that

$$\begin{aligned} \mathbf{A}_2 &= \mathbf{P}\mathbf{A}_1\mathbf{P}^{-1} \\ \mathbf{B}_2 &= \mathbf{P}\mathbf{B}_1 \\ \mathbf{C}_2 &= \mathbf{C}_1\mathbf{P}^{-1} \\ \mathbf{D}_2 &= \mathbf{D}_1 \end{aligned}$$

Similarity is important because matrices are similar if and only if they represent the same linear transformation. It is clear that similarity is an equivalence relation.

We now derive a few straightforward properties of similar LSM's.

THEOREM 2.2. Let $M_i = \langle F, n, k, l, \mathbf{A}_i, \mathbf{B}_i, \mathbf{C}_i, \mathbf{D}_i \rangle, i = 1, 2$, be LSM's. If M_1 is similar to M_2 via a nonsingular matrix $\mathbf{P}$ then,

(a) for each $q \in Q_1$, $q \equiv \mathbf{P}q$.
(b) M_1 is isomorphic to M_2.
(c) $M_1 \equiv M_2$.

Proof. Clearly (b) implies (c). To show (a), let $a_0 \cdots a_{t-1} \in F_k^+$ and $q \in Q_1$.

$$\begin{aligned} \hat{\lambda}_2(\mathbf{P}q, a_0 \cdots a_{t-1}) &= \mathbf{C}_2\mathbf{A}_2^{t-1}\mathbf{P}q + \sum_{i=0}^{t-2} \mathbf{C}_2\mathbf{A}_2^{t-i-2}\mathbf{B}_2 a_i \\ &\quad + \mathbf{D}_2 a_{t-1} \\ &= \mathbf{C}_1\mathbf{P}^{-1}(\mathbf{P}\mathbf{A}_1\mathbf{P}^{-1})^{t-1}\mathbf{P}q \\ &\quad + \sum_{i=0}^{t-2} \mathbf{C}_1\mathbf{P}^{-1}(\mathbf{P}\mathbf{A}_1\mathbf{P}^{-1})^{t-i-2}\mathbf{P}\mathbf{B}_1 a_i \\ &\quad + \mathbf{D}_1 a_{t-1} \end{aligned}$$

Since $\mathbf{A}_2 = \mathbf{P}\mathbf{A}_1\mathbf{P}^{-1}$ implies $\mathbf{A}_2^j = \mathbf{P}\mathbf{A}_1^j\mathbf{P}^{-1}$ for each $j \geq 0$, we have

$$\begin{aligned}\hat{\lambda}(\mathbf{P}q, a_0 \cdots a_{t-1}) &= \mathbf{C}_1\mathbf{A}_2^{t-1}q + \sum_{i=0}^{t-2} \mathbf{C}_1\mathbf{A}_2^{t-i-2}\mathbf{B}_1 a_i + \mathbf{D}_1 a_{t-1} \\ &= \hat{\lambda}(q, a_0 \cdots a_{t-1})\end{aligned}$$

Thus $q \equiv \mathbf{P}q$.

To show (b), let $\varphi q = \mathbf{P}q$. φ is one-to-one and onto since $\mathbf{P}$ has an inverse. By (a)

$$\lambda_1(q, x) = \lambda_2(\varphi q, x) \qquad \text{for each} \quad x \in F_k^*.$$

$$\begin{aligned}\varphi\delta_1(q, a) &= \varphi(\mathbf{A}_1 q + \mathbf{B}_1 a) = \mathbf{P}(\mathbf{A}_1 q + \mathbf{B}_1 a) \\ &= (\mathbf{P}\mathbf{A}_1\mathbf{P}^{-1})(\mathbf{P}q) + \mathbf{P}\mathbf{B}_1 a = \mathbf{A}_2\varphi q + \mathbf{B}_2 a \\ &= \delta_2(\varphi q, a).\end{aligned}$$

Thus M_1 is isomorphic to M_2. ∎

It is easy to check that not every pair of isomorphic LSM's are similar. Consider $M_1 = \langle \mathbb{Z}_5, (2), (0), (0), (0)\rangle$ and $M_2 = \langle \mathbb{Z}_5, (3), (0), (0), (0)\rangle$. M_1 is isomorphic to M_2 but (2) is not similar to (3) over $\mathbb{Z}_5$, the integers modulo 5.

Example. It is well known that every matrix $\mathbf{A}$ is similar to a direct sum of companion matrices. Thus every LSM can be (effectively, if the field is computable) assumed to be realizable as a collection of shift registers.

We turn now to finding the minimal form of an LSM. It is convenient to work with a new type of matrix in these computations.

Definition. Let $M = \langle F, n, k, l, \mathbf{A}, \mathbf{B}, \mathbf{C}, \mathbf{D}\rangle$ be an LSM. For each $i \geq 1$, define

$$\mathbf{K}_i = \begin{bmatrix} \mathbf{C} \\ \mathbf{CA} \\ \cdot \\ \cdot \\ \cdot \\ \mathbf{CA}^{i-1} \end{bmatrix}$$

Note that $\mathbf{K}_i$ has li rows and n columns. Other properties of $\mathbf{K}_i$ will now be explored.

THEOREM 2.3. Let $M = \langle F, n, k, l, \mathbf{A}, \mathbf{B}, \mathbf{C}, \mathbf{D} \rangle$ be an LSM. If* row $(\mathbf{CA}^i) \subseteq$ row $\mathbf{K}_i$, then for each $j \geq i$, row $(\mathbf{CA}^j) \subseteq$ row $\mathbf{K}_i$.

Proof. The argument is an induction on j. The basis is immediate. Suppose row $\mathbf{CA}^m \subseteq$ row $\mathbf{K}_i$. Let v be any row of $\mathbf{CA}^m$. Write $v = \sum_{r=1}^{li} d_r v_r$ for some $d_r \in F$ where v_r are the rows of $\mathbf{K}_i$. Each row of $\mathbf{CA}^{m+1}$ is of the form

$$v\mathbf{A} = \sum_r d_r(v_r\mathbf{A})$$

But the $v_r\mathbf{A} \in$ row $\mathbf{K}_i$ or $v_r\mathbf{A} \in$ row $\mathbf{CA}^i \subseteq$ row $\mathbf{K}_i$. In any event, row $(\mathbf{CA}^{m+1}) \subseteq$ row $\mathbf{K}_i$. ∎

COROLLARY 1. row $\mathbf{K}_i \subseteq$ row $\mathbf{K}_{i+1}$ and rank $\mathbf{K}_i \leq$ rank $\mathbf{K}_{i+1}$ for each i. If rank $\mathbf{K}_p$ = rank $\mathbf{K}_{p+1}$ then for each $m \geq 1$ rank $\mathbf{K}_{p+m}$ = rank $\mathbf{K}_p$.

COROLLARY 2. There exists p such that rank $\mathbf{K}_{p+1}$ = rank $\mathbf{K}_p$ and $p \leq n$.

Proof. Note that for each i, rank $\mathbf{K}_i \leq n$ since K_i has n columns. Consider $\mathbf{K}_1, \mathbf{K}_2, \ldots, \mathbf{K}_n, \mathbf{K}_{n+1}$. At worst, the rank increases once at each step, hence $p \leq n$ and rank $\mathbf{K}_{p+1}$ = rank $\mathbf{K}_p$. ∎

The development of the previous theorem and corollaries is typical of the finiteness arguments used in automata theory.

Now we turn to the problem of determining equivalent states in an LSM.

---

* row $\mathbf{A}$ denotes the row space of the matrix $\mathbf{A}$.

LEMMA 2.1. Let $M = \langle F, n, k, l, \mathbf{A}, \mathbf{B}, \mathbf{C}, \mathbf{D} \rangle$ be an LSM and $q \in F_n$. $\mathbf{CA}^i q = \mathbf{0}$ for each $i \geq 0$ if and only if $\mathbf{K}_n q = \mathbf{0}$.

Proof. Necessity is obvious. Suppose $\mathbf{K}_n q = \mathbf{0}$. Then for each i, $0 \leq i < n$, $\mathbf{CA}^i q = \mathbf{0}$. By Theorem 2.3, row $(\mathbf{CA}^i) \subseteq$ row $\mathbf{K}_n$ for $i \geq n$. Therefore $\mathbf{CA}^i q = \mathbf{0}$ for all i. ∎

The next lemma summarizes more properties of equivalent states.

LEMMA 2.2. Let $M = \langle F, n, k, l, \mathbf{A}, \mathbf{B}, \mathbf{C}, \mathbf{D} \rangle$ be an LSM and $q, q' \in F_n$. $q \equiv q'$ if and only if $\mathbf{CA}^i q = \mathbf{CA}^i q'$ for each $i \geq 0$. Moreover, $q \equiv q'$ if and only if $\mathbf{K}_n q = \mathbf{K}_n q'$. The set $E_0 = \{q \mid q \equiv 0\}$ is the null space of $\mathbf{K}_n$.

Proof. $q \equiv q'$ if and only if for each $x \in F_k^+$, $\hat{\lambda}(q, x) = \hat{\lambda}(q', x)$. By (*i*) of Theorem 2.1, this holds if and only if $\hat{\lambda}(q, \mathbf{0}^{lg(x)}) = \hat{\lambda}(q', \mathbf{0}^{lg(x)})$. Therefore $q \equiv q'$ if and only if for each $i \geq 0$, $\mathbf{CA}^i q = \mathbf{CA}^i q'$. By Lemma 2.1, $q \equiv q'$ if and only if $\mathbf{K}_n q = \mathbf{K}_n q'$. Next, $\mathbf{K}_n q = \mathbf{0}$ if and only if $q \equiv \mathbf{0}$ by the first part of the Lemma. ∎

The next proposition exhibits another property of equivalent states.

PROPOSITION 2.1. Let $M = \langle F, n, k, l, \mathbf{A}, \mathbf{B}, \mathbf{C}, \mathbf{D} \rangle$ be an LSM and $q, q' \in F_n$. We have $q \equiv q'$ if and only if $q - q' \in E_0$. M is minimal if and only if rank $\mathbf{K}_n = n$.

Proof. $q \equiv q'$ if and only if $\mathbf{K}_n(q - q') = \mathbf{0}$ which holds if and only if $q - q' \in E_0$. M is minimal if and only if $E_0 = \{\mathbf{0}\}$. Since E_0 is the null space of $\mathbf{K}_n$, this happens if and only if rank $\mathbf{K}_n = n$. ∎

We now derive a useful linearity property of equivalent states.

PROPOSITION 2.2. Let M be an LSM. If $q_i \equiv q_i'$ for $i = 1, 2$, then for any $c \in F$,

$$q_1 + cq_2 \equiv q_1' + cq_2'$$

Proof. The result follows immediately from Lemma 2.2. ▮

In a sense, we have completed our study of minimal LSM's. For now, we can show that if M is an LSM with state space F_n, then M/E_0, the quotient LSM with state space F_n/E_0 (the quotient space of F_n modulo the subspace E_0) is the minimal form of M. Thus the minimal form of an LSM is still linear. This result is not quite sufficient for our purposes. It is necessary to obtain methods for computing the matrices of the minimal linear machine. We now give such a method.

DEFINITION. Let $M = \langle F, n, k, l, \mathbf{A}, \mathbf{B}, \mathbf{C}, \mathbf{D} \rangle$ be an LSM and let rank $\mathbf{K}_n = r \leq n$. Let $\mathbf{T}$ be an $r \times n$ matrix formed from the first r linearly independent rows of $\mathbf{K}_n$. Let $\mathbf{R}$ denote an $n \times r$ right inverse* matrix of $\mathbf{T}$. Define $M' = \langle F, r, k, l, \mathbf{A}', \mathbf{B}', \mathbf{C}', \mathbf{D}' \rangle$ where

$$\mathbf{A}' = \mathbf{TAR}$$

$$\mathbf{B}' = \mathbf{TB}$$

$$\mathbf{C}' = \mathbf{CR}$$

$$\mathbf{D}' = \mathbf{D}$$

It will ultimately be shown that M' is the minimal form of M but we must first establish some relationships among these matrices.

LEMMA 2.3. Let $M = \langle F, n, k, l, \mathbf{A}, \mathbf{B}, \mathbf{C}, \mathbf{D} \rangle$ be an LSM and $M' = \langle F, r, k, l, \mathbf{A}', \mathbf{B}', \mathbf{C}', \mathbf{D}' \rangle$ be as in the preceding definition. Then,

(a) row $\mathbf{T}$ = row $\mathbf{K}_n$.
(b) null $\mathbf{K}_n$ = null $\mathbf{T}$.†
(c) null $\mathbf{T} \subseteq$ null $(\mathbf{TA})$.
(d) null $\mathbf{T} \subseteq$ null $\mathbf{C}$.

---

* $\mathbf{R}$ exists because $\mathbf{T}$ is an $r \times n$ matrix of rank r.

† For any matrix $\mathbf{A}$, null $\mathbf{A} = \{v \mid \mathbf{A}v = \mathbf{0}\}$.

Proof. (a) If obvious from the definition of $\mathbf{T}$. To see (b), first note that we can assume that the rows of $\mathbf{T}$ occur first in $\mathbf{K}_n$ (by permuting rows). Thus $\mathbf{K}_n = \mathbf{P}\begin{bmatrix}\mathbf{T}\\ \mathbf{K}\end{bmatrix}$ for some permutation matrix and some matrix $\mathbf{K}$. If $\mathbf{K}_n q = \mathbf{0}$ then $\mathbf{P}\begin{bmatrix}\mathbf{T}\\ \mathbf{K}\end{bmatrix} q = \mathbf{0}$. Since $\mathbf{P}$ is nonsingular, $\mathbf{T}q = \mathbf{0}$. Thus null $\mathbf{K}_n \subseteq$ null $\mathbf{T}$.

Conversely, every row of $\mathbf{K}_n$ is a linear combination of rows of $\mathbf{T}$ so there exists a $ln \times r$ matrix $\mathbf{P}$ so that $\mathbf{K}_n = \mathbf{PT}$. If $\mathbf{T}q = \mathbf{0}$ then $\mathbf{K}_n q = \mathbf{PT}q = \mathbf{P0} = \mathbf{0}$. Thus null $\mathbf{K}_n$ = null $\mathbf{T}$.

To see (c), note that $\mathbf{T}q = \mathbf{0}$ implies $\mathbf{K}_n q = \mathbf{0}$ by (b). By Lemma 2.2, $q \equiv \mathbf{0}$ so that $\delta(q, \mathbf{0}) = \mathbf{A}q \equiv \mathbf{0}$. Thus $\mathbf{K}_n\mathbf{A}q = \mathbf{0}$ so $\mathbf{TA}q = \mathbf{0}$. Therefore null $\mathbf{T} \subseteq$ null $\mathbf{TA}$.

Finally we suppose that $\mathbf{T}q = \mathbf{0}$, then

$$\mathbf{K}_n q = \begin{bmatrix}\mathbf{C}\\ \mathbf{K}_{n-1}\mathbf{A}\end{bmatrix} q = \begin{bmatrix}\mathbf{C}q\\ \mathbf{K}_{n-1}\mathbf{A}q\end{bmatrix} = \mathbf{0} \qquad \text{so} \quad \mathbf{C}q = \mathbf{0}. \ ▮$$

Next we relate the primed matrices to the original ones.

LEMMA 2.4. Let $M = \langle F, n, k, l, \mathbf{A}, \mathbf{B}, \mathbf{C}, \mathbf{D}\rangle$ be an LSM and $M' = \langle F, r, k, l, \mathbf{A}', \mathbf{B}', \mathbf{C}', \mathbf{D}'\rangle$ be as in the preceding definition. Then,

(a) $\mathbf{A}'\mathbf{T} = \mathbf{TA}$
(b) $(\mathbf{A}')^i = \mathbf{TA}^i\mathbf{R}$ for each $i \geq 0$
(c) $\mathbf{C}'\mathbf{T} = \mathbf{C}$
(d) $\mathbf{K}_i' = \mathbf{K}_i\mathbf{R}$ for each $i \geq 0$

Proof. Let $q \in F_n$. Define $q'' = (\mathbf{I} - \mathbf{RT})q$ so that $\mathbf{T}q'' = (\mathbf{T} - \mathbf{TRT})q = (\mathbf{T} - \mathbf{T})q = \mathbf{0}$ since $\mathbf{TR} = \mathbf{I}$. Thus any $q \in F_n$ can be written

$$q = q'' + \mathbf{RT}q \tag{1}$$

with $q'' \in$ Null $\mathbf{T}$.

(a) Multiply (1) by $\mathbf{TA}$ which yields

$$\mathbf{TA}q = \mathbf{TA}q'' + \mathbf{TART}q = \mathbf{0} + \mathbf{A}'\mathbf{T}q$$

since $q'' \in$ null $\mathbf{T} \subseteq \mathbf{TA}$, we have that $\mathbf{TA}q'' = \mathbf{0}$ using (c) of Lemma 2.3.

(b) Induction on i and skipping the basis,

$$(\mathbf{A}')^{i+1} = \mathbf{A}'\mathbf{T}\mathbf{A}^i\mathbf{R} = \mathbf{T}\mathbf{A}\mathbf{A}^i\mathbf{R} = \mathbf{T}\mathbf{A}^{i+1}\mathbf{R}$$

using (a).

(c) Multiply (1) by $\mathbf{C}$ to yield

$$\mathbf{C}q = \mathbf{C}q'' + \mathbf{CRT}q = \mathbf{0} + \mathbf{C}'\mathbf{T}q$$

since $q'' \in$ null $\mathbf{T} \subseteq$ null $\mathbf{C}$ by (d) of Lemma 2.3. Thus $\mathbf{C} = \mathbf{C}'\mathbf{T}$.

(d) Since $\mathbf{C}'(\mathbf{A}')^i = \mathbf{C}'\mathbf{T}\mathbf{A}^i R$ by (b)

$= \mathbf{C}\mathbf{A}^i\mathbf{R}$ by (c)

Therefore $\mathbf{K}'_i = \mathbf{K}_i\mathbf{R}$ for each i. ▌

Next we show that M' is in fact the minimal form of M.

THEOREM 2.4. If $M = \langle F, n, k, l, \mathbf{A}, \mathbf{B}, \mathbf{C}, \mathbf{D}\rangle$ is an LSM then M' as defined above is the minimal form of M.

Proof. We first establish that $M' \equiv M$. If $q \in F_n$ then let $q' = \mathbf{T}q$. We will show that the map $q \to \mathbf{T}q = q'$ is a homomorphism so that $q' \equiv q$. Recall that if $q'' = (\mathbf{I} - \mathbf{RT})q$ then $\mathbf{T}q'' = (\mathbf{T} - \mathbf{TRT})q = (\mathbf{T} - \mathbf{T})q = \mathbf{0}$. Thus $q'' \in$ null $\mathbf{T}$. By Lemma 2.3 (c), null $\mathbf{T} \subseteq$ null $\mathbf{TA}$ so that $\mathbf{TA}q'' = \mathbf{0}$. First we check that the map $\mathbf{T}$ preserves outputs.

$$\lambda(q, a) = \mathbf{C}q + \mathbf{D}a = \mathbf{C}(q'' + \mathbf{RT}q) + \mathbf{D}a$$

since $q = q'' + \mathbf{RT}q$.

$$\lambda(q, a) = \mathbf{C}q'' + \mathbf{CRT}q + \mathbf{D}a = \mathbf{0} + \mathbf{C}'(\mathbf{T}q) + \mathbf{D}'a = \lambda'(\mathbf{T}q, a)$$

because $\mathbf{C}q'' = \mathbf{0}$ since $q'' \in$ null $\mathbf{T} \subseteq$ null $\mathbf{C}$ by (d) of Lemma 2.3. Finally, we verify that transitions are preserved.

$$\begin{aligned} \mathbf{T}\delta(q, a) = \mathbf{T}(\mathbf{A}q + \mathbf{B}a) &= \mathbf{TA}(q'' + \mathbf{RT}q) + \mathbf{TB}a \\ &= \mathbf{0} + (\mathbf{TAR})(\mathbf{T}q) + \mathbf{B}'a \\ &= \mathbf{A}'(\mathbf{T}q) + \mathbf{B}'a = \delta'(\mathbf{T}q, a) \end{aligned}$$

Therefore $q' \equiv q$.

Next, let $q' \in F_r$. Note that state $\mathbf{R}q' \in F_n$ has the property that $\mathbf{T}(\mathbf{R}q') = q'$. Thus the map $q \to \mathbf{T}q$ is onto and $\mathbf{R}q' \equiv q'$. Therefore $M \equiv M'$.

It only remains for us to show that M' is minimal. Suppose $q_1 \equiv q_2$ in M'. Then $\mathbf{K}_r'(q_1 - q_2) = \mathbf{0}$. Since rank $\mathbf{K}_r' = r$, then* dim null $\mathbf{K}_r' = 0$ so $q_1 - q_2 = \mathbf{0}$ or $q_1 = q_2$. Thus M' is minimal. ▮

Combining our results yields the following important proposition.

THEOREM 2.5. For each LSM M, there is an LSM M' such that $M \equiv M'$ and M' is minimal. Moreover, if F is computable then M' is effectively computable.

EXAMPLE. Let $M = \langle \mathbb{Z}_2, \mathbf{A}, \mathbf{B}, \mathbf{C}, \mathbf{D} \rangle$ where

$$\mathbf{A} = \begin{bmatrix} 0 & 1 & 1 \\ 1 & 0 & 0 \\ 1 & 0 & 0 \end{bmatrix} \qquad \mathbf{B} = \begin{bmatrix} 0 \\ 1 \\ 1 \end{bmatrix}$$

$$\mathbf{C} = \begin{bmatrix} 1 & 0 & 0 \\ 1 & 1 & 1 \end{bmatrix} \qquad \mathbf{D} = \begin{bmatrix} 1 \\ 0 \end{bmatrix}.$$

We compute that $\mathbf{K}_1 = \begin{bmatrix} 1 & 0 & 0 \\ 1 & 1 & 1 \end{bmatrix}$ and that row $\mathbf{K}_2 =$ row $\mathbf{K}_1$.

Thus, $\mathbf{T} = \mathbf{K}_1$ and $\mathbf{R} = \begin{bmatrix} 1 & 0 \\ 1 & 0 \\ 0 & 1 \end{bmatrix}$

Straightforward calculations yield that

$$\mathbf{A}' = \begin{bmatrix} 1 & 1 \\ 1 & 1 \end{bmatrix} \qquad \mathbf{B}' = \begin{bmatrix} 0 \\ 0 \end{bmatrix} \qquad \mathbf{C}' = \begin{bmatrix} 1 & 0 \\ 0 & 1 \end{bmatrix}.$$

and $\mathbf{D}' = \mathbf{D}$.

---

* Recall that K_r' is a $lr \times r$ matrix of rank r. The null space of any $v \times w$ matrix of rank r has dimension $w - r$ by a standard theorem on the solution of linear equations.

We now begin to relate the concepts of similarity and equivalence.

THEOREM 2.6. Let $M = \langle F, n, k, l, \mathbf{A}, \mathbf{B}, \mathbf{C}, \mathbf{D} \rangle$ and $M' = \langle F, n, k, l, \mathbf{A}', \mathbf{B}', \mathbf{C}', \mathbf{D}' \rangle$ be LSM's with M' minimal. If for each q in M, $q \equiv \mathbf{P}q$, for some nonsingular matrix $\mathbf{P}$, then M is similar to M'.

Proof. Since $q \equiv \mathbf{P}q$, $\lambda(q, a) = \lambda'(\mathbf{P}q, a)$ for each q, a. Thus

$$\mathbf{C}q + \mathbf{D}a = \mathbf{C}'\mathbf{P}q + \mathbf{D}'a \tag{1}$$

$q \equiv \mathbf{P}q$ implies $\delta(q, a) \equiv \delta'(\mathbf{P}q, a)$. Also $\delta(q, a) \equiv \mathbf{P}\delta(q, a)$. By transivity of $\equiv$, we have $\mathbf{P}\delta(q, a) \equiv \delta'(\mathbf{P}q, a)$ and by minimality of M', $\mathbf{P}\delta(q, a) = \delta'(\mathbf{P}q, a)$. That is, for each q, a

$$\mathbf{P}(\mathbf{A}q + \mathbf{B}a) = \mathbf{A}'\mathbf{P}q + \mathbf{B}'a \tag{2}$$

It follows immediately that M is similar to M' by setting $q, a = \mathbf{0}$ in (1) and (2). ∎

THEOREM 2.7. Let $M = \langle F, n, k, l, \mathbf{A}, \mathbf{B}, \mathbf{C}, \mathbf{D} \rangle$ and $M' = \langle F, n', k, l, \mathbf{A}', \mathbf{B}', \mathbf{C}', \mathbf{D}' \rangle$ be equivalent minimal LSM's. M and M' are similar.

Proof. In view of Theorem 2.6, it suffices to show that $n' = n$ and there is a nonsingular matrix $\mathbf{P}$ such that $q \equiv \mathbf{P}q$ for each $q \in F_n$.

It follows that $n = n'$ from Theorem 1.2. For each $i \geq 0$, $\lambda(\mathbf{0}, \mathbf{0}^i) = \mathbf{0}^i = \lambda'(\mathbf{0}, \mathbf{0}^i)$ for each $i \geq 0$. Thus the $\mathbf{0}$ state in M is equivalent to the $\mathbf{0}$ state in M' and no other state in M has this property since M is minimal. Let

$$q_1 = \begin{pmatrix} 1 \\ 0 \\ \cdot \\ \cdot \\ \cdot \\ 0 \end{pmatrix}, \ldots, q_n = \begin{pmatrix} 0 \\ \cdot \\ \cdot \\ \cdot \\ 0 \\ 1 \end{pmatrix}$$

be the natural basis of F_n. Let $q_1', \ldots, q_n'$ be the states of M' such that $q_i \equiv q_i'$ for $1 \leq i \leq n$. For each $i \geq 0$, $1 \leq j \leq n$, $\hat{\lambda}(q_j, \mathbf{0}^i) = \hat{\lambda}'(q_j, \mathbf{0}^i)$. Therefore for each $i \geq 0$, $1 \leq j \leq n$ $\mathbf{CA}^i q_j = \mathbf{C}'(\mathbf{A}')^i q_j$.

Let $\mathbf{P}$ be the matrix whose columns are $q_1', \ldots, q_n'$. If we can show that $\{q_1', \ldots, q_n'\}$ is a basis of F_n, then $\mathbf{P}$ will have rank n and be nonsingular. Suppose $\sum_{i=1}^n c_i q_i' = \mathbf{0}$. By Proposition 2.2, $\sum_i c_i q_i \equiv \sum_i c_i q_i' = \mathbf{0}$. Since $\mathbf{0}$ is the only state in M equivalent to $\mathbf{0}$ in M', we have $\sum_i c_i q_i = \mathbf{0}$ which implies $c_i = 0$ for each i. Thus $\mathbf{P}$ is nonsingular.

Note that

$$\mathbf{CA}^i = \mathbf{CA}^i(q_1 \cdots q_n) = \mathbf{C}'(\mathbf{A}')^i(q_1' \cdots q_n') = \mathbf{C}'(\mathbf{A}')^i\mathbf{P}$$

Thus for each $q \in F_n$, $i \geq 0$, $\mathbf{CA}^i q = \hat{\lambda}(q, \mathbf{0}^i) = \hat{\lambda}'(\mathbf{P}q, \mathbf{0}^i) = \mathbf{C}'(\mathbf{A}')^i\mathbf{P}q$ so that $q \equiv \mathbf{P}q$. The result now follows from Theorem 2.6. ∎

From our results, we can assume that given any LSM, one can find a minimal LSM equivalent to it. Then, by placing $\mathbf{A}$ in rational canonical form, one can show that any minimal LSM can be represented as a collection of feedback shift registers. Still more can be said in the single output case. See Problem 6.

OPEN PROBLEM. Give a formula for the number of non-isomorphic LSM's over $\mathbb{Z}_p$ with the dimension of the state (input) [output space] equal to $n(k)[l]$. A formula is known for the number of nonsimilar machines.

PROBLEMS

1. Let $M = \langle F, n, k, l, \mathbf{A}, \mathbf{B}, \mathbf{C}, \mathbf{D}\rangle$ be an LSM. If $l = 1$ and M' is the minimal form of M, show that $\mathbf{K}_r' = \mathbf{I}$, the $r \times r$ identity matrix.

2. Let $M = \langle F, n, k, l, \mathbf{A}, \mathbf{B}, \mathbf{C}, \mathbf{D} \rangle$ be an LSM and let M' be its minimal form. Show that the first r linearly independent rows of $\mathbf{K}'_r$ are the rows of $\mathbf{I}$ in natural order.

3. A sequential machine $M = \langle Q, \Sigma, \Delta, \delta, \lambda \rangle$ is said to be *analyzable* if there exists $x \in \Sigma^*$ such that for each $q_1, q_2 \in Q$, $\lambda(q_1, x) = \lambda(q_2, x)$ implies $q_1 = q_2$. In other words, there is a sequence x which causes distinct states to produce distinct outputs. Relate this notion to the finiteness conditions discussed in Chapter 1.

4. Show that each minimal LSM is analyzable. (In fact, by the $\mathbf{0}$-sequence of length n.)

5. Show that each minimal LSM with $l = 1$ can be represented as a single shift register whose output is simply the output of one delay unit added to a linear boolean function of the input.

6. A *Moore model* of an LSM is a system $M = \langle F, \mathbf{A}, \mathbf{B}, \mathbf{C}, \delta, \lambda \rangle$ so that $\delta(q, a) = \mathbf{A}q + \mathbf{B}a$ and $\lambda(q) = \mathbf{C}q$. It is well known in sequential machine theory that the Moore model is equivalent to the Mealy model we have defined. Give rules for converting between these two types of LSM's.

3. Finiteness Conditions for LSM's

We shall relate the finiteness conditions of Chapter 1, Section 5, to LSM's. We begin by remarking that all the counterexamples of the previous chapter are LSM's except the one in the proof of Theorem 1.13. We shall explain this now by showing that (3) implies (4) for LSM's.

THEOREM 2.8. For LSM's, finite memory (condition 3) is equivalent to diagnosability (condition 4).

Proof. In view of Theorem 1.13, it suffices to show (3) implies (4). Suppose M is linear and (3) holds. Let $q_1, q_2 \in Q$

and $x \in \Sigma^p\Sigma^*$ and assume that $\lambda(q_1, x) = \lambda(q_2, x)$. Then $\delta(q_1, x) \equiv \delta(q_2, x)$ and for all $y \in \Sigma^*$, $\lambda(\delta(q_1, x), y) = \lambda(\delta(q_2, x), y)$. From this and the assumption that $\lambda(q_1, x) = \lambda(q_2, x)$,

$$\begin{aligned}\lambda(q_1, xy) &= \lambda(q_1, x)\lambda(\delta(q_1, x), y)\\ &= \lambda(q_2, x)\lambda(\delta(q_2, x), y) = \lambda(q_2, xy)\end{aligned}$$

Thus

$$\begin{aligned}\lambda(\mathbf{0}, xy) + \lambda(q_1, \mathbf{0}^{lg(xy)}) &= \lambda(q_1, xy) = \lambda(q_2, xy)\\ &= \lambda(\mathbf{0}, xy) + \lambda(q_2, \mathbf{0}^{lg(xy)})\end{aligned}$$

It follows that

$$\lambda(q_1, \mathbf{0}^i) = \lambda(q_2, \mathbf{0}^i) \qquad \text{for all } i \geq 0.$$

[This is clearly true for $i \geq lg(x)$; it follows for all i from the fact that λ is length preserving.] By the same identity, $\lambda(q_1, z) = \lambda(q_2, z)$ for any $z \in \Sigma^*$. Therefore $q_1 \equiv q_2$. ∎

The notion of "observability" which is discussed in system theory is another term for diagnosability for LSM's.

In Problem 4 of Chapter 1 (Section 5), we indicated that condition (2) does not imply condition (3). We now show that for LSM's the implication is valid.

THEOREM 2.9. Let M be an LSM. If condition (2) is true of M for p then condition (3) is true of M for $p + 1$. There is a finite minimal LSM which satisfies (3) for $p = 2$ but does not satisfy (2) for any $p \geq 1$.

Proof. Let M be an LSM. For each $q \in F_n$, $x \in F_k^pF_k^*$, $\delta(q, x) \equiv \delta(q, x^{(p)})$ since condition (3) holds for p. Thus for each $z \in \Sigma^+$, $\hat{\lambda}(q, xz) = \hat{\lambda}(q, x^{(p)}z)$. Choosing any $x \in \mathbf{0}^p\mathbf{0}^*$ and $z = \mathbf{0}$ gives us

$$\hat{\lambda}(q, \mathbf{0}^{p+1+i}) = \hat{\lambda}(q, \mathbf{0}^{p+1}) \qquad \text{for each } i \geq 0.$$

Now let $q_1, q_2 \in F_n$, $x \in F_k^*F_k^{p+1}$, and $i \in \mathbb{N}$ and assume $\lambda(q_1, x) = \lambda(q_2, x)$ [which implies $\hat{\lambda}(q_1, \mathbf{0}^{p+1}) = \hat{\lambda}(q_2, \mathbf{0}^{p+1+i})$].

Thus, for each $z \in \Sigma^*$

$$\begin{aligned}\hat{\lambda}(q_1, xz) &= \hat{\lambda}(q_1, \mathbf{0}^{lg(xz)}) + \hat{\lambda}(\mathbf{0}, xz)\\ &= \hat{\lambda}(q_2, \mathbf{0}^{lg(xz)}) + \hat{\lambda}(\mathbf{0}, xz)\\ &= \hat{\lambda}(q_2, xz)\end{aligned}$$

Therefore $\delta(q_1, x) \equiv \delta(q_2, x)$ and (3) has been established.

For the counterexample, let $M' = \langle \mathbb{Z}_2, \mathbf{A}, \mathbf{B}, \mathbf{C}, \mathbf{D}\rangle$ where $\mathbf{A} = \begin{bmatrix} 0 & 1 \\ 1 & 0 \end{bmatrix}$, $\mathbf{B} = \begin{bmatrix} 0 \\ 0 \end{bmatrix}$, $\mathbf{C} = (0 \quad 1)$, and $\mathbf{D} = (0)$. M' is a finite memory system, but does not satisfy condition (2) for any $p \geq 1$. ▮

We can now summarize the implications among these conditions for LSM's. We draw a graph with nodes labeled by the conditions. A directed path from i to j means condition (i) implies condition (j).

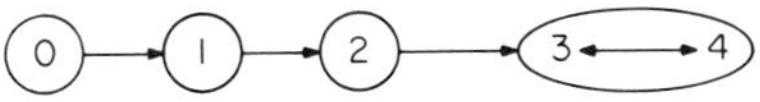

We shall next characterize when LSM's satisfy these conditions. First, we examine the feedback-free condition.

THEOREM 2.10. Let $M = \langle F, \mathbf{A}, \mathbf{B}, \mathbf{C}, \mathbf{D}\rangle$ be an LSM. M is feedback-free (more precisely, satisfies condition (0) for minimal p) if and only if $\mathbf{A}$ is nilpotent of degree p.

Proof. Let $q_1, q_2 \in F_n$ and $x \in F_k^p F_k^*$. Then

$$\delta(q_1, x) = \delta(q_2, x)$$

if and only if

$$\delta(q_1, \mathbf{0}^{lg(x)}) = \delta(q_2, \mathbf{0}^{lg(x)})$$

This holds if and only if

$$\mathbf{A}^{lg(x)} q_1 = \mathbf{A}^{lg(x)} q_2$$

Thus (0) holds (for the minimal p) if and only if $\mathbf{A}$ is nilpotent of degree p. ▮

This theorem gives a canonical form for feedback-free LSM's. See problem 1.

Next, we consider definite LSM's.

THEOREM 2.11. Let $M = \langle F, \mathbf{A}, \mathbf{B}, \mathbf{C}, \mathbf{D} \rangle$ be an LSM. M is definite [i.e., satisfies condition (1) for minimal p] if and only if p is the least positive integer such that $\mathbf{CA}^p = \mathbf{0}$.

Proof. Let $q_1, q_2 \in F_n$, $x \in F_k^p F_k^*$. Condition (1) for p holds if and only if

$$\delta(q_1, x) \equiv \delta(q_2, x)$$

By Lemma 2.2, this holds if and only if

$$\mathbf{CA}^{p+i} q_1 = \mathbf{CA}^{p+i} q_2 \qquad \text{for each } i.$$

In turn, this holds if and only if $\mathbf{CA}^p = \mathbf{0}$. ∎

Next, we characterize condition (2) for LSM's.

THEOREM 2.12. Let $M = \langle F, \mathbf{A}, \mathbf{B}, \mathbf{C}, \mathbf{D} \rangle$ be an LSM. M satisfies condition (2) for p if and only if

(i) $\mathbf{CA}^p = \mathbf{CA}^{p-1}$

and

(ii) $\mathbf{CA}^{p-1}\mathbf{B} = \mathbf{0}$.

Proof. Let $q \in F_n$ and take $x = a_0 \cdots a_{t-1}$ with $t \geq p$. We have that

$$\hat{\lambda}(q, x) = \hat{\lambda}(q, x^{(p)})$$

if and only if

$$\mathbf{CA}^{t-1} q + \sum_{i=0}^{t-2} \mathbf{CA}^{t-i-2} \mathbf{B} a_i + \mathbf{D} a_{t-1}$$
$$= \mathbf{CA}^{p-1} q + \sum_{i=t-p}^{t-2} \mathbf{CA}^{t-i-2} \mathbf{B} a_i + \mathbf{D} a_{t-1}$$

This holds if and only if

(i) $\mathbf{CA}^{p+i-1} = \mathbf{CA}^{p-1}$ for each $i \geq 0$

and

(ii) $\mathbf{CA}^{p-1}\mathbf{B} = \mathbf{0}$.

Since (i) holds if and only if $\mathbf{CA}^p = \mathbf{CA}^{p-1}$, the result follows. ▮

Next, we will show that all LSM's essentially satisfy conditions (3) and (4).

THEOREM 2.13. Let $M = \langle F, \mathbf{A}, \mathbf{B}, \mathbf{C}, \mathbf{D} \rangle$ be an LSM. M has finite memory, i.e., satisfies condition (3) for some $p \leq n$.

Proof. Let $m(x) = d_0 + d_1x + \cdots + d_{p-1}x^{p-1} + x^p$ be the minimal polynomial of $\mathbf{A}$. Suppose $q_1, q_2 \in F_n$ and $x \in F_k^p$ with $\lambda(q_1, x) = \lambda(q_2, x)$. It then follows since $\lambda(q_1, \mathbf{0}^p) = \lambda(q_2, \mathbf{0}^p)$ that

$$(*) \qquad \mathbf{CA}^j q_1 = \mathbf{CA}^j q_2 \qquad \text{for each} \qquad 0 \leq j < p$$

It suffices to prove that $\mathbf{CA}^{p+i} q_1 = \mathbf{CA}^{p+i} q_2$ for all $i \geq 0$. For if this were true and if $z \in \Sigma^*$ with $lg(z) = i$, then

$$\hat{\lambda}(q_1, \mathbf{0}^{lg(xz)}) = \mathbf{CA}^{p+i} q_1 = \mathbf{CA}^{p+i} q_2 = \hat{\lambda}(q_2, \mathbf{0}^{lg(xz)})$$

This in turn implies that for each $z \in \Sigma^*$

$$\hat{\lambda}(q_1, xz) = \hat{\lambda}(q_2, xz)$$

or $\delta(q_1, x) \equiv \delta(q_2, x)$. [Note that we have chosen x of length p. If $lg(x) > p$ then the argument is still valid by the right congruence property of $\equiv$.]

To complete the proof, we must now show that for each $i \geq 0$, $\mathbf{CA}^{p+i} q_1 = \mathbf{CA}^{p+i} q_2$. Because $\mathbf{A}$ has minimal polynomial $m(x)$, we recall (Theorem 0.6) that there exist field elements $d_j(i)$ such that

$$\mathbf{A}^{p+i} = \sum_{0 \leq j < p} d_j(i) \mathbf{A}^i$$

Then

$$\mathbf{CA}^{p+i} = \sum_{0 \leq j < p} d_j(i) \mathbf{CA}^j \qquad (*)$$

We have that

$$\mathbf{CA}^{p+i} q_1 = \sum_{0 \leq j < p} d_j(i) \mathbf{CA}^j q_1 = \sum_{0 \leq j < p} d_j(i) \mathbf{CA}^j q_2 = \mathbf{CA}^{p+i} q_2$$

by use of (*). $p \leq n$ because the degree of the minimal polynomial is at most n, the degree of the characteristic polynomial. The proof is complete. ▮

The last result of this section will show that each LSM is diagnosable.

THEOREM 2.14. Every LSM is diagnosable (i.e., satisfies condition (4) for some $p \leq n$).

Proof. The argument follows from Theorem 2.13 and Theorem 2.8. ▮

PROBLEMS

1. Show that every feedback-free linear circuit is an equivalent to a collection of unconnected shift registers without feedback paths. (Use a canonical form.)

2. Let M be an LSM. Show that a necessary and sufficient condition for M to satisfy condition (2) for minimal p is

(i) $\mathbf{CA}^p = \mathbf{CA}^{p-1}$
(ii) $\mathbf{CA}^{p-1}\mathbf{B} = \mathbf{0}$
(iii) $\mathbf{CA}^{p-1} = \mathbf{CA}^{p-2}$

Show that all these conditions are independent in the sense that no two of the conditions imply the third.

3. Give a direct proof of Theorem 2.12.

4. Controllability and LSM's with Initial States

We introduce the concept of controllability next. It will turn out that LSM's which are controllable are strongly connected and conversely. This concept is more important for continuous systems [39] where there are relations to stability theory.

DEFINITION. A sequential machine $M = \langle Q, \Sigma, \Delta, \delta, \lambda \rangle$ is said to be *p-controllable* if for each $q, q' \in Q$ there exists $x \in \Sigma^p$ so that $\delta(q, x) = q'$. M is *controllable* if it is p-controllable for some p.

In other words, M is p-controllable if any state of M is reachable from any other state by a sequence of length p.

It is clear that any p-controllable sequential machine is strongly connected but not conversely as the following example shows.

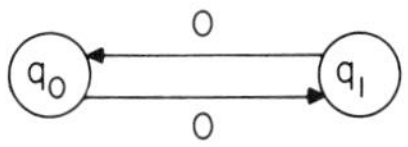

There is no way to get both from q_0 to q_0 and from q_0 to q_1 in k steps for any k.

NOTATION. Let $M = \langle F, \mathbf{A}, \mathbf{B}, \mathbf{C}, \mathbf{D} \rangle$ be an LSM. For each $i \geq 1$, define

$$\mathbf{L}_i = (\mathbf{A}^{i-1}\mathbf{B}, \mathbf{A}^{i-2}\mathbf{B}, \ldots, \mathbf{AB}, \mathbf{B}).$$

The construction of $\mathbf{L}_i$ is very similar to that of $\mathbf{K}_i$. We list, without proof, some of the properties of $\mathbf{L}_i$.

(i) $\mathbf{L}_i$ has n rows and ik columns.

(ii) If the degree of the minimum polynomial of $\mathbf{A}$ is p, then* col $(\mathbf{L}_p)$ = col $(\mathbf{L}_{p+1}) = \cdots =$ col $(\mathbf{L}_n)$ and rank $\mathbf{L}_p$ = rank $\mathbf{L}_{p+1} = \cdots =$ rank $\mathbf{L}_n$.

(iii) If p is as in (ii), then col $\mathbf{L}_p$ = col $\mathbf{L}_n$ is an $\mathbf{A}$-invariant subspace.

(iv) $\mathbf{L}_n y' = q$ where $y' = \begin{bmatrix} a_0 \\ \cdot \\ \cdot \\ \cdot \\ a_{n-1} \end{bmatrix}$, $a_i \in F_k$ if and only if

$$\delta(\mathbf{0}, y) = q \text{ where } y = a_0 \cdots a_{n-1}.$$

* For any matrix $\mathbf{L}$, col $\mathbf{L}$ denotes the column space of $\mathbf{L}$.

Before characterizing controllable LSM's, we prove the following lemma.

LEMMA 2.5. Let $\mathbf{L}$ be an $n \times p$ matrix over F. For each $v' \in F_n$, there exists $v \in F_p$, such that $v' = \mathbf{L}v$ if and only if rank $\mathbf{L} = n$.

Proof. The condition is that the linear transformation described by $\mathbf{L}$ is all of F_n (i.e., the range has dimension n). This holds if and only if rank $\mathbf{L} = n$. ∎

We now give a necessary and sufficient condition for an LSM to be controllable.

THEOREM 2.15. Let $M = \langle F, \mathbf{A}, \mathbf{B}, \mathbf{C}, \mathbf{D} \rangle$ be an LSM. M is p-controllable if and only if rank $\mathbf{L}_p = n$. If F is computable, one can effectively decide if M is controllable.

Proof. For each $q_1, q_2 \in F_n$, there exists $x = a_0 \cdots a_{p-1} \in F_k^p$ such that $\delta(q_1, x) = q_2$ if and only if

$$q_2 = \mathbf{A}^p q_1 + \sum_{i=0}^{p-1} \mathbf{A}^{p-i-1} \mathbf{B} a_i$$

This holds if and only if

$$q_2 - \mathbf{A}^p q_1 = \mathbf{L}_p x' \tag{1}$$

where $x' = \begin{bmatrix} a_0 \\ \cdot \\ \cdot \\ \cdot \\ a_{p-1} \end{bmatrix}$. Since q_1 and q_2 are arbitrary, M is controllable if and only if for each q there exists $y \in F_k^p$ so that

$$q = \mathbf{L}_p y'$$

By Lemma 2.5, this holds if and only if rank $\mathbf{L}_p = n$. ∎

COROLLARY 1. Let M be an LSM. If M is p-controllable and $q \geq p$, then M is q-controllable.

Proof. rank $\mathbf{L}_p$ = rank $\mathbf{L}_q = n$. ∎

COROLLARY 2. Let $M = \langle F, n, k, l, \mathbf{A}, \mathbf{B}, \mathbf{C}, \mathbf{D} \rangle$ be an LSM. If M is p-controllable then M is m-controllable and n-controllable where m is the degree of the minimum polynomial of $\mathbf{A}$.

Proof. See the properties of $\mathbf{L}_i$. ∎

COROLLARY 3. An LSM $M = \langle F, n, k, l, A, B, C, D \rangle$ is controllable if and only if M is n-controllable.

We now show that an LSM is strongly connected if and only if it is controllable.

THEOREM 2.16. Let $M = \langle F, n, k, l, \mathbf{A}, \mathbf{B}, \mathbf{C}, \mathbf{D} \rangle$ be an LSM. M is strongly connected if and only if M is controllable.

Proof. Suppose M is strongly connected. First we will show that for each $q \in F_n$, there exists $x_q \in F_k^n$ so that $\delta(q, x_q) = \mathbf{0}$. This follows since M is strongly connected, we must have $\delta(\mathbf{0}, z) = q$ for some $z \in F_k^i$. Thus $q \in \text{col } \mathbf{L}_i \subseteq \text{col } \mathbf{L}_n$ (even when $i > n$). Since col $\mathbf{L}_n$ is an $\mathbf{A}$-invariant subspace, we also have $-\mathbf{A}_q^n \in \text{col } \mathbf{L}_n$ or $\mathbf{0} = \mathbf{A}_q^n \vdash \mathbf{L}_n x_q'$. Therefore $\delta(q, x_q) = \mathbf{0}$ and $lg(x_q) = n$.

By an analogous argument whose proof we omit, we can show that for each $q' \in F_n$, there exists $y_{q'} \in F_k^n$ so that $\delta(\mathbf{0}, y_{q'}) = q'$. Now let $p = 2n$.

We claim that M is p-controllable. Choose $q, q' \in F_n$. Let $z = x_q \mathbf{0}^r y_{q'}$ where $r = p - lg(x_q) - lg(y_{q'})$ and note that $lg(z) = p$.

$$\begin{aligned}\delta(q, z) &= \delta(\delta(q, x_q), \mathbf{0}^r y_{q'}) \\ &= \delta(\mathbf{0}, \mathbf{0}^r y_{q'}) = \delta(\delta(\mathbf{0}, \mathbf{0}^r), y_{q'}) \\ &= \delta(\mathbf{0}, y_{q'}) = q'. \ ∎\end{aligned}$$

It is often convenient to associate an initial state q_0 with a sequential machine. The formalism becomes $M = \langle Q, \Sigma, \Delta, \delta, \lambda, q_0\rangle$ where $q_0 \in Q$ and everything else has its customary meaning. In this case, $F(M) = \{\lambda_{q_0}\}$ is one function.

DEFINITION. A sequential machine with initial state $M = \langle Q, \Sigma, \Delta, \delta, \lambda, q_0\rangle$ is said to be *connected* if for each $q \in Q$ there is some $x \in \Sigma^*$ such that $\delta(q_0, x) = q$.

If M is any sequential machine with initial state, then one can form a connected submachine by deleting the states not reachable from q_0. This is done in detail in [22] for the finite case.

The situation is somewhat different for LSM's. Due to the constraints of linearity, arbitrary starting states are not usually encountered. The most common case is when an LSM is started in the $\mathbf{0}$ state. Since $q = \delta(\mathbf{0}, x)$ and $q' = \delta(\mathbf{0}, y)$ implies† $q + cq' = \delta(\mathbf{0}, x + cy)$, we have the connected submachine of M with initial state $\mathbf{0}$ is also an LSM. Let M_0 denote the connected submachine with initial state $\mathbf{0}$.

We remark in passing that M_0 can be effectively constructed from M if the field is computable (see problem 5).

THEOREM 2.17. Let $M = \langle F, n, k, l, \mathbf{A}, \mathbf{B}, \mathbf{C}, \mathbf{D}\rangle$ be an LSM with $q \in F_n$. If there is $x \in F_k^*$ so that $\delta(\mathbf{0}, x) = q$ then there exists $y \in F_k^*$ so that $\delta(q, y) = \mathbf{0}$.

Proof. There is a least positive integer p so that rank $\mathbf{L}_p$ = rank $\mathbf{L}_{p+1} = \cdots =$ rank $\mathbf{L}_n$. If $q = \delta(\mathbf{0}, x)$, then $q \in$ col $\mathbf{L}_p$. Because col $\mathbf{L}_p$ is an $\mathbf{A}$ invariant subspace (cf property (iii) of $\mathbf{L}_i$), we have that $\mathbf{A}^p q \in \text{col}\,(\mathbf{A}^p\mathbf{L}_p) = \text{col}\,\mathbf{L}_p$. Therefore, $-\mathbf{A}^p q \in \text{col}\,\mathbf{L}_p$ so that

$$\mathbf{0} - \mathbf{A}^p q = \mathbf{L}_p y'$$

† To be complete, assume $lg(x) = lg(y)$. Otherwise, if $r = lg(x) - lg(y) > 0$, replace y by $\mathbf{0}^r y$.

for some $y' = \begin{bmatrix} a_0 \\ \cdot \\ \cdot \\ \cdot \\ a_{p-1} \end{bmatrix}$ with $a_i \in F_k$. By property (iv) of $\mathbf{L}_p$,

$$\delta(q, y) = \mathbf{0}$$

where $y = a_0 \cdots a_{p-1}$. ▮

It is important to note that the converse of Theorem 2.17 is false. For a counterexample, take $\mathbf{A} = \mathbf{B} = (0)$. In continuous systems, the converse is valid and so this is a case in which the continuous and discrete theories are different.

COROLLARY. Let $M = \langle F, n', k, l, \mathbf{A}', \mathbf{B}', \mathbf{C}', \mathbf{D}' \rangle$ be an LSM. The submachine M_0 is a strongly connected (equivalently controllable) LSM.

Proof. By construction $M_0 = \langle F, n, k, l, \mathbf{A}, \mathbf{B}, \mathbf{C}, \mathbf{D} \rangle$ is connected. Let $q, q' \in F_n$ and suppose $\delta(q, x) = \mathbf{0}$ and $\delta(\mathbf{0}, y) = q'$. [$x$ exists by the theorem and y by connectivity of M_0.] Let $p = \max \{lg(x), lg(y)\}$. Define $x' = x\mathbf{0}^{p-lg(x)}$ and $y' = \mathbf{0}^{p-lg(y)}y$. Clearly $lg(x') = lg(y') = p$. Moreover $\delta(q, x) = \delta(q, x') = \mathbf{0}$ and $\delta(\mathbf{0}, y) = \delta(\mathbf{0}, y') = q'$. Finally $\delta(q, x' + y') = \delta(q, x') + \delta(\mathbf{0}, y') = \mathbf{0} + q' = q'$. Thus M_0 is strongly connected. ▮

Next, it is shown that these notions can be applied to produce a decomposition of the state space of an LSM.

DEFINITION. Let $M = \langle F, n, k, l, \delta, \lambda \rangle$ be an LSM. $q \in F_n$ is said to be *controllable* if $\delta(q, x) = \mathbf{0}$ for some $x \in F_k^*$. A state $q \in F_n$ is said to be *unobservable* if $q \equiv \mathbf{0}$.

We have already seen that the set of unobservable states is a subspace U of F_n (see Lemma 2.2). The same is also true of the set of controllable states.

PROPOSITION 2.3. Let $M = \langle F, n, k, l, \delta, \lambda \rangle$ be an LSM. The set $K = \{q \mid q \in F_n \text{ is controllable}\}$ is a subspace.

Proof. Let q, $q' \in F_n$. Then there exist x, $y \in F_k^*$ so that $\delta(q, x) = \mathbf{0}$ and $\delta(q, y) = \mathbf{0}$. Let $p = \max\{lg(x), lg(y)\}$ and $x' = x\mathbf{0}^{p-lg(x)}$ and $y' = y\mathbf{0}^{p-lg(y)}$. Then $lg(x') = lg(y') = p$. For any $c \in F$,

$$\delta(q + cq', x' + y') = \delta(q, x') + c\delta(q', y') = \mathbf{0}. \blacksquare$$

We now proceed to give a decomposition of F_n.

DEFINITION. Let M be an LSM with state space F_n. Let K and U be as above. Define V_1, V_2, V_3, V_4 by

$$V_1 = K \cap U$$
$$K = V_1 \oplus V_2$$
$$U = V_1 \oplus V_3$$
$$F_n = V_1 \oplus V_2 \oplus V_3 \oplus V_4$$

Note that M determines (uniquely) the vector spaces, K, U, and V_1. The subspaces V_2, V_3, and V_4 are not in general unique.

The point of this decomposition should now be clear. F_n is split into four pieces, $F_n = V_1 \oplus V_2 \oplus V_3 \oplus V_4$ such that

(i) V_1 is the set of states which are controllable but unobservable.
(ii) V_2 consists of states which are controllable and observable.
(iii) V_3 consists of states which are unobservable and uncontrollable.
(iv) V_4 consists of states which are uncontrollable and observable.

Next, we check these spaces for invariance under $\mathbf{A}$.

PROPOSITION 2.4. Let $M = \langle F, n, k, l, \mathbf{A}, \mathbf{B}, \mathbf{C}, \mathbf{D}\rangle$ be an LSM whose state space is decomposed as above. Then each of the subspaces U, K, and V_1 are $\mathbf{A}$ invariant.

Proof. U is $\mathbf{A}$-invariant because $\equiv$ is a right congruence. If $q \in K$, then $\delta(q, x) = \mathbf{0}$ for some $x \in F_k^*$ with $lg(x) = r$. Then $\mathbf{0} = \mathbf{A}^r q + \mathbf{L}_r x'$. This yields $-\mathbf{A}^r q = \mathbf{L}_r x'$ or $-\mathbf{A}^r q \in \operatorname{col} \mathbf{L}_r \subseteq \operatorname{col} \mathbf{L}_n$. But then $-\mathbf{A}^{r+1} q \in \operatorname{col} \mathbf{L}_n$ since $\operatorname{col} \mathbf{L}_n$ is $\mathbf{A}$-invariant. Therefore if $r \geq n$

$$\mathbf{0} = \mathbf{A}^r(\mathbf{A}q) + \mathbf{L}_r y'$$

and $\delta(\mathbf{A}q, y) = \mathbf{0}$.

If $r < n$, $-\mathbf{A}^r q \in \operatorname{col} \mathbf{L}_r$ implies $-\mathbf{A}^{n+1} q \in \operatorname{col} \mathbf{L}_n$ so that

$$\mathbf{0} = \mathbf{A}^n(\mathbf{A}q) + \mathbf{L}_n z'$$

which implies that $\delta(\mathbf{A}q, z) = \mathbf{0}$.

Finally V_1 is $\mathbf{A}$-invariant since both U and K are. ∎

We now recall a simple lemma from linear algebra.

LEMMA 2.6. Let α be a linear transformation on a vector space V of dimension n. If V_1 is a subspace of dimension k which is α-invariant and $V = V_1 \oplus V_2$, then α can be represented by a matrix $\mathbf{A}$ where

$$\mathbf{A} = \begin{bmatrix} \mathbf{P} & \mathbf{Q} \\ \mathbf{0} & \mathbf{R} \end{bmatrix}$$

where $\mathbf{P}$ is $k \times k$, $\mathbf{Q}$ is $k \times (n - k)$ and $\mathbf{R}$ is $(n - k) \times (n - k)$.

Proof. Let $\{v_1, \ldots, v_k\}$ be a basis of V_1 and $\{v_{k+1}, \ldots, v_n\}$ a basis of V_2. Since $V = V_1 \oplus V_2$, $\{v_1, \ldots, v_n\}$ is a basis of V. If $v \in V_1$ then $v\alpha \in V_1$ which implies that the (2, 1) submatrix is $\mathbf{0}$. ∎

We now give the decomposition theorem associated with controllable states.

THEOREM 2.18. Let $M = \langle F, \mathbf{A}, \mathbf{B}, \mathbf{C}, \mathbf{D} \rangle$ be an LSM. The state space of M can be decomposed into a direct sum of four spaces. That is $M \equiv M' = \langle F, \mathbf{A}', \mathbf{B}', \mathbf{C}', \mathbf{D}' \rangle$ where

$$\mathbf{A}' = \begin{bmatrix} \mathbf{A}_{11} & \mathbf{A}_{12} & \mathbf{A}_{13} & \mathbf{A}_{14} \\ \mathbf{0} & \mathbf{A}_{22} & \mathbf{0} & \mathbf{A}_{24} \\ \mathbf{0} & \mathbf{0} & \mathbf{A}_{33} & \mathbf{A}_{34} \\ \mathbf{0} & \mathbf{0} & \mathbf{0} & \mathbf{A}_{44} \end{bmatrix}$$

$$\mathbf{B}' = \begin{bmatrix} \mathbf{B}_1 \\ \mathbf{B}_2 \\ \mathbf{0} \\ \mathbf{0} \end{bmatrix} \qquad \mathbf{C}' = [\mathbf{0} \quad \mathbf{C}_2 \quad \mathbf{0} \quad \mathbf{C}_4]$$

$$\mathbf{D}' = \mathbf{D}.$$

Proof. One chooses a basis for F_n by taking the union of the bases for the subspaces. Next we check the pattern of zero submatrices.

$$\lambda(q, a) = \mathbf{C} \begin{bmatrix} q_1 \\ q_2 \\ q_3 \\ q_4 \end{bmatrix} + \mathbf{D}a$$

$$= \mathbf{D}a + \mathbf{C}_1 q_2 + \mathbf{C}_2 q_2 + \mathbf{C}_3 q_3 + \mathbf{C}_4 q_4$$

But states in V_1 or V_3 which are unobservable give only a zero output so that

$$\lambda'(q, a) = \mathbf{C}'q + \mathbf{D}'a = \lambda(q, a)$$

The argument for $\delta(q, a)$ is similar. Since $K = V_1 \oplus V_2$ is $\mathbf{A}$-invariant, we have (by Lemma 2.6) that $\mathbf{A}_{31}$, $\mathbf{A}_{32}$, $\mathbf{A}_{41}$, and $\mathbf{A}_{42}$ are all zero matrices. Since $U = V_1 \oplus V_3$ is $\mathbf{A}$-invariant, it follows that $\mathbf{A}_{21}$, $\mathbf{A}_{23}$, $\mathbf{A}_{41}$, and $\mathbf{A}_{43}$ are also zero matrices.

To see that $\mathbf{B}_3$ and $\mathbf{B}_4$ are zero, suppose the contrary. Let $q = \delta(\mathbf{0}, a)$ where

$$q = \mathbf{B}a = \begin{bmatrix} \mathbf{B}_1 a \\ \mathbf{B}_2 a \\ \mathbf{B}_3 a \\ \mathbf{B}_4 a \end{bmatrix}$$

and a is chosen so that $\mathbf{B}_3 a \neq \mathbf{0}$ or $\mathbf{B}_4 a \neq \mathbf{0}$. q is a controllable state (by Theorem 2.17). But then $q \in V_1 \oplus V_2$ which means that

$$q = \begin{bmatrix} q_1 \\ q_2 \\ \mathbf{0} \\ \mathbf{0} \end{bmatrix}$$

This contradicts that $\mathbf{B}_3 a \neq \mathbf{0}$ or $\mathbf{B}_4 a \neq 0$. ▮

PROBLEMS

1. Let $M = \langle F, n, 1, l, \mathbf{A}, \mathbf{B}, \mathbf{C}, \mathbf{D} \rangle$ be an LSM with one input terminal. Show that M is controllable if and only if $\mathbf{L}_n$ is nonsingular. Moreover the least such p for which M is p-controllable must be n.

2. Is the proof of Theorem 2.16 constructive?

3. Let $M = \langle F, \mathbf{A}, \mathbf{B}, \mathbf{C}, \mathbf{D} \rangle$ be an LSM. Show that if rank $\mathbf{B} = n$ then M is 1-controllable.

4. Let $M = \langle F, \mathbf{A}, \mathbf{B}, \mathbf{C}, \mathbf{D} \rangle$ be a controllable LSM. Show that if rank $\mathbf{B} = 1$ then $\mathbf{A}$ describes a cyclic transformation. Is the converse true?

5. Let M be an LSM. Give an effective construction (assuming the computability of F) of M_0. Can you say more if $k = 1$ (the single input case)?

6. Let M be any sequential machine and M_q the connected submachine with initial state q. Let α_q be the map which takes M into M_q. Show that if M_i are sequential machines with q_i in M_i then $q_1 \equiv q_2$ implies $\alpha_{q_1} M_1$ is isomorphic to $\alpha_{q_2} M_2$. Moreover, show that if μ is the map which carries M onto its minimal form, then $\alpha_q \mu = \mu \alpha_q$. In other words, it does not matter which simplification process is applied first.

7. Let $M = \langle F, n, k, l, \delta, \lambda \rangle$ be an LSM and let P be a one place predicate such that either V_P or $V_{\sim P}$ is a subspace of F_n where

$$V_P = \{q \mid Pq\} \qquad \text{and} \qquad V_{\sim P} = \{q \mid \text{not } Pq\}.$$

Let Q be another predicate with the same "subspace property." Show that every LSM possesses a decomposition of F_n into four subspaces which can be identified with states which have

(i) properties P and Q.
(ii) property P but not property Q.
(iii) property Q but not property P.
(iv) neither property P nor property Q.

Does Theorem 2.18 hold for all such decompositions?

Chapter 3

Relations and Decision Problems for LSM's

In this chapter, the input-output relations of LSM's are explored. A basic connection between these relations and minimality is established in Section 1. In Section 2, it is shown that for LSM's, relational equivalence implies functional equivalence. The rest of this chapter is devoted to the formulation of decision questions for LSM's. It is shown that one can decide of two LSM's whether or not they are equivalent. Other decision results are derived.

1. Input-Output Relations of LSM's

In this section, we establish an interesting property of the relations of LSM's with a single input and output. We shall show that minimal LSM's of dimension n have relations which contain all input-output sequences of length n but not length $n + 1$. The least such n is the state dimension of the minimal machine of M.

We begin with a theorem that relates this property to $\mathbf{K}_i$ of Chapter 2, Section 3.

THEOREM 3.1. Let $M = \langle F, n, 1, 1, \mathbf{A}, \mathbf{B}, \mathbf{C}, \mathbf{D} \rangle$ be an LSM. $(F \times F)^n \subseteq R(M)$ if and only if rank $\mathbf{K}_n = n$ where

$$\mathbf{K}_n = \begin{bmatrix} \mathbf{C} \\ \mathbf{CA} \\ \cdot \\ \cdot \\ \cdot \\ \mathbf{CA}^{n-1} \end{bmatrix}$$

Proof. Let $(x, y) \in (F \times F)^n$, $(x, y) \in R(M)$ if and only if $\lambda(q, x) = y$ for some $q \in F_n$. This holds, if and only if

$$\lambda(q, x) = \lambda(q, \mathbf{0}^n) + \lambda(\mathbf{0}, x) \qquad \text{for some } q \in F_n.$$

Thus, $(x, y) \in R(M)$ if and only if $\lambda(q, \mathbf{0}^n) = y - \lambda(\mathbf{0}, x) = z$ for some $q \in F_n$. Since x and y are arbitrary elements of F^n, the condition becomes that for each $z \in F^n$ there exists $q \in F_n$ such that

$$\lambda(q, \mathbf{0}^n) = z \qquad \text{and} \qquad z' = \mathbf{K}_n q \qquad \text{where if } z = b_0 \cdots b_{n-1},$$

then

$$z' = \begin{bmatrix} b_0 \\ \cdot \\ \cdot \\ \cdot \\ b_{n-1} \end{bmatrix}$$

This holds if and only if rank $\mathbf{K}_n = n'$ by Lemma 2.5. ∎

COROLLARY. Let $M = \langle F, n, 1, 1, \delta, \lambda \rangle$ be an LSM. $(F \times F)^{n+1} \nsubseteq R(M)$.

Proof. Suppose $(F \times F)^{n+1} \subseteq R(M)$. Then rank $\mathbf{K}_{n+1} = n + 1$ which is impossible since $\mathbf{K}_{n+1}$ has only n columns. ∎

Now we state and prove the main theorem of this section.

THEOREM 3.2. Let M be an LSM and let n be the dimension of the state space of the minimal form of M. Then $(F \times F)^n \subseteq R(M)$ and $(F \times F)^{n+1} \nsubseteq R(M)$.

Proof. Let M be an LSM and M' be its minimal form. Since $M \equiv M'$, $R(M) = R(M')$ and n is the dimension of the state space of M'. Since M' is minimal, rank $\mathbf{K}'_n = n$ by Proposition 2.1. It now follows from Theorem 3.1, its corollary and $R(M') = R(M)$ that

$$(F \times F)^n \subseteq R(M) \qquad \text{and} \qquad (F \times F)^{n+1} \nsubseteq R(M). \quad \blacksquare$$

This theorem is one of the few results known concerning the structure of the relation of an LSM.

OPEN PROBLEM. Give necessary and sufficient conditions for a relation (function) to be the relation (function) of an LSM.

In the finite case, there is the following problem.

OPEN PROBLEM. Let M be a finite LSM. Characterize the behavior (relation) of M as a regular (transduction) expression.

Another important open problem is the following.

OPEN PROBLEM. Give necessary and sufficient conditions for a monoid to be the monoid of an LSM.

PROBLEMS

1. Let $M = \langle F, n, 1, 1, \delta, \lambda \rangle$ be an LSM. Show that M is minimal if and only if $\bigcup_{i=0}^{n} (F \times F)^i \subseteq R(M)$ and $(F \times F)^{n+1} \nsubseteq R(M)$.

2. Show by an example that Theorem 3.2 is not valid for LSM's with $k > 1$ and $l > 1$.

3. Is Theorem 3.2 valid for LSM's with $k > 1$ and $l = 1$?

2. Relational Equivalence Implies Functional Equivalence for LSM's

We have already seen that relational equivalence does not imply functional equivalence for sequential machines in general. It is very interesting that this implication is valid for LSM's. This result supports our view that the input-output relation is an important way of specifying a sequential machine.

We begin with a simple lemma concerning finite memory machines. No assumption of finiteness of the state set is used.

LEMMA 3.1. Let $M_i = \langle Q_i, \Sigma, \Delta, \delta_i, \lambda_i \rangle, i = 1, 2$, be sequential machines. Let M_2 have finite memory p. If $R(M_1) = R(M_2)$ and if there exist $q_1 \in Q_1$, $q_2 \in Q_2$, and, $x \in \Sigma^p\Sigma^*$ such that $\lambda_1(q_1, x) = \lambda_2(q_2, x)$, then $\delta_1(q_1, x) \equiv \delta_2(q_2, x)$.

Proof. Let q_1, q_2, x satisfy the hypothesis of the lemma and suppose that $\delta_1(q_1, x) \not\equiv \delta_2(q_2, x)$. Then $\lambda_1(\delta_1(q_1, x), z) \neq \lambda_2(\delta_2(q_2, x), z)$ for some $z \in \Sigma^*$. Thus

$$\lambda_1(q_1, xz) \neq \lambda_2(q_2, xz) \tag{1}$$

Since $(xz, \lambda_1(q_1, xz)) \in R(M_1)$ and $R(M_1) = R(M_2)$, we have

$$\lambda_1(q_1, xz) = \lambda_2(q_2', xz) \tag{2}$$

for some $q_2' \in Q_2$. Thus $\lambda_1(q_1, x) = \lambda_2(q_2', x)$. By hypothesis, $\lambda_1(q_1, x) = \lambda_2(q_2, x)$ and therefore $\lambda_2(q_2, x) = \lambda_2(q_2', x)$. Since $lg(x) \geq p$ and M_2 has finite memory,

$$\delta_2(q_2, x) \equiv \delta_2(q_2', x)$$

But this and $\lambda_2(q_2, x) = \lambda_2(q_2', x)$ imply that

$$\lambda_2(q_2, xz) = \lambda_2(q_2', xz)$$

From (2)

$$\lambda_1(q_1, xz) = \lambda_2(q_2, xz)$$

But this contradicts (1) and proves the lemma. ▮

The next lemma is required to show that two relationally equivalent LSM's have a pair of equivalent states.

LEMMA 3.2. Let $M_i = \langle Q_i, \Sigma, \Delta, \delta_i, \lambda_i \rangle$ be LSM's for $i = 1, 2$. If $R(M_1) = R(M_2)$, then there exist $q \in Q_1$ and $q' \in Q_2$ such that $q \equiv q'$.

Proof. Since M_2 is linear, it has finite memory p for some p. Choose $q_1 \in Q_1$, and any positive integer $t > p$. Since $R(M_1) = R(M_2)$,

$$\lambda_1(q_1, \mathbf{0}^t) = \lambda_2(q_2, \mathbf{0}^t)$$

for some $q_2 \in Q_2$. By Lemma 3.1,

$$\delta_1(q_1, \mathbf{0}^t) \equiv \delta_2(q_2, \mathbf{0}^t).$$

Let $q = \delta_1(q_1, \mathbf{0}^t)$ and $q' = \delta_2(q_2, \mathbf{0}^t)$ and the proof is complete. ∎

We now prove the main theorem of this section which relates functional equivalence and relational equivalence for LSM's.

THEOREM 3.3. Let $M_i = \langle Q_i, \Sigma, \Delta, \delta_i, \lambda_i \rangle$ be LSM's for $i = 1, 2$. If $R(M_1) = R(M_2)$, then $F(M_1) = F(M_2)$.

Proof. If M_1 and M_2 are relationally equivalent, there is no loss in generality in assuming that they are minimal. We shall show that M_1 is isomorphic to M_2. Let p_1 and p_2 be their finite memories respectively. By Lemma 3.2, there exist $q_1 \in Q_1$ and $q_2 \in Q_2$ such that $q_1 \equiv q_2$.

Our first step is to show that the zero-states in M_1 and M_2 are equivalent. Since $q_1 \equiv q_2$,

$$\lambda_1(q_1, x) = \lambda_2(q_2, x)$$

for each $x \in \Sigma^*$. Therefore

$$\lambda_1(\mathbf{0}, x) + \lambda_1(q_1, \mathbf{0}^{lg(x)}) = \lambda_2(\mathbf{0}, x) + \lambda_2(q_2, \mathbf{0}^{lg(x)})$$

Since $\lambda_1(q_1, \mathbf{0}^{lg(x)}) = \lambda_2(q_2, \mathbf{0}^{lg(x)})$, we have

$$\lambda_1(\mathbf{0}, x) = \lambda_2(\mathbf{0}, x) \tag{1}$$

and we have shown that the zero-states of the respective machines are equivalent.

Next, we show that for each $q_1' \in Q_1$, there is a state $q_2' \in Q_2$ since that $q_1' \equiv q_2'$. Let $q_1' \in Q_1$ and choose $p > \max\{p_1, p_2\}$. Since $R(M_1) = R(M_2)$, there exists $q_2' \in Q_2$ such that

$$\lambda_1(q_1', \mathbf{0}^p) = \lambda_2(q_2', \mathbf{0}^p)$$

By Lemma 3.1

$$\delta_1(q_1', \mathbf{0}^p) \equiv \delta_2(q_2', \mathbf{0}^p)$$

so that for each i,

$$\lambda_1(q_1', \mathbf{0}^i) = \lambda_2(q_2', \mathbf{0}^i)$$

Using this fact and (1), we have for each $x \in \Sigma^*$

$$\lambda_1(q_1', \mathbf{0}^{lg(x)}) + \lambda_1(\mathbf{0}, x) = \lambda_2(q_2', \mathbf{0}^{lg(x)}) + \lambda_2(\mathbf{0}, x)$$

Therefore $\lambda_1(q_1', x) = \lambda_2(q_2', x)$ for each x and thus

$$q_1' \equiv q_2'.$$

Select $q_2 \in Q_2$ and since the hypotheses are symmetric with respect to M_1 and M_2, one can find $q_1 \in Q_1$ such that $q_1 \equiv q_2$.

Thus $M_1 \equiv M_2$ and $F(M_1) = F(M_2)$. ▮

COROLLARY. If M_1 and M_2 are minimal relationally equivalent LSM's, then M_1 is isomorphic to M_2.

PROBLEMS

1. Prove the following assertion.

PROPOSITION. Let M_1 and M_2 be minimal LSM's such that $R(M_1) = R(M_2)$. If $\varphi = \equiv \subseteq Q_1 \times Q_2$ where Q_i is the state set of M_i, then

(a) φ is a function
(b) φ is one-to-one
(c) φ in onto
(d) φ is linear
(e) $\lambda_1(q, a) = \lambda_2(\varphi q, a)$ for each $(q, a) \in F_{n_1} \times F_k$
(f) $\varphi\delta_1(q, a) = \delta_2(\varphi q, a)$ for each $(q, a) \in F_{n_1} \times F_k$

2. Prove that if M_1 and M_2 are LSM's (not necessarily minimal) with $R(M_1) = R(M_2)$, then there is a homomorphism of M_1 into M_2 and vice versa. Can you assume that the homomorphisms are linear?

3. Decidability and Computable Fields

In the theory of finite automata, there are many natural decision questions. One can provide algorithms for the solution of many of these problems. Informally, an algorithm is a procedure or recipe for carrying out a process. Each step in the procedure is sufficiently simple that it can be carried out mechanically. A familiar example is the method for adding two natural numbers expressed in their decimal expansions. An example of a non-algorithm is the following set of directions to a motorist. "Go straight down this road and turn left after crossing the last bridge."

Formally, one identifies algorithms with recursive functions or Turing machines. We will assume that the reader has had some exposure to this theory in what follows. For those without this background, the results will be stated in such a way that one can use one's intuition about algorithms.

In order to consider decision problems for LSM's, we must first ask, "What is a computable field?" To do this, we need to ask in what manner the field is given. For instance, the usual constructions of the real numbers render them algorithmically intractable. We must somehow restrict the range of fields to be used. The following definition is due to Rabin [32] and identifies a class of fields for which this sort of theory has meaning.

DEFINITION. An *indexing* of a set S is a one-to-one mapping i of S into the positive integers such that $i(S)$ is a recursive set.* Let $F = \langle F, +, \cdot, 0, 1 \rangle$ be a field. An indexing i of F is said to be *admissible* if both the corresponding addition function $s(j, k)$ [defined by $a_j + a_k = a_{s(j,k)}$] and the multiplication function $m(j, k)$ [given by $a_j \cdot a_k = a_{m(j,k)}$] are computable functions from $i(F) \times i(F)$ into $i(F)$. A field F is *computable* if it has at least one admissible indexing.

EXAMPLES. Clearly, each finite field is computable. Of course, the real field $\mathbb{R}$ and the complex field $\mathbb{C}$ are not computable since they are too "big." The field $\mathbb{Q}$ of rational numbers is a computable field also.

Note that an effective description of a field F consists of three computable functions

(i) A computable function f so that $f(n) = 1$ if $n \in i(F)$ and 0 otherwise.
(ii) A computable function s (for $+$).
(iii) A computable function m (for $\cdot$).

Many of the methods of ordinary linear algebra are algorithmic. In particular, if F is a computable field and $\mathbf{A}$ is an $m \times n$ matrix and b is an $m \times 1$ vector, it is decidable whether or not there exists x such that $\mathbf{A}x = b$.

We now mention two important decision questions concerning computable fields.

Finiteness. It is possible to decide if a given computable field is finite?

* Recursive sets and functions are defined in [14,32].

Equality. Is it possible to decide if two given computable fields are equal?

In both cases, the answer is no. S. A. Cook has proven the following theorem which is stated without proof. Full details can be found in [7].

THEOREM 3.4. It is recursively unsolvable to determine whether or not

(a) a computable field is finite.
(b) two computable fields are isomorphic.

PROBLEMS

1. Given a computable field (by the three algorithms), show that one can effectively calculate $i(0)$ and $i(1)$. Moreover, show that given an element $i(a)$, one can effectively compute $i(-a)$ and $i(a^{-1})$.

2. Give an algorithm for solving the system of linear equations $\mathbf{A}x = b$ over a computable field F.

4. The Equivalence Problem for LSM's is Decidable

We will now show that if we have two LSM's given over the same computable field, then one can decide whether or not the LSM's are equivalent (relationally equivalent).

We start by proving an interesting lemma.

LEMMA 3.3. Let $M = \langle F, n, k, l, \mathbf{A}, \mathbf{B}, \mathbf{C}, \mathbf{D} \rangle$ and $M' = \langle F, n, k, l, \mathbf{A}', \mathbf{B}', \mathbf{C}', \mathbf{D}' \rangle$ be minimal LSM's. M is similar to M' if and only if

(i) there is a $n \times n$ matrix $\mathbf{P}$ such that $\mathbf{K}_n = \mathbf{K}'_n\mathbf{P}$,
(ii) there is a $n \times n$ matrix $\mathbf{P}'$ such that $\mathbf{K}'_n = {}_n\mathbf{KP}'$,
(iii) $\mathbf{K}_n\mathbf{B} = \mathbf{K}'_n\mathbf{B}'$,

and

(iv) $\mathbf{D} = \mathbf{D}'$.

Proof. If M is similar to M', there is a nonsingular matrix $\mathbf{P}$ such that $\mathbf{A}'\mathbf{P} = \mathbf{PA}$, $\mathbf{B}' = \mathbf{PB}$, $\mathbf{C} = \mathbf{C}'\mathbf{P}$, and $\mathbf{D}' = \mathbf{D}$. It is easy to verify that (i)–(iv) are satisfied. Conversely, (i) and (ii) imply that

$$\mathbf{K}_n'\mathbf{PP}' = \mathbf{K}_n\mathbf{P}' = \mathbf{K}_n'.$$

Thus $\mathbf{PP}' = \mathbf{I}$ so $\mathbf{P}$ is nonsingular and hence $\mathbf{P}' = \mathbf{P}^{-1}$. We note that (i) and (iii) are equivalent to

(i′) $\mathbf{K}_i = \mathbf{K}_i'\mathbf{P}$ for each $i \geq 0$.
(ii′) $\mathbf{K}_i\mathbf{B} = \mathbf{K}_i'\mathbf{B}'$ for each $i \geq 0$.

[This follows from the techniques of Chapter 2 which involve the minimum polynomials of $\mathbf{A}$ and $\mathbf{A}'$.] Consider $\lambda(q, a_0 \cdots a_t) = \mathbf{CA}^{t-1}q + \sum_{i=0}^{t-2} \mathbf{CA}^{t-i-2}\mathbf{B}a_i + \mathbf{D}a_{t-1}$. Since $\mathbf{CA}^{t-1} = \mathbf{C}'(\mathbf{A}')^{t-1}\mathbf{P}$ (from (i′), $\mathbf{CA}^{t-i-2}\mathbf{B} = \mathbf{C}'(\mathbf{A}')^{t-i-2}\mathbf{B}'$ (from (ii′)), and $\mathbf{D} = \mathbf{D}'$, we have

$$\begin{aligned}\lambda(q, a_0 \cdots a_{t-1}) &= \mathbf{C}'(\mathbf{A}')^{t-1}\mathbf{P}q + \sum_{i=0}^{t-2} \mathbf{C}'(\mathbf{A}')^{t-i-2}\mathbf{B}'a_i + \mathbf{D}'a_{t-1} \\ &= \lambda'(\mathbf{P}q, a_0 \cdots a_{t-1})\end{aligned}$$

Therefore $\mathbf{P}q \equiv q$ and since $\mathbf{P}$ is nonsingular, $M \equiv M'$. Since both M and M' are minimal, they are similar. ▮

We now state and prove the main theorem of this section.

THEOREM 3.5. Let M and M' be LSM's over the same computable field F. It is decidable whether or not $M \equiv M'$. [M is relationally equivalent to M'.]

Proof. We may assume, without loss of generality, that M and M' are minimal. Let $M = \langle F, n, k, l, \mathbf{A}, \mathbf{B}, \mathbf{C}, \mathbf{D}\rangle$ and $M' = \langle F, n, k, l, \mathbf{A}', \mathbf{B}', \mathbf{C}', \mathbf{D}'\rangle$. $M \equiv M'$ if and only if

(i) $\mathbf{D} = \mathbf{D}'$
(ii) $\mathbf{K}_n\mathbf{B} = \mathbf{K}_n'\mathbf{B}'$
(iii) There is a $n \times n$ matrix $\mathbf{P}$ such that $\mathbf{K}_n = \mathbf{K}_n'\mathbf{P}$
(iv) There is a $n \times n$ matrix $\mathbf{P}'$ such that $\mathbf{K}_n' = \mathbf{K}_n\mathbf{P}'$

Conditions (i) and (ii) are easily checked. To establish conditions (iii) and (iv), one decides whether or not a system of linear equations has a solution. ▮

PROBLEMS

1. Let $M_i = \langle \mathbb{Q}, \mathbf{A}_i, \mathbf{B}_i, \mathbf{C}_i, \mathbf{D}_i \rangle$ be LSM's for $i = 1, 2$ where

$$\mathbf{A}_1 = \begin{bmatrix} 1 & 1 \\ 1 & 1 \end{bmatrix}, \quad \mathbf{A}_2 = \begin{bmatrix} 2 & 0 \\ 0 & 0 \end{bmatrix}, \quad \mathbf{B}_1 = \mathbf{B}_2 = \begin{bmatrix} 0 \\ 0 \end{bmatrix},$$

$\mathbf{C}_1 = \mathbf{C}_2 = \begin{bmatrix} 1 & 0 \\ 0 & 1 \end{bmatrix}$, $\mathbf{D}_1 = \mathbf{D}_2 = \begin{bmatrix} 1 \\ 0 \end{bmatrix}$, where $\mathbb{Q}$ denotes the field of rational numbers. Decide whether or not $M_1 \equiv M_2$ using the method given in the proof of Theorem 3.4.

2. Repeat problem 1 where the matrices are the same except $\mathbf{C}_1 = \begin{bmatrix} 1 & 1 \\ 1 & -1 \end{bmatrix}$ and $\mathbf{C}_2 = \begin{bmatrix} 1 & 0 \\ 0 & 1 \end{bmatrix}$.

5. Other Decision Questions

We will now investigate other decision questions for LSM's. These are of less importance than the results of Section 4 on equivalence. In Section 6, we consider an important decision problem concerned with transitions from one state to another.

We begin with a simple decision question. The problem concerns an LSM over a computable field with a single output. We ask how one decides if there are infinitely many inputs which produce an output 1.

THEOREM 3.6. There is an algorithm for deciding whether or not for a given LSM $M = \langle F, n, k, l, \mathbf{A}, \mathbf{B}, \mathbf{C}, \mathbf{D} \rangle$ the set $U = \{x \in F_k^+ \mid \hat{\lambda}(q, x) = 1 \text{ for some } q \in F_n\}$ is infinite provided we know whether F is finite or infinite.

Proof. If F is finite, there are well-known techniques for deciding this question (for then, U is a regular set). Let us suppose F is infinite.

If $\mathbf{D} \neq \mathbf{0}$, choose $q = \mathbf{0}$. Let $x = a_0 \cdots a_t$ where $a_0 = \cdots = a_{t-1} = 0$, and choose a_t such that $\mathbf{D}a_t = 1$. (This is always possible since $\mathbf{D} \neq \mathbf{0}$.) Clearly there are infinitely many such x.

If $\mathbf{D} = \mathbf{0}$, but $\mathbf{C} \neq \mathbf{0}$, then there is $q \in F_n$ such that $\mathbf{C}q = 1$. Then for each $a \in F_k$, $\hat{\lambda}(q, a) = \mathbf{C}q + \mathbf{D}a = 1$. Since F is infinite, there are infinitely many such a.

If $\mathbf{C} = \mathbf{0}$ and $\mathbf{D} = \mathbf{0}$, then clearly

$$\hat{\lambda}(q, x) = \mathbf{0} \quad \text{for all} \quad q \in F_n,\ x \in F_k^*$$

Thus, we conclude: If F is infinite, U is infinite if and only if $\mathbf{D} \neq \mathbf{0}$ or $\mathbf{C} \neq \mathbf{0}$. ▌

The next decision result states that the relations of LSM's are recursive sets [32].

THEOREM 3.7. Let $M = \langle F, n, k, l, \mathbf{A}, \mathbf{B}, \mathbf{C}, \mathbf{D} \rangle$ be an LSM with F a computable field and (x, y) be in $F_k^* \times F_l^*$. It is decidable whether or not $(x, y) \in R(M)$.

Proof. If $lg(x) \neq lg(y)$, then $(x, y) \notin R(M)$. Suppose $lg(x) = lg(y) = t$. Then write

$$x = a_0 \cdots a_{t-1}, \qquad y = b_0 \cdots b_{t-1}$$

where $(a_i, b_i) \in F_k \times F_l$ for $0 \leq i < t$. $(x, y) \in R(M)$ if and only if there is some q so that $\hat{\lambda}(q, a_i \cdots a_{i-1}) = b_{i-1}$ for $1 \leq i \leq t$. This condition is equivalent to the following set of conditions for $1 \leq i \leq t$

$$\mathbf{C}\mathbf{A}^{i-1}q = b_{i-1} - \sum_{j=0}^{i-2} \mathbf{C}\mathbf{A}^{i-j-2}\mathbf{B}a_j - \mathbf{D}a_{i-1}$$

Thus we have a system of $t \times l$ equations in the unknowns which are the coordinates of q. It is decidable whether or not a solution exists. $(x, y) \in R(M)$ if and only if such a solution exists. ▌

By the elementary properties of sequential relations,† dom $R(M) = F_k^*$. For LSM's, we always have that ran $R(M)$ is infinite [because $(\mathbf{0}^k, \mathbf{0}^k) \in R(M)$ for each k]. By another property of sequential relations (extendability), for each $x \in F_k^*$, there is some $y \in F_l^*$ such that $(x, y) \in R(M)$. Next, we consider the reverse problem, given y, is there an x such that $(x, y) \in R(M)$?

THEOREM 3.8. Let $M \in \langle F, n, k, l, \mathbf{A}, \mathbf{B}, \mathbf{C}, \mathbf{D}\rangle$ be an LSM over a computable field F and let $y \in F_l^*$. It is decidable whether there is some $x \in F_k^*$ such that $(x, y) \in R(M)$.

Proof. Write $y = b_0 \cdots b_{t-1}$. We wish to decide whether there exists $q \in F_n$, $a_0 \cdots a_{t-1} \in F_k^t$ such that for $1 \leq i \leq t$

$$\mathbf{CA}^{i-1}q + \sum_{j=0}^{i-2} \mathbf{CA}^{i-j-2}\mathbf{B}a_j + \mathbf{D}a_{i-1} = b_{i-1}$$

This is a system of $t \times l$ equations in the $n + tk$ unknowns which are the coordinates of $q, a_0, \ldots, a_{t-1}$. It is decidable whether or not such a system of nonhomogeneous equations has a solution. [Note that if $b_i = \mathbf{0}$ for $0 \leq i < t$, then the equations always have a solution by the fundamental theorem on linear equations. In this case, $(\mathbf{0}^t, \mathbf{0}^t) \in R(M)$.] ∎

There is a variant of the problem discussed in the previous theorem. The problem is so similar that we merely state the result without justification.

THEOREM 3.8′. Let $M = \langle F, n, k, l, \mathbf{A}, \mathbf{B}, \mathbf{C}, \mathbf{D}\rangle$ be an LSM and let $y \in F_l^*$, $q \in F_n$ be fixed. It is decidable whether or not there exists $x \in F_k^*$ such that $\lambda(q, x) = y$.

Next, we consider a decision problem which involves a pair of LSM's M_1 and M_2. We will give a decision procedure for

† For any relation $R \subseteq \Sigma^* \times \Delta^*$, we write dom $R = \{x \mid (x, y) \in R$ for some $y\}$ and ran $R = \{y \mid (x, y) \in R$ for some $x\}$.

deciding if two fixed states exist which give the same output for some input sequence.*

THEOREM 3.9. Let $M_i = \langle F, n_i, k, l, \mathbf{A}_i, \mathbf{B}_i, \mathbf{C}_i, \mathbf{D}_i \rangle$ be LSM's over a computable field and let $q_i \in F_{n_i}$ be fixed for $i = 1, 2$. It is decidable whether or not there is some $x \in F_k^+$ such that $\lambda_1(q_1, x) = \lambda_2(q_2, x)$.

Proof. Clearly such an $x \in F_k^+$ exists if and only if there exists $a \in F_k$ such that $\lambda_1(q_1, a) = \lambda_2(q_2, a)$. This happens if and only if the system

$$(\mathbf{D}_1 - \mathbf{D}_2)a = \mathbf{C}_2 q_2 - \mathbf{C}_1 q$$

of l linear equations in the k unknowns which are the coordinates of a has a solution. Since it is decidable whether a system of linear equations is solvable, the theorem follows. ▮

There is another decision problem of a slightly different character with which we shall now deal.

THEOREM 3.10. Let $M_i = \langle F, n_i, k, l, \mathbf{A}_i, \mathbf{B}_i, \mathbf{C}_i, \mathbf{D}_i \rangle$ be LSM's over a computable field and let $q_i \in F_{n_i}$ be fixed for $i = 1, 2$. Let $t > 0$ be fixed. It is decidable whether or not there exists $a_0, \ldots, a_t \in F_k$ such that $\lambda_1(q_1, a_0 \cdots a_t \mathbf{0}^j) = \lambda_2(q_2, a_0 \cdots a_t \mathbf{0}^j)$ for all $j \geq 1$.

Proof. Let $m_i(x)$ be the minimum polynomial of $\mathbf{A}_i$ for $i = 1, 2$ and assume the degree of $m_i(x)$ is p_i. Let $m(x) = m_1(x)m_2(x)$ and let $n = \deg m(x) = p_1 + p_2$. Thus there exist $b_j \in F$ for $0 \leq j < n$ so that

$$\mathbf{A}_i^n = \sum_{j=0}^{n-1} b_j \mathbf{A}_i^j \qquad \text{for} \qquad i = 1, 2$$

* If the starting states were not fixed, it is easy to see that the problem would be to decide if $R(M_1) \cap R(M_2) = \emptyset$. The answer is always no since $\{(\mathbf{0}^k, \mathbf{0}^k) \mid k \geq 0\} \subseteq R(M)$ for any LSM M.

Recall that for each $r \geq n$, there exist $b_j(r)$ so that

$$\mathbf{A}_i^r = \sum_{j=0}^{n-1} b_j(r)\mathbf{A}_i^j \tag{1}$$

For any $a_0, \ldots, a_t \in F_k$

$$\lambda_1(q_1, a_0 \cdots a_t\mathbf{0}^j) = \lambda_2(q_2, a_0 \cdots a_t\mathbf{0}^j) \qquad \text{for all} \qquad j \geq 1$$

if and only if

$$\lambda_1(q_1, a_0 \cdots a_t) = \lambda_2(q_2, a_0 \cdots a_t)$$

and $\hat{\lambda}_1(\delta_1(q_1, a_0 \cdots a_t), \mathbf{0}^j) = \hat{\lambda}_2(\delta_2(q_2, a_0 \cdots a_t), \mathbf{0}^j)$ for all $j \geq 1$. Let $q_i' = \delta_i(q_i, a_0 \cdots a_t)$ for $i = 1, 2$. Then

$$\hat{\lambda}_i(q_i', \mathbf{0}^j) = \mathbf{C}_i\mathbf{A}_i^{j-1}q_i' \tag{2}$$

We claim that if

$$\hat{\lambda}_1(q_1', \mathbf{0}^j) = \hat{\lambda}_2(q_2', \mathbf{0}^j) \qquad \text{for} \qquad 1 \leq j \leq n,$$

then

$$\hat{\lambda}_1(q_1', \mathbf{0}^j) = \hat{\lambda}_2(q_2', \mathbf{0}^j) \qquad \text{for all} \qquad j \geq 1.$$

[For if $j \leq n$, there is nothing to show. If $j > n$, we use (1) and (2) to verify that

$$\begin{aligned}\hat{\lambda}_1(q_1', \mathbf{0}^j) = \mathbf{C}_1\mathbf{A}_1^j q_1' &= \sum_{u=0}^{n-1} b_u(j)\mathbf{C}_1\mathbf{A}_1^u q_1' \\ &= \sum_{u=0}^{n-1} b_u(j)\mathbf{C}_2\mathbf{A}_2^u q_2' = \mathbf{C}_2\mathbf{A}_2^j q_2' = \hat{\lambda}_2(q_2', \mathbf{0}^j).]\end{aligned}$$

We can conclude that there exist $a_0, \ldots, a_t \in F_k$ such that

$$\lambda_1(q_1, a_0 \cdots a_t\mathbf{0}^j) = \lambda_2(q_2, a_0 \cdots a_t\mathbf{0}^j)$$

for all j, if and only if the following set of $(t + 1 + n)l$ linear equations in the $(t + 1)k$ unknowns which are the coordinates of $a_0, \ldots, a_t$ has a solution:

$$\begin{aligned}(\mathbf{D}_1 - \mathbf{D}_2)a_j + \sum_{u=0}^{j-1} (\mathbf{C}_1\mathbf{A}_2^{j-u-1}\mathbf{B}_1 - \mathbf{C}_2\mathbf{A}_2^{j-u-1}\mathbf{B}_2)a_u \\ = \mathbf{C}_2\mathbf{A}_2^j q_2 - \mathbf{C}_1\mathbf{A}_1^j q_1 \qquad \text{for} \qquad 0 \leq j \leq t\end{aligned}$$

$$\begin{aligned}\sum_{u=0}^{t} (\mathbf{C}_1\mathbf{A}^{j-u-1}\mathbf{B}_1 - \mathbf{C}_2\mathbf{A}_2^{j-u-1}\mathbf{B}_2)a_u \\ = \mathbf{C}_2\mathbf{A}_2^j q_2 - \mathbf{C}_1\mathbf{A}_1^j q_1 \qquad \text{for} \qquad t < j \leq t + n\end{aligned}$$

Since it is decidable if solutions of linear equations exist, the result follows. ▮

We close this section with the following unresolved question.

OPEN PROBLEM. Let $M_i = \langle F, n_i, k, l, \mathbf{A}_i, \mathbf{B}_i, \mathbf{C}_i, \mathbf{D}_i \rangle$ be LSM's over a computable field and let $q_i \in F_{n_i}$ for $i = 1, 2$. Is it decidable whether or not there exists $x \in F_k^+$ such that $\lambda_1(q_1, x\,\mathbf{0}^j) = \lambda_2(q_2, x\mathbf{0}^j)$ for each $j \geq 0$?

6. Accessibility

In this section, we consider one last decision problem which is of great interest but is substantially harder than those in Section 5. Given two states q_1 and q_2 in an LSM, does there exist an input x such that $\delta(q_1, x) = q_2$?

We shall show that (for computable fields) this problem is equivalent to a seemingly simpler problem concerned with matrices. We shall discuss a further simplification of the problem and state the assumptions under which we found a solution. The general problem remains unsolved.

We shall make use of the following simple lemma which is a variant of Theorem 2.2.

LEMMA 3.4. Let $M = \langle F, n, k, l, \mathbf{A}, \mathbf{B}, \mathbf{C}, \mathbf{D} \rangle$ be a LSM and $\mathbf{P}$ be an $n \times n$ nonsingular matrix. If M is similar to M' where $M' = \langle F, n, k, l, \mathbf{PAP}^{-1}, \mathbf{PB}, \mathbf{CP}^{-1}, \mathbf{D} \rangle$. Then, for any $q_1, q_2 \in F_n$, $x \in F_k^*$

$$q_2 = \delta(q_1, x)$$

if and only if

$$\mathbf{P}q_2 = \delta'(\mathbf{P}q_1, x)$$

THEOREM 3.11. Let F be any computable field. The following two problems are equivalent.

(1) Give a decision procedure which for any LSM $M = \langle F, n, k, l, \mathbf{A}, \mathbf{B}, \mathbf{C}, \mathbf{D} \rangle$ and any $q_1, q_2 \in F_n$ will tell us whether there exists an $x \in F_k^*$ such that

$$q_2 = \delta(q_1, x)$$

(2) Give a decision procedure which for any $n \times n$ matrix $\mathbf{A}$ and any $q_1, q_2 \in F_n$ will tell us whether there exists an integer t such that

$$q_2 = \mathbf{A}^t q_1$$

Proof. Suppose we have the algorithm required in (1). Let $\mathbf{A}$ be a given $n \times n$ matrix. We define an LSM to be $M = \langle F, n, 1, 1, \mathbf{A}, \mathbf{0}, \mathbf{0}, \mathbf{0} \rangle$. Then for any $q_1 \in F_n$ and $x \in F_k^t$

$$\delta(q_1, x) = \mathbf{A}^t q_1$$

Hence for any $q_2 \in F_n$

$$q_2 = \delta(q_1, x) \qquad \text{if and only if} \qquad q_2 = \mathbf{A}^t q_1$$

and we have the algorithm required in (2).

Conversely, suppose we have the algorithm required in (2). Let $M = \langle F, n, k, l, \mathbf{A}, \mathbf{B}, \mathbf{C}, \mathbf{D} \rangle$ be the given LSM and let q_1 and q_2 be the given states.

We define $W \subseteq F_n$ by $W = \text{col } \mathbf{L}_n$. W is the set of states of the $\mathbf{0}$ submachine of M. It is clear that W can be effectively constructed. Let $d = \text{rank } \mathbf{L}_n$.

Let us denote the d linearly independent columns of $\mathbf{L}_n$, by $p_1, p_2, \ldots, p_d$. It could be that $d = n$, but if not, then we can effectively find some $p_{d+1}, \ldots, p_n$ such that $\{p_i \mid 1 \leq i \leq n\}$ is a basis of F_n, let $\mathbf{P}$ be the $n \times n$ matrix whose ith column is p_i. We can effectively find the inverse $\mathbf{P}^{-1}$ of $\mathbf{P}$.

Recalling that W is $\mathbf{A}$-invariant and that all the columns of $\mathbf{B}$ belong to W we see that $\mathbf{PAP}^{-1}$ is of the form $\begin{bmatrix} \mathbf{A}_1 & \mathbf{A}_2 \\ \mathbf{0} & \mathbf{A}_3 \end{bmatrix}$ where $\mathbf{A}_1$ is a $d \times d$ matrix, $\mathbf{A}_2$ is a $d \times (n - d)$ matrix while $\mathbf{A}_3$ is an $(n - d) \times (n - d)$ matrix and $\mathbf{PB}$ is of the form $\begin{pmatrix} \mathbf{B}_1 \\ \mathbf{0} \end{pmatrix}$ where $\mathbf{B}_1$ is a $d \times k$ matrix.

Let $M' = \langle F, n, k, l, \mathbf{PAP}^{-1}, \mathbf{PB}, \mathbf{CP}^{-1}, \mathbf{D} \rangle$. Then $q_2 = \delta(q_1, x)$ if and only if $\mathbf{P}q_2 = \delta(\mathbf{P}q_1, x)$ (by Lemma 3.4).

Let us write every element q of F_n in the form $\begin{bmatrix} s \\ r \end{bmatrix}$ where $s \in F_d$ and $r \in F_{n-d}$. (The case when $n = d$ is discussed later.) Then the set of all states accessible from the $\mathbf{0}$ state in M' is

$$W' = \left\{ \begin{bmatrix} s' \\ r' \end{bmatrix} \middle| \, r' = \mathbf{0} \right\}$$

Furthermore

$$\delta'(q', a) = \begin{bmatrix} \mathbf{A}_1 & \mathbf{A}_2 \\ \mathbf{0} & \mathbf{A}_3 \end{bmatrix} \begin{bmatrix} s' \\ r' \end{bmatrix} + \begin{bmatrix} \mathbf{B}_1 \\ \mathbf{0} \end{bmatrix} a$$
$$= \begin{bmatrix} \mathbf{A}_1 s' + \mathbf{A}_2 r' + \mathbf{B}_1 a \\ \mathbf{A}_3 r' \end{bmatrix}$$

So for any sequence x of length t, $\delta'(q_1', x)$ is of the form $\begin{bmatrix} \sigma \\ \mathbf{A}_3^t r' \end{bmatrix}$.

Therefore, if $q_2' = \delta'(q_1', x)$ for some $x \in F_k^t$, then $r_2' = \mathbf{A}_3^t r_1'$.

We are now in a position to describe the algorithm required in (1) assuming that we have the algorithm required in (2).

We are given LSM $M = \langle F, n, k, l, \mathbf{A}, \mathbf{B}, \mathbf{C}, \mathbf{D} \rangle$ and $q_1, q_2 \in F_n$.

(i) Find $d = \operatorname{rank} \mathbf{L}_n$. If $d = n$ then there exists an $x \in F_k^*$ such that

$$q_2 = \delta(q_1, x)$$

This is because rank $\mathbf{L}_n = n$ and by Corollary 3 of Theorem 2.15.

(ii) If $d \neq n$, then $d < n$. Then we can effectively find $\mathbf{P}$ and M' as described above. Also we can work out $q_1' = \mathbf{P} q_1$ and $q_2' = \mathbf{P} q_2$ and so find r_1' and r_2'. Using the algorithm required by (2) we can find out whether or not there exists a t such that

$$r_2' = \mathbf{A}_3^t r_1'$$

If there is no such t, then there exists no $x \in F_k^*$ such that

$$q_2 = \delta(q_1, x)$$

(iii) If there is such a t, then using the algorithm required by (2) we can find out whether or not there exists a t' such that

$$r_2' = \mathbf{A}_3^{t'}(\mathbf{A}_3 r_2')$$

If there exists such a t', then there exists an $x \in F_k^*$ such that

$$q_2 = \delta(q_1, x)$$

This is because the existence of such a t' implies that there exist arbitrarily large t's such that

$$r_2' = \mathbf{A}_3^t r_2'$$

If we choose such a t which is greater than n, then any state q' which is accessible from the $\mathbf{0}$ state in M' will be accessible from the $\mathbf{0}$ state in M' using a sequence of length t. Let

$$q' = q_2' - \delta'(q_1', \mathbf{0}^t) = \begin{pmatrix} s_2' \\ r_2' \end{pmatrix} - \begin{pmatrix} \sigma \\ \mathbf{A}_3^t r_1' \end{pmatrix} = \begin{pmatrix} s_2' - \sigma \\ \mathbf{0} \end{pmatrix}$$

for some $\sigma \in F_d$. Hence $q' \in W'$ and there exists an x of length t such that $q' = \delta'(\mathbf{0}, x)$. Therefore $\delta'(\mathbf{0}, x) = q_2' - \delta'(q_1', \mathbf{0}^t)$ or $\delta'(q_1', x) = q_2'$.

(iv) If there exists no t' of the type desired in (iii), then the t such that $r_2' = \mathbf{A}_3^t r_1'$ is unique. We can find its value by working out $\mathbf{A}_3^i r_1'$ for $i = 0, 1, 2, \ldots$ and comparing it with r_2'. When we have found the value of t we consider the system of n linear equations

$$\sum_{i=0}^{t-1} \mathbf{A}^{t-i-1}\mathbf{B}a_i = q_2 - \mathbf{A}^t q_1$$

in the $t \times k$ unknowns which are the coordinates of $a_0, \ldots, a_{t-1}$. This system of equations has a solution if and only if there exists an $x \in F_k^*$ such that $q_2 = \delta(q_1, x)$. ▮

Further simplifications of the problem are possible. An example of such a simplification is the following:

THEOREM 3.12. Let F be any computable field. Problems (1) and (2) of Theorem 3.11 are also equivalent to the following problem:

(3) Give a decision algorithm which for any $n \times n$ companion matrix $\mathbf{A}$ and any $q_1, q_2 \in F_n$ will tell us whether there exists an integer t such that

$$q_2 = \mathbf{A}^t q_1$$

Proof. That the algorithm required in (2) will also do the work of the algorithm required in (3) is obvious.

Conversely, suppose we have the algorithm required in (3). Let $\mathbf{A}$ be the given matrix. One can effectively find the rational canonical form of $\mathbf{A}$, say $\mathbf{A}'$, and a nonsingular matrix $\mathbf{P}$ so that $\mathbf{A}' = \mathbf{PAP}^{-1}$. Let us write

$$\mathbf{A}' = \mathbf{C}_{p_1} \oplus \cdots \oplus \mathbf{C}_{p_r}$$

where the $\mathbf{C}_{p_i}$ are companion matrices. Thus $q_2 = \mathbf{A}^t q_1$ if and only if

$$q_2' = (\mathbf{A}')^t q_1' \quad \text{where} \quad q_1' = \mathbf{P}q_1 \quad \text{and} \quad q_2' = \mathbf{P}q_2.$$

So if we have an algorithm which will tell us for any $n \times n$ matrix $\mathbf{A}$ which is a direct sum of companion matrices and any $q_1, q_2 \in F_n$ whether there exists an integer t such that

$$q_2 = \mathbf{A}^t q_1$$

then we also have the algorithm required in (2).

From now on we assume that $\mathbf{A}$ is a direct sum of companion matrices $\mathbf{C}_1, \mathbf{C}_2, \ldots, \mathbf{C}_r$, i.e.,

$$\mathbf{A} = \begin{bmatrix} \mathbf{C}_1 & & & & \\ & \mathbf{C}_2 & & & \\ & & \cdot & & \\ & & & \cdot & \\ & & & & \cdot \\ & & & & & \mathbf{C}_r \end{bmatrix}$$

If $r = 1$, $\mathbf{A}$ is a companion matrix itself, and the algorithm required in (3) will also be the algorithm required in (2).

Let us now assume that we have the algorithm required in (2) for all matrices $\mathbf{A}$ for which $1 \leq r < m$. If we can now produce an algorithm for $r = m$ as well, then the proof is complete by induction. Let

$$\mathbf{A}_1 = \mathbf{C}_1 \quad \text{and} \quad \mathbf{A}_2 = \begin{bmatrix} \mathbf{C}_2 & & & \\ & \cdot & & \\ & & \cdot & \\ & & & \cdot \\ & & & & \mathbf{C}_m \end{bmatrix}$$

and write each $q \in F_n$ as

$$q = \begin{pmatrix} s \\ r \end{pmatrix}$$

Then $q_2 = \mathbf{A}^t q_1$ if and only if

$$\begin{pmatrix} s_2 \\ r_2 \end{pmatrix} = \begin{pmatrix} \mathbf{A}_1^t & 0 \\ 0 & \mathbf{A}_2^t \end{pmatrix} \begin{pmatrix} s_1 \\ r_1 \end{pmatrix}$$

if and only if

$$s_2 = \mathbf{A}_1^t s_1 \quad \text{and} \quad r_2 = \mathbf{A}_2^t r_1$$

By induction hypothesis we can find out whether or not there exist a t_1 and a t_2 such that

$$s_2 = \mathbf{A}_1^{t_1} s_1 \quad \text{and} \quad r_2 = \mathbf{A}_2^{t_2} r_1$$

If either t_1 or t_2 does not exist, then there is no t such that $q_2 = \mathbf{A}^t q_1$.

If both t_1 and t_2 exist then we can effectively find the least t_1 and t_2 satisfying the conditions. We can also effectively decide whether or not there exist a u_1 and a u_2 such that

$$s_2 = \mathbf{A}_1^{u_1}(\mathbf{A}_1 s_2) \quad \text{and} \quad r_2 = \mathbf{A}_2^{u_2}(\mathbf{A}_2 r_2)$$

If there is no such u_1, then t_1 is unique and there exists a t such that $q_2 = \mathbf{A}^t q_1$ if and only if $q_2 = \mathbf{A}^{t_1} q_1$.

Similarly if there is no such u_2.

If both u_1 and u_2 exist we can find the least such u_1 and u_2. Then there exists a t such that $q_2 = \mathbf{A}^t q_1$ if and only if the equation

$$t_1 + x_1(u_1 + 1) = t_2 + x_2(u_2 + 1)$$

has an integer solution x_1 and x_2, that is if and only if the greatest common divisor of $u_1 + 1$ and $u_2 + 1$ divides $t_2 - t_1$. ∎

Although these theorems help us to simplify the problem it remains unsolved.

OPEN PROBLEM. Let F be a computable field with $q, q' \in F_n$ and $\mathbf{A}$ an $n \times n$ matrix over F. Is it decidable whether or not there exists such that $q' = \mathbf{A}^t q$?

We have found algorithms for certain special cases (making assumptions about the field F).

It should be pointed out that we have no algorithm even for the case $n = 1$ for arbitrary computable fields. For recursively ordered fields, for fields with certain types of recursive valuation, and for quotient fields of integral domains which have a recursive unique factorization the problem has been solved.

PROBLEMS

1. It is very restrictive to demand algorithms for the solution of these problems under the assumption that F is computable. Let us suppose that the underlying system is the set of numbers $a + bi$ where $i^2 = -1$ and a, b are rational. Addition and multiplication are as for complex numbers. What sort of algebraic system is this?

2. Using the algebraic system of Problem 1, can you solve the decision problem: does there exist an algorithm to determine the existence of a nonnegative integer i such that $\mathbf{A}^i q = q'$?

3. Give an example (with $n = 1$) to show that it is impossible to bound the length of the input which carries one state to

another in an LSM. In other words, for each $N_0 \in \mathbb{N}$, there exist states q, q', and $x \in \Sigma^*$ so that $\delta(q, x) = q'$ with $lg(x) > N_0$ and x has minimal length among all sequences for which $\delta(q, x) = q'$.

4. In this section, we used the fact that one can effectively compute the rational canonical form of a matrix over a computable field. Is the same result true for the classical canonical form?

Chapter 4

Realizations and Their Properties

In this chapter we introduce a general notion of realizations of LSM's. Some basic properties of these realizations are given in Section 1. Section 2 is devoted to a machine which has no linear realization. Section 3 concerns an algorithm for deciding if a finite sequential machine has a linear realization. In Section 4, it is proven that the algorithm of Section 3 is valid. Finally, Section 5 is devoted to considering field changes in the underlying field.

1. Definitions and Basic Facts about Realizations

In this section, we consider the basic definitions concerning realizations. We will show that "state splitting" is not helpful in obtaining linear realizations.

DEFINITION. Let $M = \langle Q, \Sigma, \Delta, \delta, \lambda\rangle$ and $M' = \langle Q', \Sigma', \Delta', \delta', \lambda'\rangle$ be two sequential machines. M' *realizes* M if there exist three mappings α, β, and φ such that

(i) α maps Σ into Σ'.
(ii) β maps Δ into Δ' and β is one-to-one.

(iii) φ maps Q into nonempty subsets of Q'.
(iv) For each $(q, a) \in Q \times \Sigma$ and $q' \in \varphi q$

$$\delta'(q', \alpha a) \in \varphi\delta(q, a).$$

(v) For each $(q, a) \in Q \times \Sigma$ and $q' \in \varphi q$

$$\lambda'(q', \alpha a) = \beta\lambda(q, a).$$

Furthermore if $|\varphi q| = 1$ for each $q \in Q$, then M' *realizes* M *without state splitting*. We write $\varphi q = q'$ instead of $\varphi q = \{q'\}$ in this case.

Next, we consider linear realizations.

DEFINITION. A sequential machine M is said to be *linearly realizable over a field* F if there exists an LSM M' over F which is a realization of M.

Next we see that the functions involved in a realization correspond for all input sequences, not just for input symbols.

THEOREM 4.1. Let $M = \langle Q, \Sigma, \Delta, \delta, \lambda\rangle$ and $M' = \langle Q', \Sigma', \Delta', \delta', \lambda'\rangle$ be sequential machines such that M' is a realization of M (with mappings α, β, and φ such that α is extended to be a homomorphism). Then for all $q \in Q$, $x \in \Sigma^+$ and $q' \in \varphi q$

$$\hat{\lambda}'(q', \alpha x) = \beta\hat{\lambda}(q, x)$$

Proof. The argument is an induction on $lg(x)$. The basis, $lg(x) = 1$, is guaranteed by (v) of the definition. Assume the result holds for all sequences of length $\leq t$. Suppose $(q, a, x) \in Q \times \Sigma \times \Sigma^t$ and $q' \in \varphi q$. Then

$$\begin{aligned}\hat{\lambda}'(q', \alpha(ax)) &= \hat{\lambda}'(q', (\alpha a)(\alpha x)) \\ &= \hat{\lambda}'(\delta'(q', \alpha a), \alpha x) \\ &= \hat{\lambda}'(q'', \alpha x)\end{aligned}$$

where $q'' = \delta'(q', \alpha a) \in \varphi\delta(q, a)$ by (iv). Using the induction hypothesis,

$$\begin{aligned}\hat{\lambda}'(q', \alpha(ax)) &= \beta\hat{\lambda}(\delta(q, a), x) \\ &= \beta\hat{\lambda}(q, ax)\end{aligned}$$

This completes the induction. ▮

COROLLARY 1. Let M and M' be as in the theorem. Extend both α and β to be homomorphisms. Then for each $q \in Q$, $x \in \Sigma^+$, and $q' \in \varphi q$

$$\lambda'(q', \alpha x) = \beta\lambda(q, x)$$

Proof. Assume $q \in Q$, $q' \in \varphi q$, and let $x = a_1 \cdots a_m$ be in Σ^*. Then

$$\lambda(q, x) = \hat{\lambda}(q, a_1) \cdots \hat{\lambda}(q, a_1 \cdots a_m)$$

and since β is a homomorphism

$$\beta\lambda(q, x) = \beta\hat{\lambda}(q, a_1) \cdots \beta\hat{\lambda}(q, a_1 \cdots a_m)$$

By the theorem,

$$\begin{aligned}\beta\lambda(q, x) &= \hat{\lambda}'(q', \alpha a_1) \cdots \hat{\lambda}'(q', \alpha(a_1 \cdots a_m)) \\ &= \lambda'(q', \alpha x)\end{aligned}$$ ▮

COROLLARY 2. If, in addition, α is onto then for each $q \in Q$; $q_1, q_2 \in \varphi q$ implies $q_1 \equiv q_2$.

Proof. Let $q \in Q$; $q_1, q_2 \in \varphi q$ and $x \in (\Sigma')^+$. Since α is onto, there exists $y \in \Sigma^*$ so that $\alpha y = x$. Then

$$\begin{aligned}\lambda'(q_1, x) &= \lambda_1(q_1, \alpha y) \\ &= \beta\lambda(q, y) \\ &= \lambda'(q_2, \alpha y) \\ &= \lambda'(q_2, x)\end{aligned}$$

Since x was arbitrary, $q_1 \equiv q_2$. ▮

This corollary indicates that if M' is a realization of M with α onto and β one-to-one then there exists a machine M'' which is equivalent to M' and which is a realization of M without state splitting (and with the same α and β). In the case of realizations by LSM's we have the same result without any restriction on α.

COROLLARY 3. If the machine M' in Theorem 4.1 is linear, then for all $q \in Q$, if $q_1, q_2 \in \varphi q$ then $q_1 \equiv q_2$.

Proof. By Theorem 2.4, M' satisfies condition (4), the diagnosability condition for $p = n$. That is, for each $x \in (\Sigma')^n(\Sigma')^*$, q_1, $q_2 \in Q'$; $\lambda'(q_1, x) = \lambda'(q_2, x)$ implies $q_1 \equiv q_2$. Let $a \in \Sigma$ and using α, we have that $\alpha a \in \Sigma'$ so $(\alpha a)^n \in (\Sigma')^n(\Sigma')^*$

$$\begin{aligned}\lambda'(q_1, (\alpha a)^n) &= \lambda'(q_1, \alpha(a^n)) \\ &= \beta\lambda(q, a^n) && \text{(Corollary 1)} \\ &= \lambda'(q_2, \alpha(a^n)) && \text{(Corollary 1)} \\ &= \lambda'(q_2, (\alpha a)^n)\end{aligned}$$

Hence $q_1 \equiv q_2$. ∎

We remark that Corollary 2 would still be true if we replaced "linear" by "diagnosable."

Now we state an important result which is peculiar to linear machines. Very few other classes of sequential machines exhibit this property.

THEOREM 4.2. Let $M = \langle Q, \Sigma, \Delta, \delta, \lambda\rangle$ be a minimal sequential machine. If M is linearly realizable over F by an LSM $M_1 = \langle F, n, k, l, \delta_1, \lambda_1\rangle$ (via maps α, β, and φ), then M is linearly realizable without state splitting by the minimal form, $M' = \langle F, r, k, l, \delta', \lambda'\rangle$ of M_1 under maps α, β, and ψ where ψ is one-to-one.

Proof. M_1 is a linear realization of M under mappings α, β, and φ. $|\varphi q| = 1$ for each $q \in Q$ [for if $q_1, q_2 \in \varphi q$, then $q_1 \equiv q_2$

and we get a new realization by choosing one element in each $\varphi q]$. Let M' be the minimal form of M_1. Let τ be the map which takes M_1 into its minimal form M'. (Actually, this map carries q in F_n into $\mathbf{T}q$ in F_r where $\mathbf{T}$ is constructed as in Chapter 2.) M is linearly realized by M' with maps α, β, and ψ where $\psi q = \tau\varphi q$. It is easy to see that $\beta\lambda(q, a) = \lambda'(\psi q, \alpha a)$ and $\psi\delta(q, a) = \delta'(\psi q, \alpha a)$. Suppose that $\psi q = \psi q'$. Since M' is an LSM, $q \equiv q'$ by Corollary 3 of Theorem 4.1. Since M is minimal $q = q'$ and ψ is one-to-one. ▮

Our final result in this section has shown that a minimal sequential machine which is linearly realizable may be assumed to have such a realization without state splitting by a one-to-one map into a minimal LSM. Henceforth we shall always assume that this is the case.

It should be noted that if M' is a linear realization of M with α and β the identity mappings on F_k and F_l respectively, then in general $R(M) \subseteq R(M')$ and $F(M) \subseteq F(M')$. Usually, these containments are proper.

PROBLEMS

1. Show that if β is not one-to-one in the definition of a realization, then every sequential machine is realized (over any field) by the "zero" LSM.

2. Show that any submachine or homomorphic image of a linearly realizable machine is also linearly realizable. Give an example of a sequential machine which is not an LSM but is linearly realizable.

3. Let M be a sequential machine and M' be a realization of M with maps α, β, and φ. Extend α and β to be homomorphisms and define $R_{\alpha\beta}(M) = \{(\alpha x, \beta y) \mid (x, y) \in R(M)\}$. Show that $R_{\alpha,\beta}(M) \subseteq R(M')$.

4. Let M and M' be sequential machines. Let M' be a realization of M via maps α, β, and φ with the additional property that all of α, β, and φ are onto. Show that $R_{\alpha,\beta}(M) = R(M)$.

5. Let M and M' be sequential machines. If M' is a realization of M with maps α, β, φ such that α is one-to-one onto and φ is onto. Show that $F(M') = \beta F(M)\alpha^{-1}$.

6. Construct a monoid G which is the monoid of a sequential machine M which is not an LSM and find an LSM with monoid G. Is M linearly realizable?

2. A Nonlinear Machine

We have seen a number of machines which are not linear. We shall now present a machine which is very nonlinear, because it cannot be linearly realized over any field using any maps α and β.

DEFINITION. Let N be the following sequential machine.

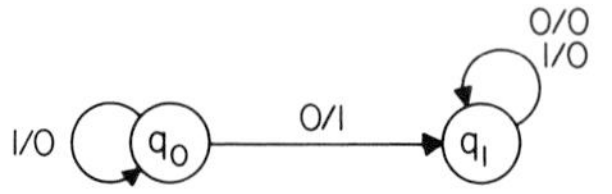

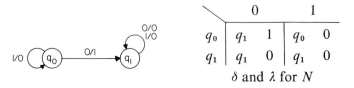

	0		1	
q_0	q_1	1	q_0	0
q_1	q_1	0	q_1	0

δ and λ for N

THEOREM 4.3. Let N be the sequential machine of the previous definition. N is not linearly realizable over any field F.

Proof. Suppose N is linearly realizable by an LSM $M' = \langle F, n, k, l, \mathbf{A}, \mathbf{B}, \mathbf{C}, \mathbf{D}, \delta', \lambda' \rangle$. From Theorem 4.2, we may suppose there exist maps α from $\{0, 1\}$ into F_k, β from $\{0, 1\}$ into F_l with β one-to-one, and φ from $\{q_0, q_1\}$ into F_n.

Since β is one-to-one

$$\beta 0 \neq \beta 1 \tag{1}$$

From the definition of a realization and from N

$$\beta 1 = \beta\lambda(q_0, 0) = \lambda'(\varphi q_0, \alpha 0) = \mathbf{C}\varphi q_0 + \mathbf{D}\alpha 0$$

or

$$\beta 1 = \mathbf{C}\varphi q_0 + \mathbf{D}\alpha 0 \tag{2}$$

Similar reasoning leads to

$$\beta 0 = \mathbf{C}\varphi q_0 + \mathbf{D}\alpha 1 \tag{3}$$

$$\beta 0 = \mathbf{C}\varphi q_1 + \mathbf{D}\alpha 0 \tag{4}$$

$$\beta 0 = \mathbf{C}\varphi q_1 + \mathbf{D}\alpha 1 \tag{5}$$

Equating (4) and (5) proves that

$$\mathbf{D}\alpha 0 = \mathbf{D}\alpha 1 \tag{6}$$

From (2), (6), and (3)

$$\beta 1 = \mathbf{C}\varphi q_0 + \mathbf{D}\alpha 0 = \mathbf{C}\varphi q_0 + \mathbf{D}\alpha 1 = \beta 0$$

we have just proved $\beta 1 = \beta 0$ which contradicts (1) and establishes that N is not linearly realizable over any field. ▌

PROBLEMS

*1. Characterize the state graphs of finite LSM's.

2. Show that the machine N of this section cannot have a linear state realization with a one-to-one state assignment.

3. An Algorithm for Obtaining Finite Realizations

We now consider the problem of deciding if a given *finite* sequential machine is linearly realizable over a finite field F. We shall present the algorithm in detail and work several examples. After we are familiar with the details, the proof will be given.

Algorithm 4.1. Let $M = \langle Q, F_k, F_l, \delta, \lambda\rangle$ be a finite minimal sequential machine and F a finite field. Let α and β be the identity maps.

1. We form a sequence of matrices $\mathbf{J}_1, \mathbf{J}_2, \ldots$ as follows. $\mathbf{J}_m$ will have $|Q|$ columns labelled by the states of M. The entry in ith block (of l rows) and column q_j will be $\hat{\lambda}(q_j, \mathbf{0}^i)$. Matrix $\mathbf{J}_m$ is formed of rows $\hat{\lambda}(q_j, \mathbf{0}^i)$ for $i \leq m$.

2. One forms $\mathbf{J}_1, \ldots, \mathbf{J}_p$ until rank $\mathbf{J}_p =$ rank $\mathbf{J}_{p+1} = r$. Henceforth only $\mathbf{J}_p$ is needed.

3. $\mathbf{J}_p$ has r linearly independent rows. The first set of r such rows are checked off and removed to form an $r \times |Q|$ matrix $\mathbf{\Phi}$ of rank r.

4. $\mathbf{\Phi}$ determines the state assignment φ for φq_j is the jth column of $\mathbf{\Phi}$.

5. Let $v_1, \ldots, v_r$ be r linearly independent columns of $\mathbf{\Phi}$ which correspond to states $q^{(i)}$, that is $\varphi q^{(i)} = v_i$. Let $\mathbf{V} = [v_1 \cdots v_r]$. Note that $\mathbf{V}$ is an $r \times r$ nonsingular matrix.

6. To determine $\mathbf{A}$, form

$$\mathbf{Q}_0 = [\varphi\delta(q^{(1)}, \mathbf{0}) \cdots \varphi\delta(q^{(r)}, \mathbf{0})] = \mathbf{A}[v_1 \cdots v_r] = \mathbf{AV}$$

Then $\mathbf{A} = \mathbf{Q}_0\mathbf{V}^{-1}$.

7. $\mathbf{C}$ is found similarly. We take

$$\mathbf{\Delta}_0 = [\lambda(q^{(1)}, \mathbf{0}) \cdots \lambda(q^{(r)}, \mathbf{0})] = \mathbf{CV}$$

or

$$\mathbf{C} = \mathbf{\Delta}_0\mathbf{V}^{-1}$$

8. To determine $\mathbf{B}$, let $u_1, \ldots, u_k$ be the natural basis of F_k, i.e., u_i has k rows and one column with a 1 in the ith row and zeros elsewhere. $\mathbf{B}$ can be solved for from the equations.

$$[\varphi\delta(q, u_1) \cdots \varphi\delta(q, u_k)] = \mathbf{A}[\varphi q \cdots \varphi q] + \mathbf{B}$$

where $q \in Q$. Note that if $\varphi q = \mathbf{0}$ for some q, the computations are simplified.

9. $\mathbf{D}$ is determined similarly from the equations.

$$[\lambda(q, u_1) \cdots \lambda(q, u_k)] = \mathbf{C}[\varphi q \cdots \varphi q] + \mathbf{D}$$

for each $q \in Q$.

10. One must check whether or not

$$\varphi\delta(q, a) = \mathbf{A}\varphi q + \mathbf{B}a$$

$$\lambda(q, a) = \mathbf{C}\varphi q + \mathbf{D}a$$

for all $(q, a) \in Q \times \Sigma$. If this test fails, for some (q, a), then M is not linearly realizable. Otherwise, the algorithm has produced a linear realization.

It is clear that this procedure is an algorithm which always terminates if M is a finite sequential machine. It is not immediately obvious that this algorithm works but we shall prove this later.

We illustrate the algorithm by several examples.

EXAMPLE. Let M be given by the following table and $F = \mathbb{Z}_2$.

	0	1	0	1
a	a	c	e_0	e_2
b	c	a	e_3	e_1
c	b	d	e_1	e_3
d	d	b	e_2	e_0

$$e_0 = \begin{bmatrix} 0 \\ 0 \end{bmatrix} \qquad e_1 = \begin{bmatrix} 0 \\ 1 \end{bmatrix}$$

$$e_2 = \begin{bmatrix} 1 \\ 0 \end{bmatrix} \qquad e_3 = \begin{bmatrix} 1 \\ 1 \end{bmatrix}$$

Clearly M is minimal. We form

$$\mathbf{J}_1 = \begin{bmatrix} 0 & 1 & 0 & 1 \\ 0 & 1 & 1 & 0 \end{bmatrix}$$

and then

$$\mathbf{J}_2 = \left[\begin{array}{cccc} 0 & 1 & 0 & 1 \\ 0 & 1 & 1 & 0 \\ \hdashline 0 & 0 & 1 & 1 \\ 0 & 1 & 1 & 0 \end{array}\right]$$

Since rank $\mathbf{J}_2$ = rank $\mathbf{J}_1$, $r = 2$ and

$$\boldsymbol{\Phi} = \begin{pmatrix} 0 & 1 & 0 & 1 \\ 0 & 1 & 1 & 0 \end{pmatrix}$$

Thus

$$\varphi a = \begin{pmatrix} 0 \\ 0 \end{pmatrix}, \quad \varphi b = \begin{pmatrix} 1 \\ 1 \end{pmatrix}, \quad \varphi c = \begin{pmatrix} 0 \\ 1 \end{pmatrix} \quad \text{and} \quad \varphi d = \begin{pmatrix} 1 \\ 0 \end{pmatrix}$$

We form $\mathbf{V} = (\varphi d \quad \varphi c) = \mathbf{I}$ and obtain

$$\mathbf{AV} = \mathbf{A} = (\varphi\delta(d, \mathbf{0})\, \varphi\delta(c, \mathbf{0})) = \begin{pmatrix} 1 & 1 \\ 0 & 1 \end{pmatrix}$$

Similarly

$$\mathbf{C} = (\lambda(d, \mathbf{0})\, \lambda(c, \mathbf{0})) = \begin{pmatrix} 1 & 0 \\ 0 & 1 \end{pmatrix}$$

Next we take $q = a$

$$\mathbf{B} = \varphi\delta(a, 1) - \mathbf{A0} = \varphi c = \begin{pmatrix} 0 \\ 1 \end{pmatrix}$$

and

$$\mathbf{D} = \lambda(a, 1) = e_2 = \begin{pmatrix} 1 \\ 0 \end{pmatrix}$$

Thus $M' = \langle \mathbb{Z}_2, \mathbf{A}, \mathbf{B}, \mathbf{C}, \mathbf{D} \rangle$ is a linear realization because M satisfies all the conditions of Step 10.

EXAMPLE. Let M be given below and $F = \mathbb{Z}_2$.

	0	1	0	1
q_0	q_0	q_1	0	0
q_1	q_2	q_3	0	0
q_2	q_0	q_1	1	1
q_3	q_2	q_3	1	0

M is clearly minimal. One forms

$$\mathbf{J}_3 = \begin{pmatrix} 0 & 0 & 1 & 1 \\ 0 & 1 & 0 & 1 \\ 0 & 0 & 0 & 0 \end{pmatrix}$$

Thus

$$\mathbf{\Phi} = \begin{pmatrix} 0 & 0 & 1 & 1 \\ 0 & 1 & 0 & 1 \end{pmatrix}$$

and

$$\varphi q_0 = \begin{pmatrix} 0 \\ 0 \end{pmatrix}, \quad \varphi q_1 = \begin{pmatrix} 0 \\ 1 \end{pmatrix}, \quad \varphi q_2 = \begin{pmatrix} 1 \\ 0 \end{pmatrix} \quad \text{and} \quad \varphi q_3 = \begin{pmatrix} 1 \\ 1 \end{pmatrix}$$

Solving for the matrices leads to

$$\mathbf{A} = \begin{pmatrix} 0 & 1 \\ 0 & 0 \end{pmatrix}, \quad \mathbf{B} = \begin{pmatrix} 0 \\ 1 \end{pmatrix}, \qquad \mathbf{C} = (1 \quad 0) \quad \text{and} \quad \mathbf{D} = (0)$$

When we check all possibilities, we find that

$$\lambda(q_3, 1) = 0 \neq 1 = (1 \quad 0)\begin{pmatrix} 1 \\ 1 \end{pmatrix} + (0)1$$

Thus M has a linear state realization but is not realizable by an LSM.

EXAMPLE. Our last example shows how realizations can involve submachines. Suppose M is the following Moore machine over $\mathbb{Z}_2$.

	0	1	
q_0	q_1	q_3	$\begin{pmatrix} 0 \\ 0 \end{pmatrix}$
q_1	q_2	q_0	$\begin{pmatrix} 0 \\ 1 \end{pmatrix}$
q_2	q_3	q_1	$\begin{pmatrix} 1 \\ 1 \end{pmatrix}$
q_3	q_0	q_2	$\begin{pmatrix} 1 \\ 0 \end{pmatrix}$

We form

$$\mathbf{J}_3 = \begin{bmatrix} 0 & 0 & 1 & 1 \\ 0 & 1 & 1 & 0 \\ \hdashline 0 & 1 & 1 & 0 \\ 1 & 1 & 0 & 0 \\ \hdashline 1 & 1 & 0 & 0 \\ 1 & 0 & 0 & 1 \end{bmatrix}$$

From this, we select

$$\mathbf{\Phi} = \begin{bmatrix} 0 & 0 & 1 & 1 \\ 0 & 1 & 1 & 0 \\ 1 & 1 & 0 & 0 \end{bmatrix}$$

so

$$\varphi q_0 = \begin{bmatrix} 0 \\ 0 \\ 1 \end{bmatrix} \quad \varphi q_1 = \begin{bmatrix} 0 \\ 1 \\ 1 \end{bmatrix} \quad \varphi q_2 = \begin{bmatrix} 1 \\ 1 \\ 0 \end{bmatrix} \quad \varphi q_3 = \begin{bmatrix} 1 \\ 0 \\ 0 \end{bmatrix}$$

Let

$$\mathbf{V} = (\varphi q_3 \, \varphi q_1 \, \varphi q_0) = \begin{bmatrix} 1 & 0 & 0 \\ 0 & 1 & 0 \\ 0 & 1 & 1 \end{bmatrix}$$

and $\mathbf{V}^{-1} = \mathbf{V}$. Then $\mathbf{AV} = \begin{bmatrix} 0 & 1 & 0 \\ 0 & 1 & 1 \\ 1 & 0 & 1 \end{bmatrix}$

so

$$\mathbf{A} = \begin{bmatrix} 0 & 1 & 0 \\ 0 & 0 & 1 \\ 1 & 1 & 1 \end{bmatrix}$$

By the same technique,

$$\mathbf{CV} = \begin{bmatrix} 1 & 0 & 0 \\ 0 & 1 & 0 \end{bmatrix}$$

which implies that

$$\mathbf{C} = \begin{bmatrix} 1 & 0 & 0 \\ 0 & 1 & 0 \end{bmatrix}$$

We observe that

$$\begin{bmatrix} 1 \\ 0 \\ 0 \end{bmatrix} = \mathbf{A} \begin{bmatrix} 0 \\ 0 \\ 1 \end{bmatrix} + \mathbf{B}$$

implies

$$\mathbf{B} = \begin{bmatrix} 1 \\ 1 \\ 1 \end{bmatrix}$$

and

$$\mathbf{D} = \begin{bmatrix} 0 \\ 0 \end{bmatrix} - \mathbf{C} \begin{bmatrix} 0 \\ 0 \\ 1 \end{bmatrix} = \begin{bmatrix} 0 \\ 0 \end{bmatrix}$$

It is easily checked that this is a linear realization of M. It is instructive to construct the state graph of M. Note that although M is linearly realizable it is not isomorphic to any LSM. Moreover, $F(M)$ is properly contained in the set of functions of the LSM. This suggests the following problem.

OPEN PROBLEM. Characterize the relations of linearly realizable sequential machines.

PROBLEMS

1. Decide if the following sequential machine is linearly realizable over $\mathbb{Z}_2$.

	0	1	0	1
q_1	q_1	q_2	0	1
q_1	q_2	q_0	1	0
q_2	q_0	q_1	1	1

If M is not linearly realizable over $\mathbb{Z}_2$, can you change the output function so that M is still minimal yet is linearly realizable?

2. Would the algorithm of this section be equally valid if α and β were one-to-one linear onto maps?

3. Does the realization algorithm work for nonminimal sequential machines? Explain and extend if necessary.

4. Proof That the Realization Algorithm Works

Now, we turn to proving that the realization algorithm of Section 3 is valid. We begin with a lemma which will be used in our main proof.

LEMMA 4.1. Let $M_i = \langle Q_i, \Sigma_i, \Delta_i, \delta_i, \lambda_i \rangle$ be sequential machines for $i = 1, 2, 3$. If M_{i+1} is a realization of M_i for $i = 1, 2$ without state splitting, then M_3 is a realization of M_1 without state splitting.

Proof. Let M_{i+1} realize M_i by maps $(\alpha_i, \beta_i, \varphi_i)$ for $i = 1, 2$. It is easy to verify that M_3 realizes M_1 under maps $(\alpha_2\alpha_1, \beta_2\beta_1, \varphi_2\varphi_1)$. ∎

The next lemma plays the key role in our proof that the algorithm works.

LEMMA 4.2. If $M = \langle Q, F_k, F_l, \delta, \lambda \rangle$ is a submachine (not necessarily an LSM) of a minimal finite LSM $M_1 = \langle F, n, k, l, \mathbf{A}_1, \mathbf{B}_1, \mathbf{C}_1, \mathbf{D}_1, \delta_1, \lambda_1 \rangle$, then M' obtained by Algorithm 4.1 is a linear realization of M.

Proof. We apply Algorithm 4.1 to M and produce an LSM $M' = \langle F, r, k, l, \mathbf{A}, \mathbf{B}, \mathbf{C}, \mathbf{D}, \delta', \lambda' \rangle$. We must prove that M' is a linear realization of M, that is, for each $(q, a) \in Q \times F_k$

$$\varphi\delta(q, a) = \delta'(\varphi q, a)$$
$$\lambda(q, a) = \lambda'(\varphi q, a)$$

We begin by noting that since M is a submachine of M_1, for each $(q, a) \in Q \times F_k$,

$$\delta(q, a) = \delta_1(q, a) = \mathbf{A}_1 q + \mathbf{B}_1 a$$

and

$$\lambda(q, a) = \lambda_1(q, a) = \mathbf{C}_1 q + \mathbf{D}_1 a$$

The algorithm produces $\mathbf{\Phi}$ of rank r. Let s be the number of linearly independent states in Q.

CLAIM. $r = s$.

Proof of Claim.

$$\text{Let } \mathbf{K}_i = \begin{bmatrix} \mathbf{C}_1 \\ \cdot \\ \cdot \\ \cdot \\ \mathbf{C}_1\mathbf{A}_1^{i-1} \end{bmatrix}$$

Since $\mathbf{J}_i = \mathbf{K}_i[q_1 \cdots q_{|Q|}]$, we compute

$$\mathbf{J}_n = \mathbf{K}_n[q_1 \cdots q_{|Q|}] \qquad (*)$$

Then we have (because rank $(\mathbf{AB}) \leq \min\{\text{rank } \mathbf{A}, \text{rank } \mathbf{B}\}$ and M_1 is minimal, i.e., rank $\mathbf{K}_n = n$)

$$r = \text{rank } \mathbf{J}_p = \text{rank } \mathbf{J}_n = \text{rank } (\mathbf{K}_n[q_1 \cdots q_{|Q|}])$$
$$\leq \min\{n, s\} = s$$

Thus $r \leq s$.

Recall Sylvester's inequality [15] states that if $\mathbf{A}$ is a $m \times n$ matrix and $\mathbf{B}$ is a $n \times q$ matrix then

$$\text{rank } \mathbf{A} + \text{rank } \mathbf{B} - n \leq \text{rank } (\mathbf{AB})$$

It then follows that

$$\text{rank } \mathbf{K}_n + \text{rank } [q_1 \cdots q_{|Q|}] - n = n + s - n \leq \text{rank } \mathbf{J}_n = r$$

Thus $r \geq s$ and therefore $r = s$.

Returning to the main proof, we will next show certain properties of the matrices. Recall that $v_1, \ldots, v_r$ are r linearly independent columns of $\mathbf{\Phi}$ and the states which correspond to them are $q^{(1)}, \ldots, q^{(r)}$ and $\varphi q^{(i)} = v_i$. Since $\{q^i \mid 1 \leq i \leq r\}$ spans* Q, we have that for each $q \in Q$

$$q = \sum_{i=1}^{r} c_i q^{(i)}$$

and

$$\varphi q = \sum_{i=1}^{r} c_i \varphi q^{(i)} = \sum_{i=1}^{r} c_i v_i$$

Thus,

$$\mathbf{V} \begin{bmatrix} c_1 \\ \cdot \\ \cdot \\ \cdot \\ c_r \end{bmatrix} = \varphi q \tag{1}$$

or

$$\mathbf{V}^{-1} \varphi q = \begin{bmatrix} c_1 \\ \cdot \\ \cdot \\ \cdot \\ c_r \end{bmatrix}$$

Turning to the **A** matrix, we find that

$$\mathbf{A} \varphi q = \mathbf{A}\mathbf{V} \begin{bmatrix} c_1 \\ \cdot \\ \cdot \\ \cdot \\ c_r \end{bmatrix} = \mathbf{Q}_0 \begin{bmatrix} c_1 \\ \cdot \\ \cdot \\ \cdot \\ c_r \end{bmatrix}$$

using both (1) and Step 5 of the algorithm. Thus,

$$\mathbf{A} \varphi q = \sum_{i=1}^{r} c_i \varphi \delta(q^{(i)}, \mathbf{0}) = \sum_{i=1}^{r} c_i \varphi(\mathbf{A}_1 q^{(i)}) = \varphi(\mathbf{A}_1 q)$$

---

* Recall that M is a submachine of an LSM and its states are vectors. Also note that φ is a linear function.

since φ is a linear function. This argument has shown that

$$\mathbf{A}\varphi q = \varphi \mathbf{A}_1 q \tag{2}$$

Next we work with **B**.

$$\mathbf{B}a = \mathbf{B}\begin{bmatrix} a_1 \\ \cdot \\ \cdot \\ \cdot \\ a_k \end{bmatrix} = [\varphi\delta(q, u_1) \cdots \varphi\delta(q,u_k)]\begin{bmatrix} a_1 \\ \cdot \\ \cdot \\ \cdot \\ a_k \end{bmatrix}$$

$$- [\varphi(\mathbf{A}_1 q) \cdots \varphi(\mathbf{A}_1 q)]\begin{bmatrix} a_1 \\ \cdot \\ \cdot \\ \cdot \\ a_k \end{bmatrix}$$

$$= a_1\varphi(\mathbf{A}_1 q + \mathbf{B}_1 u_1) + \cdots + a_k\varphi(\mathbf{A}_1 q + \mathbf{B}_1 u_k)$$

$$- a_1\varphi(\mathbf{A}_1 q) - \cdots - a_k\varphi(\mathbf{A}_1 q)$$

$$= a_1\varphi\mathbf{B}_1 u_1 + \cdots + a_k\varphi\mathbf{B}_1 u_k = \varphi\mathbf{B}_1 a$$

We have shown that

$$\mathbf{B}a = \varphi\mathbf{B}_1 a \tag{3}$$

Combining (2) and (3) yields

$$\varphi\delta(q, a) = \varphi(\mathbf{A}_1 q + \mathbf{B}_1 a) = \mathbf{A}\varphi q + \mathbf{B}a = \delta'(\varphi q, a)$$

for each $(q, a) \in Q \times F_k$.

The proofs for the **C** and **D** matrices are so similar to those already given that they are omitted. The argument gives that

$$\mathbf{C}\varphi q = \mathbf{C}_1 q \tag{4}$$

and

$$\mathbf{D}a = \mathbf{D}_1 a \tag{5}$$

Combining (4) and (5) leads to

$$\lambda(q, a) = \lambda_1(q, a) = \mathbf{C}_1 q + \mathbf{D}_1 a = \mathbf{C}\varphi q + \mathbf{D}a = \lambda'(\varphi q, a)$$

for each $(q, a) \in Q \times F_k$.

Thus M' has been shown to be a linear realization of M and the proof is complete. ▮

We now prove the main result of this section.

THEOREM 4.4. A finite minimal sequential machine $M = \langle Q, F_k, F_l, \delta, \lambda \rangle$ is linearly realizable (with α and β the identity maps) if and only if the LSM M' produced by Algorithm 4.1 is a linear realization of M.

Proof. Clearly if M' is a linear realization, then M is linearly realizable.

Conversely, suppose that M is linearly realizable by an LSM M_1. By Theorem 4.2, M_1 may be assumed to be minimal and the state assignment is a one-to-one mapping (no state splitting). Thus there is a submachine M_2 (not necessarily linear) of M_1 which is isomorphic to M. In fact, M_2 is a realization of M. By Lemma 4.2, there is an LSM M_3 which linearly realizes M_2. By Lemma 4.1, M_3 linearly realizes M. Since M and M_2 are isomorphic, the tables $\mathbf{J}_i$ are the same for both machines. Thus the LSM M' is identical to M_3.* We have therefore shown that if a linear realization exists, then M' as given in Algorithm 4.1 yields a linear realization of M. ▮

One of the limitations of the algorithm is that no provision is available for determining α and β. While some partial results are known, no satisfactory algorithm exists.

OPEN PROBLEM. Find an algorithm which will decide of a given sequential machine M whether or not M is linearly realizable without state splitting and using one-to-one onto maps α and β.

PROBLEMS

1. Let M be a linearly realizable finite sequential machine given by its table. Show that the states in one row and one

* M' will be identical to M_3 if one chooses the same set of r rows from the matrix $\mathbf{J}_p$. Otherwise, M' will only be isomorphic to M_3.

column of the table (both the transition function and the output function part of the table) form subspaces. Show that each row or column forms a coset.

2. Is Lemma 4.1 valid if the phrase "without state splitting" is removed?

3. Show that φ is a linear function in the proof of Lemma 4.2.

5. Change of Ground Fields

We shall now investigate the effect on realizations of changing the base field. The first observation is immediate.

PROPOSITION 4.1. If a sequential machine M is linearly realizable over a field F, and if F' is a superfield of F, then M is linearly realizable over F'.

The problem of realizations over a subfield is much more interesting. When a realization over a subfield is possible, it is usually preferable if the field operations are simpler to compute. For example, multiplication is simpler to compute over the reals than over the complex numbers. We now present a general theorem which presents a solution to this problem when the larger field is a finite extension* of the smaller. Later, infinite extensions will be discussed.

LEMMA 4.3. Let F and F' be fields with F a finite extension of F'. Let $\gamma_1, \ldots, \gamma_r$ in F be a basis of F over F'. Define $c_{ijk} \in F'$ for $i \leq i, j, k \leq r$ by

$$\gamma_i \gamma_j = \sum_{k=1}^{r} c_{ijk} \gamma_k$$

---

* Let F and F' be fields. If $F' \subseteq F$, then F is an *extension* of F'. Note that F is a vector space over F'. F is a *finite extension* if dim F is finite; otherwise F is an *infinite extension.*

Let

$$v = \begin{bmatrix} v_1 \\ \cdot \\ \cdot \\ \cdot \\ v_s \end{bmatrix}$$

be an s-dimensional column vector over F where $v_k = \sum_{i=1}^{r} v_{ki}\gamma_i$. Let $\Gamma(v)$ be the sr dimensional vector over F' defined by

$$\begin{aligned} \Gamma(v) &= \Gamma((v_1, \ldots, v_s)^T) \quad * \\ &= \Gamma\left(\left[\sum_1^r v_{1i}\gamma_i, \ldots, \sum_1^r v_{si}\gamma_i\right]^T\right) \\ &= (v_{11}, \ldots, v_{1r} \ldots, v_{s1} \ldots, v_{sr})^T \end{aligned}$$

Let $\mathbf{H} = (h_{fe})$ be a $t \times s$ matrix over F. Let $\Theta(\mathbf{H})$ be the $tr \times sr$ matrix over F' obtained by replacing each element

$$h_{fe} = \sum_{i=1}^{r} h_{fei}\gamma_i$$

of $\mathbf{H}$ by the $r \times r$ matrix whose (i, k) element is

$$\sum_{j=1}^{r} h_{fej}c_{jki}$$

Then, for each such v and $\mathbf{H}$,

$$\Gamma(\mathbf{H}v) = \Theta(\mathbf{H})\Gamma(v)$$

Proof. Both $\Theta(\mathbf{H})\Gamma(v)$ and $\Gamma(\mathbf{H}v)$ are rt dimensional column vectors. The $(a-1)r + b$ element $(1 \le a \le t,$

---

* We write $(v_1, \ldots, v_r)^T$ for the *transpose* of $(v_1, \ldots, v_r)$. The transpose is used only for typographic simplicity.

$1 \leq b \leq r$) of $\Theta(\mathbf{H})\Gamma(v)$ is computed as follows:

$$\left[\sum_{j=1}^{r} h_{a1j}c_{j1b}, \ldots, \sum_{j=1}^{r} h_{a1j}c_{jrb}, \ldots, \sum_{j=1}^{r} h_{asj}c_{j1b}, \ldots, \sum_{j=1}^{r} h_{asj}c_{jrs}\right]$$

$$\times \begin{bmatrix} v_{11} \\ \cdot \\ \cdot \\ \cdot \\ v_{1r} \\ \cdot \\ \cdot \\ \cdot \\ v_{s1} \\ \cdot \\ \cdot \\ \cdot \\ v_{sr} \end{bmatrix} = \sum_{l=1}^{r} \sum_{d=1}^{r} \sum_{j=1}^{r} h_{alj}c_{jdb}v_{ld}$$

Next we compute the $(a - 1)r + b$ element of $\Gamma(\mathbf{H}v)$. First it is necessary to compute the ath element of $\mathbf{H}v$. This is

$$\begin{aligned}
\sum_{l=1}^{r} h_{al}v_i &= \sum_{l=1}^{s} \left[\sum_{j=1}^{r} h_{alj}\gamma_j\right]\left[\sum_{d=1}^{r} v_{ld}\gamma_d\right] \\
&= \sum_{l=1}^{s} \sum_{j=1}^{r} \sum_{d=1}^{r} h_{alj}v_{ld}\gamma_j\gamma_d \\
&= \sum_{l=1}^{s} \sum_{d=1}^{r} \sum_{j=1}^{r} h_{alj}v_{ld} \sum_{b=1}^{r} c_{jdb}\gamma_b \\
&= \sum_{b=1}^{r} \left[\sum_{l=1}^{s} \sum_{j=1}^{r} \sum_{d=1}^{r} h_{alj}v_{ld}c_{jdb}\right]\gamma_b
\end{aligned}$$

Therefore the $(a - 1)r + b$ element of both matrices agree and the proof is complete. ▮

We now state the main theorem of this section.

THEOREM 4.5. Let $M = \langle F, n, k, l, \mathbf{A}, \mathbf{B}, \mathbf{C}, \mathbf{D}\rangle$ be an LSM over F and let F' be a subfield of F. If F is a finite extension of F' then there is an LSM $M' = \langle F', n', k', l', \mathbf{A}', \mathbf{B}', \mathbf{C}', \mathbf{D}' \rangle$ which realizes M.

Proof. F is a finite extension of F', hence F is a finite dimensional vector space over F'. Let $\gamma_1, \ldots, \gamma_r$ be a basis of F over F'. There is a natural one-to-one onto map ψ between elements of F and r-tuples of elements of F'. This is defined by

$$\psi(a_1\gamma_1 + \cdots + a_r\gamma_r) = (a_1, \ldots, a_r)$$

Define c_{ijk}, Γ, Θ as in the previous lemma. Define $M' = \langle F', nr, kr, lr, \Theta(\mathbf{A}), \Theta(\mathbf{B}), \Theta(\mathbf{C}), \Theta(\mathbf{D}) \rangle$. To show that M' realizes M, define

$$\begin{aligned} \alpha a &= \Gamma(a) && \text{for each } a \in F_k. \\ \beta b &= \Gamma(b) && \text{for each } b \text{ in } F_l. \\ \varphi q &= \Gamma(q) && \text{for each } q \in F_n. \end{aligned}$$

To complete the proof, we must show that these mappings have the required properties. Since Γ is linear,

$$\begin{aligned} \varphi\delta(q, a) &= \varphi(\mathbf{A}q + \mathbf{B}a) \\ &= \Gamma(\mathbf{A}q + \mathbf{B}a) \\ &= \Gamma(\mathbf{A}q) + \Gamma(\mathbf{B}a) \end{aligned}$$

Using Lemma 4.3

$$\begin{aligned} \varphi\delta(q, a) &= \Theta(\mathbf{A})\Gamma(q) + \Theta(\mathbf{B})\Gamma(a) \\ &= \Theta(\mathbf{A})\varphi q + \Theta(\mathbf{B})\alpha a \\ &= \delta'(\varphi q, \alpha a) \end{aligned}$$

Finally, we check the β mapping.

$$\begin{aligned} \beta\lambda(q, a) &= \Gamma(\mathbf{C}q + \mathbf{D}a) \\ &= \Gamma(\mathbf{C}q) + \Theta(\mathbf{D}a) \\ &= \Theta(\mathbf{C})\Gamma(q) + \Theta(\mathbf{D})\Gamma(a) \\ &= \Theta(\mathbf{C})\varphi q + \Theta(\mathbf{D})\alpha a \\ &= \lambda'(\varphi q, \alpha a) \quad \blacksquare \end{aligned}$$

COROLLARY. Let M be an LSM over a finite field F. For any subfield F' of F, there exists an LSM M' which is a realization of M.

Proof. Any finite field is a finite extension of any of its subfields. ∎

Theorem 4.5 does not deal with the case in which F is an infinite extension of F'. In this case, F must be infinite. If the cardinality of F is greater than that of F', then there exists an LSM M over F for which there is no machine M' over F' which is a linear realization of M. A concrete example is $M = \langle F, (0), (0), (0), (1) \rangle$ which computes the identity function on F. Since the cardinality of F is greater than that of F' (and is infinite), it is also greater than the cardinality of F'_r for any finite r. Hence there cannot be a function β from F into F'_r which is one-to-one. These considerations lead to the following important proposition.

THEOREM 4.6. Given any LSM M over the real numbers or complex numbers, it is impossible to find an LSM over the rational numbers which realizes M.

This indicates that the usual practice of system theorists of approximating the real numbers by the rational numbers is not consistent with preserving realizations.

The method described in the previous paragraphs does not work when the infinite extension F has the same cardinality as F'.

There is an open problem which we shall state here and with which we shall conclude this chapter.

OPEN PROBLEM. Give a synthesis procedure for linearly realizing a given relation. It would be natural to assume the relation is given as in [21].

Chapter 5

Decompositions of LSM's

In this chapter, we will consider decompositions of LSM's into series and parallel connections of LSM's. A necessary and sufficient condition for each type of decomposition will be given.

We will consider only state realizations here although additional results of a more general nature will be stated without proof in the last section of this chapter.

1. Preliminaries of Linear Realizations

We begin our studies of realizations of LSM's. The special implications involved with linear realizations are first discussed and then a sufficient condition for such realizations is derived.

DEFINITION. An LSM M has a (*nontrivial*) *linear parallel* (*series*) *decomposition* if M has a (nontrivial) state realization by $M_1 \circledparallel \cdots \circledparallel M_k$ (respectively $M_k \ominus \cdots \ominus M_1$) for some LSM's $M_1, \ldots, M_k$ in which $n_i < n$ for each i.

We begin with some preliminary results.

THEOREM 5.1. Let $M = \langle F, n, k, \delta \rangle$ be an LSM* without output and let R be a right congruence relation on F_n. If R

* Since we will be dealing with LSM's without outputs, we will often shorten the notation by writing $\langle F, n, k, \delta \rangle$ or $\langle F, \mathbf{A}, \mathbf{B} \rangle$.

induces a coset partition on F_n (considered as an additive group), then M/R is also an LSM.

Proof. Let W be a subspace of F_n such that the cosets $\{q + W \mid q \in F_n\}$ are the equivalence classes of R. The quotient space F_n/W is isomorphic to F_r for some r and hence $M/R = \langle F, r, k, \delta' \rangle$ where $\delta'(q + W, a) = \delta(q, a) + W$. It is easily checked that M/R is an LSM without output. ∎

Our next result is very simple.

LEMMA 5.1. Let V be a finite dimensional vector space with a subspace W. The coset partition induced by W can be described by $a_0 + W, a_1 + W, \ldots, a_k + W$ where $a_0 = \mathbf{0}$ and $k \leq \infty$. There is a choice of representatives so that $\{a_0, \ldots, a_k\}$ is a vector space.

Proof. Let W be a subspace of dimension m of V where $\dim V = n$. There exists a subspace X where $V = W \oplus X$ and $\dim X = n - m$. Each element x in X is in some coset (namely $x + W$). Distinct elements of X are in distinct cosets [if $x_1 + w_1 = x_2 + w_2$ then $x_1 - x_2 = w_2 - w_1$ but then we have an element in $W \cap X$ so $x_1 - x_2 = w_2 - w_1 = \mathbf{0}$]. ∎

Next we turn to finding a sufficient condition for linear decompositions.

THEOREM 5.2. Let $M = \langle F, n, k, l, \mathbf{A}, \mathbf{B}, \mathbf{C}, \mathbf{D} \rangle$ be an LSM. If the classical canonical form (using elementary divisors) of $\mathbf{A}$ has at least two blocks, then M has a nontrivial linear parallel (serial) decomposition.

Proof. Let $\mathbf{A}' = \mathbf{A}_1 \oplus \mathbf{A}_2$ be the classical canonical form of $\mathbf{A}$ where $\mathbf{A}_1$ is an $m \times m$ matrix and $\mathbf{A}_2$ is an $r \times r$ matrix $(m + r = n)$. There is a nonsingular matrix $\mathbf{P}$ such that $\mathbf{A}' = \mathbf{PAP}^{-1}$. Let us write $q = \begin{pmatrix} q_1 \\ q_2 \end{pmatrix}$ where $q_1 \in F_m$ and $q_2 \in F_r$.

Define two right congruence relations R_1 and R_2 on F_n by, for $i = 1, 2$, $(q, q') \in R_i$ if and only if $\mathbf{P}q = \begin{bmatrix} r_1 \\ r_2 \end{bmatrix}$, $\mathbf{P}q' = \begin{bmatrix} r_1' \\ r_2' \end{bmatrix}$ and $r_i = r_i'$; $r_1, r_1' \in F_m$; $r_2, r_2' \in F'$. It is immediately verified that both R_1 and R_2 are right congruence relations. Moreover, they induce coset partitions. To see that $R_1 \cap R_2 = 0$, suppose that $(q, q') \in R_1 \cap R_2$. Then $\mathbf{P}q = \mathbf{P}q'$ and $q = q'$ since $\mathbf{P}$ is nonsingular.

Thus, M admits a parallel decomposition by Theorem 1.3. This decomposition is linear by Theorem 5.1. M also has a serial decomposition by Theorem 1.4. To see that this is a linear decomposition, note that one of the machines is M/R where R is a coset partition. Thus this machine is linear by Theorem 5.1. The other machine is constructed by choosing representatives. Thus this machine is linear by Lemma 5.1. ▌

We shall conclude this section by considering the serial and parallel connections of LSM's. It is necessary to compute the exact forms of such connections.

THEOREM 5.3. Let $M_i = \langle F, n_i, k, \mathbf{A}_i, \mathbf{B}_i \rangle$ be LSM's for $i = 1, 2$. Then $M = \langle F, n_1 + n_2, k, \mathbf{A}, \mathbf{B} \rangle$ where $\mathbf{A} = \mathbf{A}_1 \oplus \mathbf{A}_2$ and $\mathbf{B} = \begin{bmatrix} \mathbf{B}_1 \\ \mathbf{B}_2 \end{bmatrix}$ is state isomorphic to $M_1 \circledcirc M_2$.

Proof. Let $\varphi: (q_1, q_2) \to \begin{bmatrix} q_1 \\ q_2 \end{bmatrix}$. Clearly φ is a state isomorphism of $M_1 \circledcirc M_2$ onto M. ▌

The previous result could be extended to include outputs. Next we focus on serial connections.

THEOREM 5.4. Let $M_1 = \langle F, n_1, k_1, l_1, \mathbf{A}_1, \mathbf{B}_1, \mathbf{C}_1, \mathbf{D}_1 \rangle$ and

$M_2 = \langle F, n_2, l_1, \mathbf{A}_2, \mathbf{B}_2 \rangle$ be two LSM's. The LSM $M = \langle F, n_1 + n_2, k_1, \mathbf{A}, \mathbf{B} \rangle$ where $\mathbf{A} = \begin{bmatrix} \mathbf{A}_1 & \mathbf{0} \\ \mathbf{B}_2\mathbf{C}_1 & \mathbf{A}_2 \end{bmatrix}$ and $\mathbf{B} = \begin{bmatrix} \mathbf{B}_1 \\ \mathbf{B}_2\mathbf{D}_1 \end{bmatrix}$ is state isomorphic to $M_2 \ominus M_1$.

Proof. Define a map $\varphi(q_2, q_1) = \begin{bmatrix} q_1 \\ q_2 \end{bmatrix}$ from $M_2 \ominus M_1$ into M. φ is onto $F_{n_1+n_2}$ and is one-to-one. It follows immediately that $\delta'((q_2, q_1), a) = \delta(\varphi(q_2, q_1), a)$ where δ' is the transition function of $M_2 \ominus M_1$. ∎

Now we turn to a useful result which concerns certain subspaces in LSM's.

THEOREM 5.5. Let $M = \langle F, n, k, \mathbf{A}, \mathbf{B} \rangle$ and $M' = \langle F, n', k, \mathbf{A}', \mathbf{B}' \rangle$ be LSM's without outputs such that M' state realizes M (under a one-to-one map φ). There is a linear one-to-one map ψ between* col $\mathbf{L}_n$ and col $\mathbf{L}'_{n'}$.

Proof. Suppose $\varphi\mathbf{0} = q'$ where φ is the one-to-one assignment. We claim that there is another assignment ψ of M into M' for which $\psi\mathbf{0} = \mathbf{0}$. To see this, note that

$$q' = \varphi\mathbf{0} = \varphi\delta(\mathbf{0}, \mathbf{0}) = \delta'(\varphi\mathbf{0}, \mathbf{0}) = \mathbf{A}'q'$$

Thus

$$\mathbf{A}'q' = q' \tag{1}$$

Now we define $\psi q = \varphi q - q'$ for each $q \in F_n$. To confirm that ψ is an assignment, note first that ψ is one-to-one since φ is. Furthermore it is easy to see that:

$$\mathbf{A}'\varphi q = \mathbf{A}'\psi q + q' \tag{2}$$

[For $\varphi q = \psi q + q'$ implies

$$\mathbf{A}'\varphi q = \mathbf{A}'\psi q + \mathbf{A}'q' = \mathbf{A}'\psi q + q'$$

* Recall that in an LSM, col $\mathbf{L}_n$ is the "zero-submachine" which consists of the states reachable from the zero-state.

using (1).] We compute that

$$\psi\delta(q, a) = \varphi\delta(q, a) - q' = \delta'(\varphi q, a) - q' = \mathbf{A}'\varphi q + \mathbf{B}'a - q'$$

Using (2), we see that

$$\psi\delta(q, a) = \mathbf{A}'\psi q + q' + \mathbf{B}'a - q' = \delta'(\psi q, a)$$

Thus ψ is an assignment which is homogeneous, i.e. $\psi\mathbf{0} = \mathbf{0}$.

To complete the proof, we need only to show that ψ is linear on $W = \operatorname{col} \mathbf{L}_n$. We know that $W = \{\delta(\mathbf{0}, x) \mid x \in F_k^*\}$ so if $q_1, q_2 \in W$, then there exist $x_1, x_2 \in F_k^*$ so that $\delta(\mathbf{0}, x_i) = q_i$ for $i = 1, 2$. Suppose, without loss of generality that $lg(x_1) = lg(x_2)$, and compute, for $c \in F$

$$\begin{aligned} \psi(\delta(\mathbf{0}, x_1) + c\delta(\mathbf{0}, x_2)) &= \psi\delta(\mathbf{0}, x_1 + cx_2) \\ &= \delta'(\psi\mathbf{0}, x_1 + cx_2) \\ &= \delta'(\mathbf{0}, x_1 + cx_2) \\ &= \delta'(\mathbf{0}, x_1) + c\delta'(\mathbf{0}, x_2) \\ &= \psi\delta(\mathbf{0}, x_1) + c\psi\delta(\mathbf{0}, x) \end{aligned}$$

Thus ψ is linear on W and the proof is complete. ▮

COROLLARY. Let M and M' be LSM's and suppose M' state realizes M. If M is strongly connected (i.e., controllable) then there is a linear assignment from M into M'.

PROBLEM

Extend Theorems 5.3 and 5.4 to the case where there are outputs.

2. Parallel Decompositions I

In this section, a systematic investigation of linear parallel decompositions is begun. Ultimately, necessary and sufficient conditions will be given for such decompositions to exist. The development will break into a number of cases which are dependent on the algebraic structure of the LSM.

One of the first concepts of importance concerns indecomposable matrices.

DEFINITION. Let $\mathbf{A}$ be a square matrix over a field F and having minimum (characteristic) polynomial $m(x)$ (respectively $\varphi(x)$). $\mathbf{A}$ is *indecomposable over* $\mathbf{F}$ if $m(x) = \varphi(x) = (p(x))^e$ where $p(x)$ is irreducible over F.

It is easy to verify the following facts.

REMARKS. (1) A matrix $\mathbf{A}$ is indecomposable if and only if $\mathbf{A}$ is not similar to a direct sum of matrices. (2) An indecomposable and non-nilpotent matrix is nonsingular.

One of the reasons for considering indecomposable matrices is the following lemma.

LEMMA 5.2. Let V be an n dimensional vector space and $\mathbf{A}$ an $n \times n$ indecomposable matrix. If $V = V_1 \oplus V_2$ with V_1 and V_2 both $\mathbf{A}$ invariant subspaces then $V_1 = \{\mathbf{0}\}$ or $V_2 = \{\mathbf{0}\}$.

Proof. Assume for the sake of contradiction, that dim $V_1 > 1$ and dim $V_2 > 1$. Since V_1 and V_2 are $\mathbf{A}$ invariant subspaces, $\mathbf{A}$ is similar to $\mathbf{A}' = \mathbf{A}_1 \oplus \mathbf{A}_2$. Then

$$\varphi_{\mathbf{A}'} = \varphi_{\mathbf{A}_1}\varphi_{\mathbf{A}_2} = \varphi_{\mathbf{A}} = m_{\mathbf{A}} = m_{\mathbf{A}'} = [p(x)]^e$$

CLAIM. $m_{\mathbf{A}'} = m_{\mathbf{A}_1}$ or $m_{\mathbf{A}'} = m_{\mathbf{A}_2}$. Note that $m_{\mathbf{A}'} = \langle m_{\mathbf{A}_1}, m_{\mathbf{A}_2}\rangle = [p(x)]^e$. Since $m_{\mathbf{A}_i} \mid \varphi_{\mathbf{A}_i}$, $m_{\mathbf{A}_i} = [p(x)]^{e_i}$. Let $e^* = \max\{e_1, e_2\}$ and $m_{\mathbf{A}'} = [p(x)]^e = [p(x)]^{e^*}$ so $e_1 = e$ or $e_2 = e$ which implies the result.

Suppose $m_{\mathbf{A}'} = m_{\mathbf{A}_1}$. Then $m_{\mathbf{A}'} = m_{\mathbf{A}_1} = m_{\mathbf{A}} = \varphi_{\mathbf{A}}$. But $\deg m_{\mathbf{A}_1} \leq n_1 < n = \deg \varphi_{\mathbf{A}}$ so this is a contradiction. Thus dim $V_1 = 0$ or dim $V_2 = 0$ and the result follows. ∎

Another preliminary lemma will be required.

LEMMA 5.3. If an LSM $M = \langle F, n, k, \mathbf{A}, \mathbf{B} \rangle$ has a nontrivial linear parallel decomposition by $M_1 \oplus M_2 = \langle F, n', k, \mathbf{A}', \mathbf{B}' \rangle$ and $\mathbf{A}$ is indecomposable, then $n' > n$.

Proof. Since the state assignment is one-to-one into, $n' \geq n$. By Theorem 5.3, $\mathbf{A}' = \mathbf{A}_1 \oplus \mathbf{A}_2$ where $\mathbf{A}_1$ and $\mathbf{A}_2$ are the matrices of M_1 and M_2 respectively. If $n' = n$, $F_{n'} = F_n = F_{n_1} \oplus F_{n_2}$ where n_i is the size of $\mathbf{A}_i$. The map φ from F_n into $F_{n'} = F_n$ is one-to-one and onto so that φ^{-1} exists and is also one-to-one and onto. It is easily checked that φ^{-1} is also a state assignment mapping. Let $V_1 = \varphi^{-1}(F_{n_1} \oplus \{\mathbf{0}\})$ and $V_2 = \varphi^{-1}(\{\mathbf{0}\} \oplus F_{n_2})$. Since* $F_{n_1} \oplus \{\mathbf{0}\}$ and $\{\mathbf{0}\} \oplus F_{n_2}$ are invariant under $\mathbf{A}'$, it is clear that V_1 and V_2 are $\mathbf{A}$ invariant subspaces of F_n. Using properties of φ that were established in the proof of Theorem 5.5, one verifies† that $F_n = V_1 \oplus V_2$. This contradicts Lemma 5.2 since the decomposition must be nontrivial. ▮

Our next result is important and uses a number of auxiliary concepts. The proof is presented in the Appendix to maintain readability.

THEOREM 5.6. If an LSM $M = \langle F, n, k, \mathbf{A}, \mathbf{B} \rangle$ has a nontrivial linear parallel decomposition and if $\mathbf{A}$ is indecomposable, then the assignment φ is not linear.

COROLLARY. Let M be an LSM whose $\mathbf{A}$ matrix is indecomposable. If M is strongly connected, there is no nontrivial linear parallel decomposition.

---

* In other words, $F_{n_1} \oplus \{\mathbf{0}\}$ is a column vector space of n-tuples of the form $\begin{bmatrix} v \\ \mathbf{0} \end{bmatrix}$ where $v \in F_{n_1}$ and $\mathbf{0}$ is a zero vector of dimension $n - n_1$.

† This proof is needed since φ may not be a linear mapping.

Proof. Corollary to Theorem 5.5 and the present theorem. ▮

Our investigation into linear parallel decompositions will now break into a number of special cases. We may assume that the matrix **A** is indecomposable (because of Theorem 5.2). The cases to be considered are when $m(x) = \varphi(x) = (p(x))^e$ with $p(x)$ irreducible and

1. **A** nilpotent.
2. **A** non-nilpotent, $e = 1$, and $\mathbf{B} \neq \mathbf{0}$.
3. **A** non-nilpotent, $e = 1$, $\mathbf{B} = \mathbf{0}$, and F is finite.
4. **A** non-nilpotent, $e > 1$, $\mathbf{B} = \mathbf{0}$, and F is finite.
5. **A** non-nilpotent, $e > 1$, $\mathbf{B} \neq \mathbf{0}$, and F is finite.

We shall dispose of many of these cases quickly although Case 5 is very long. We now dispatch Case 1.

THEOREM 5.7. If $M = \langle F, n, k, \mathbf{A}, \mathbf{B} \rangle$ is an LSM with **A** indecomposable and nilpotent, then M has no nontrivial linear parallel realization.

Proof. Since **A** is indecomposable and nilpotent, we have that

$$m_{\mathbf{A}}(x) = \varphi_{\mathbf{A}}(x) = x^n$$

Suppose $M' = M_1 \textcircled{\scriptsize ||} M_2$ is an LSM state realizing M, and $\mathbf{A}' = \mathbf{A}_1 \oplus \mathbf{A}_2$. $\mathbf{A}^n = \mathbf{0}$. Thus $\mathbf{A}^n q = \mathbf{0}$ for all $q \in F_n$ and there is a state q_0 such that $\mathbf{A}^i q_0 = \mathbf{0}$ holds if and only if $i \geq n$ (otherwise $m_{\mathbf{A}}(x) \mid x^{n-1}$). Then $(\mathbf{A}')^i \varphi q_0 = \mathbf{0}$ holds if and only if $i \geq n$. Writing $\varphi q_0 = \begin{bmatrix} q_1 \\ q_2 \end{bmatrix}$ we have that $\mathbf{A}_1^i q_1 = \mathbf{0}$ holds if and only if $i \geq n$ or $\mathbf{A}_2^i q_2 = \mathbf{0}$ holds if and only if $i \geq n$. Then the minimum annihilating polynomial for q_1 (or q_2) is x^n; it divides $m_{\mathbf{A}_1}(x)$ (or $m_{\mathbf{A}_2}(x)$). Thus size $\mathbf{A}_1$ (or $\mathbf{A}_2$) $\geq$ degree $m_{\mathbf{A}_1}(x)$ (or deg $m_{\mathbf{A}_2}(x)$) $\geq n$. This leads to a trivial decomposition. ▮

Next, we deal with Case 2. Note that the proof does not depend on whether **A** is nilpotent.

THEOREM 5.8. Let $M = \langle F, n, k, \mathbf{A}, \mathbf{B}\rangle$ be an LSM with $\mathbf{A}$ indecomposable and $\mathbf{B} \neq \mathbf{0}$. Let the minimum polynomial of $\mathbf{A}$ be $m(x)$ which is irreducible. M has no nontrivial linear parallel decomposition.

Proof. Since $m(x)$ is irreducible, the only $\mathbf{A}$ invariant subspaces of F_n are $\mathbf{0}$ and F_n (cf. Lemma 5.2). Since $\mathbf{B} \neq \mathbf{0}$, $F_n = \text{col } \mathbf{L}_n$ and by Theorem 5.5 there is a linear one-to-one map between col $\mathbf{L}_n$ and col $\mathbf{L}'_{n'}$ (the state space of the zero submachine of M'). But this contradicts Theorem 5.6. ∎

PROBLEMS

1. Prove the remarks at the beginning of the section.
2. Suppose that $\mathbf{A} = \mathbf{A}_1 \oplus \mathbf{A}_2$. Show that $m_{\mathbf{A}} = \langle m_{\mathbf{A}_1}, m_{\mathbf{A}_2}\rangle$ where $\langle a, b\rangle$ is the least common multiple of a and b.

3. Parallel Decompositions II ($\mathbf{B} = \mathbf{0}$)

In this section, we shall deal with Cases 3 and 4. It will be necessary to assume that the field is finite and a number of auxiliary concepts will be needed.

Since we wish to consider Cases 3 and 4 where $\mathbf{B} = \mathbf{0}$, we need only consider an LSM as an $\mathbf{A}$ matrix. Henceforth, assume that F is finite and of characteristic p. Thus G_M or $G_{\mathbf{A}}$ denotes the monoid of the LSM and is finite. Since $\mathbf{A}$ is not nilpotent and is indecomposable, $\mathbf{A}$ is nonsingular so G_M is a group. In fact, $G_{\mathbf{A}}$ is the cyclic group generated by $\mathbf{A}$.

If M' state realizes M then G_M is isomorphic to some subgroup $G_{M''}$ of $G_{M'}$. (Theorem 1.8.) Let T be the order of G_M (and of $G_{M''}$). Thus $|G_{M'}| = jT$ for some number j. (This is Lagrange's Theorem.) In a linear parallel decomposition, $\mathbf{A}' = \mathbf{A}_1 \oplus \cdots \oplus \mathbf{A}_k$ and $G_{\mathbf{A}'}$ is a normal subgroup of $G_{\mathbf{A}_1} \times \cdots \times G_{\mathbf{A}_k}$ (cf. Problem 1). The order of $G_{\mathbf{A}'}$ is $\langle T_1, \ldots, T_k\rangle$, the least common multiple of $T_1, \ldots, T_k$ and where T_i is the order of $G_{\mathbf{A}_i} = G_{M_i}$. Thus we have shown the following:

REDUCTION 1. Let $\mathbf{B} = \mathbf{0}$ and let F be finite. M (or $\mathbf{A}$) has a linear parallel decomposition only if there exist matrices $\mathbf{A}_1, \ldots, \mathbf{A}_k$ so that for some j, $jT = \langle T_1, \ldots, T_k \rangle$ where $T = |G_\mathbf{A}|$ and $T_i = |G_{\mathbf{A}_i}|$.

Before continuing, some new concepts are needed.

DEFINITION. Let F be a finite field. For each $p(x) \in F[x]$ so that $x \nmid p(x)$, the *exponent* of $p(x)$ is the least positive integer k so that $p(x) \mid x^k - 1$. If $\mathbf{A}$ is a matrix, the exponent of $\mathbf{A}$ is the exponent of $m_\mathbf{A}$. We will write exp $p(x)$ or exp $\mathbf{A}$ to denote the exponent.†

The exponent of $c \in F$ is 1. This definition is based on a theorem of field theory which states for any such $p(x)$, the exponent exists [37]. With this definition, one can derive the following fact.

PROPOSITION 5.1. Let $\mathbf{A}$ be a nonsingular matrix; then the order of $G_\mathbf{A}$ is exp $\mathbf{A}$.

Next, we can further reduce the problem to the case where $j = 1$.

REDUCTION 2. Let $\mathbf{B} = \mathbf{0}$ and let F be finite. M (or $\mathbf{A}$) has a linear parallel decomposition only if there exist matrices $\mathbf{A}_1, \ldots, \mathbf{A}_k$ so that $T = \langle T_1, \ldots, T_k \rangle$ where $T = |G_\mathbf{A}|$ and $T_i = |G_{\mathbf{A}_i}|$.

Proof. If there is such a decomposition, let $\mathbf{A}' = \mathbf{A}_1 \oplus \cdots \oplus \mathbf{A}_k$ with $jT = \langle T_1, \ldots, T_k \rangle$. Define $(\mathbf{A}')^* = (\mathbf{A}')^j = \mathbf{A}_1^j \oplus \cdots \oplus \mathbf{A}_k^j$. Now $|G_{(\mathbf{A}')^*}| = T = \langle T_1', \ldots, T_k' \rangle$ where T_i' is the order of $G_{\mathbf{A}_i^j}$. ∎

† There is no danger of confusion with the exponential function since this latter concept does not appear in this book.

Before proving the main result, it is necessary to introduce some combinatorial machinery. Since we are dealing with a nonsingular matrix **A** over a finite field F, the vector space is broken into cycles by the action of **A**. It will be important to be able to compute these cycle structures.

DEFINITION. Let F be a finite field of characteristic p and **A** a nonsingular $n \times n$ matrix over F. The *cycle structure of* **A** is denoted by $f_1^{j_1} \cdots f_{p^n}^{j_{p^n}}$ if **A** induces j_i cycles of length i.

EXAMPLE. $F = \mathbb{Z}_2$ and $\mathbf{A} = \begin{pmatrix} 0 & 1 \\ 1 & 1 \end{pmatrix}$. The state diagram of **A** is

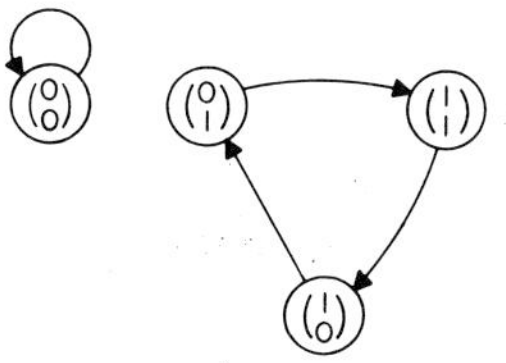

and so the cycle structure is $f_1 f_3$. Note that if the cycle structure of **A** is $f_1^{j_1} \cdots f_{p^n}^{j_{p^n}}$, we must have that

$$\sum_{i=1}^{p^n} i j_i = p^n$$

since every element is in one and only one cycle.

We shall expand our notion of cycle structure to include the cycle structure of a monic polynomial.

DEFINITION. Let $f(x)$ be a monic polynomial of degree h. The *cycle structure* of $f(x)$ is the cycle structure induced by the companion matrix $\mathbf{C}_f$.

EXAMPLE. If $F = \mathbb{Z}_2$ and $f(x) = x^2 + x + 1$, then

$$\mathbf{C}_f = \begin{pmatrix} 0 & 1 \\ 1 & 1 \end{pmatrix}$$

which is the matrix **A** of the previous example. Thus the cycle structure of $f(x)$ is $f_1 f_3$.

We must be able to compute with cycle structures. The following important definition is common in combinatorial analysis [22, 23].

DEFINITION. Let $a = f_1^{j_1} \cdots f_m^{j_m}$ and $b = f_1^{k_1} \cdots f_n^{k_n}$ be cycle structures. The *cross operation* is defined to be

$$a \times b = \left[\prod_{r=1}^{m} f_r^{j_r}\right] \times \left[\prod_{s=1}^{n} f_s^{k_s}\right] = \prod_{r=1}^{m} \prod_{s=1}^{n} f_{\langle r,s\rangle}^{j_r k_s (r,s)}$$

where $\langle r, s\rangle$ is the least common multiple of r and s while (r, s) is their greatest common divisor.

EXAMPLE. Let $a = f_1 f_3$ and $b = f_1 f_2^2$. Then

$$\begin{aligned} a \times b &= (f_1 f_3) \times (f_1 f_2^2) \\ &= (f_1 \times f_1)(f_1 \times f_2^2)(f_3 \times f_1)(f_3 \times f_2^2) \\ &= f_1 f_2^2 f_3 f_6^2 \end{aligned}$$

Next, we note why the cross operation is natural.

LEMMA 5.4. Let $\mathbf{A}_1$ and $\mathbf{A}_2$ be nonsingular matrices over a finite field of characteristic p and having cycle structures a_1 and a_2. Then the cycle structure of $\mathbf{A}_1 \oplus \mathbf{A}_2$ is $a_1 \times a_2$.

Proof. Any element q of $F_{n_1+n_2}$ will be of the form $q = \begin{bmatrix} q_1 \\ q_2 \end{bmatrix}$ with $q_i \in F_{n_i}$. If $q_1(q_2)$ is in a cycle of length $r(s)$, then q is in a cycle of length $\langle r, s\rangle$. The number of such cycles must be $j_r j_s (r, s)$ (which is the exponent in $a_1 \times a_2$), since $(r, s)\langle r, s\rangle = rs$. Thus

$$\sum_r \sum_s \langle r, s\rangle (r, s) j_r j_s = \sum_r r j_r \sum_s s j_s = p^{n_1} p^{n_2} = p^{n_1+n_2}$$

as is required. ∎

The next step in our investigation into cycle structures is to derive the cycle structure of a given polynomial. This will be done for primary polynomials and extended to arbitrary polynomials by the use of the cross operation. We state this result now without proof [11, 16]. See Problem 4.

THEOREM 5.9. Let $f(x) = [p(x)]^e$ where $p(x)$ is irreducible over a finite field of characteristic p. Let h be the degree of $p(x)$. The cycle structure of $f(x)$ (or $\mathbf{C}_f$) is

$$f_1 f_{T_1}^{(p^h-1)/T_1} f_{T_2}^{(p^{2h}-p^h)/T_2} \cdots f_{T_e}^{(p^{eh}-p^{(e-1)h})/T_e}$$

where $T_i = \exp [p(x)]^i$. Moreover $T_i = p^{r_i}T_1$ where r_i is the least integer so that $p^{r_i} \geq i$.

COROLLARY 1. For each $1 \leq i \leq e$,

$$T_i \mid (p^{ih} - p^{(i-1)h})$$

Note that $(T_1, p) = 1$.

COROLLARY 2. If $e = 1$, the cycle structure is

$$f_1 f_T^{(p^h-1)/T}$$

and $T \mid (p^h - 1)$. Note that $(T, p) = 1$ and $T = \exp p(x)$.

We will often refer to T_1 as the basic period, since all the others are derived from it.

We now have the necessary background to settle Case 3.

THEOREM 5.10. Let F be a finite field of characteristic p and $\mathbf{A}$ an indecomposable nonsingular matrix with $m(x) = p(x)$ of degree h. [This is Case 3 where $\mathbf{A}$ is non-nilpotent, $e = 1$, and $\mathbf{B} = \mathbf{0}$.] M (or $\mathbf{A}$) has a nontrivial parallel linear decomposition if and only if there exist $k (k > 1)$ irreducible polynomials $p_1(x), \ldots, p_k(x)$ with exponents $T_1, \ldots, T_k$ and degrees $h_1, \ldots, h_k$ respectively, such that $T = \langle T_1, \ldots, T_k \rangle$ where $T = \exp p(x)$. Finally $h_i < h$ for each i, $i = 1, \ldots, k$.

Proof. If there is such a decomposition, we have seen that there exist matrices $\mathbf{A}_1, \ldots, \mathbf{A}_k$ so that $T = \langle T_1, \ldots, T_k \rangle$ where

$T = |G_{\mathbf{A}}|$ and $T_i = |G_{\mathbf{A}_i}|$. Using Proposition 5.1, we know that $T = \exp m(x)$ while $T_i = \exp m_{\mathbf{A}_i}$ for $i = 1, \ldots, k$. It is clear that the $m_{\mathbf{A}_i}$ can be taken to be irreducible. We must have that $h_i < h$ for $1 \leq i \leq k$ for if (say) $h_1 \geq h$, then $\deg m_{\mathbf{A}_1}(x) = h_1 \geq h$ and hence $\mathbf{A}_1$ is larger than or equal to an $h \times h$ matrix so that the decomposition is trivial.

Conversely, suppose that T is prime. Then there is no decomposition. If T is not prime, $(T, p) = 1$ because of Corollary 2. Therefore $(T_i, p) = 1$ for $i = 1, \ldots, k$ [for if $(T_i, p) = d > 1$, then $d \mid \langle T_1, \ldots, T_k \rangle$ and $d \mid p$ implies $d \mid 1$]. Let the cycle structure of $\mathbf{A}$ be $C_{\mathbf{A}}$ and

$$C_{\mathbf{A}} = f_1 f_T^{(p^h-1)/T}$$

where T is the exponent of $p(x)$. Let C_i be the cycle structure of $\mathbf{A}_i$ for $i = 1, \ldots, k$ then define $\mathbf{A}' = \mathbf{A}_1 \oplus \cdots \oplus \mathbf{A}_k \oplus \mathbf{I}$ where $\mathbf{I}$ is an identity matrix of size t which will be specified shortly. $\mathbf{A}_i$ is the companion matrix of $p_i(x)$. There will be cycles of length T_i in $C_{\mathbf{A}_i}$. We can show that $\mathbf{A}'$ is a linear parallel decomposition of $\mathbf{A}$ by showing that every cycle of $\mathbf{A}$ is a cycle of $\mathbf{A}'$. To do this, we choose t so large that

$$p^t(T_1, \ldots, T_k)a_1 \cdots a_k > (p^h - 1)/T$$

where a_i is the number of T_i cycles in $C_{\mathbf{A}_i}$. [This number is the number of cycles of length T induced by $\mathbf{A}'$. Note that $a_1, \ldots, a_k \geq 1$.] Thus every cycle of $\mathbf{A}$ is a cycle of $\mathbf{A}'$ and the argument is complete. ∎

We now turn to a consideration of Case 4. There is always a decomposition in this instance.

THEOREM 5.11. Let M be an LSM with $\mathbf{B} = \mathbf{0}$, $\mathbf{A}$ a nonsingular indecomposable matrix with $m(x) = [p(x)]^e$ with $e > 1$ and $\deg p(x) = h$ where $p(x)$ is irreducible. There is a nontrivial linear parallel decomposition of M (or $\mathbf{A}$).

Proof. Define $\mathbf{A}_1 = \mathbf{C}_{p(x)}$, $\mathbf{A}_2 = \mathbf{C}_{(x-1)^e}$, and $\mathbf{A}' = \mathbf{A}_1 \oplus \mathbf{A}_2 \oplus \mathbf{I}$ where the size t of $\mathbf{I}$ is chosen so that the size of $\mathbf{A}'$ is 1 plus the size of $\mathbf{A}$, i.e.

$$t + h + e = he + 1 \qquad \text{so} \qquad t = (h - 1)(e - 1)$$

To show that $\mathbf{A}'$ realizes $\mathbf{A}$, we show that the cycle structure of $\mathbf{A}$ is contained in the cycle structure induced by $\mathbf{A}'$. The argument will be an induction on e.

Basis: $e = 2$, $C = f_1 f_T^{(p^h-1)/T} f_{pT}^{(p^{2h}-p^h)/pT}$, $C_{\mathbf{A}_1} = f_1 f_T^{(p^h-1)/T}$, $C_{\mathbf{A}_2} = f_1^p f_p^{(p-1)}$, and $C_{\mathbf{I}} = f_1^{p^{h-1}}$. Using $(T, p) = 1$, we find that the exponent x of the term f_{pT}^x in $C_{\mathbf{A}'}$ is

$$x = \frac{(p - 1)(p^h - 1)(p^{h-1})}{T}$$

It is a straightforward matter to verify that

$$x \geq (p^{2h} - p^h)/pT$$

Induction Step. Assume the result for all values less than e_1 and let $e = e_1 > 1$. If $[p(x)]^{e-1}$ induces cycle structure C and $[p(x)]^e$ induces cycle structure $\tilde{C}$, then

$$\tilde{C} = C f_{p^{j_1}T}^{(p^{he_1}-p^{h(e_1-1)})/p^{j_1}T}$$

where j_1 satisfies $p^{j_1-1} < e_1 \leq p^{j_1}$. (See Theorem 5.9.) In passing from $\mathbf{A}'$ for $e_1 - 1$ to $\mathbf{A}'$ for e_1, note that

(1) $\mathbf{A}_1$ is unchanged,
(2) the size of $\mathbf{A}_2$ is increased by 1, and
(3) the size of $\mathbf{A}$ increases by $h - 1$.

We must check that at least $(p^{he_1} - p^{h(e_1-1)})/p^{j_1}T$ new cycles of length $p^{j_1}T$ are added. The least number to be added corresponds to a cycle structure product of the exponent x of f_T^x induced by $\mathbf{A}_1$ times the new exponent from $\mathbf{A}_2$ (which is $f_{p^j}^{(p^{e_1}-p^{(e_1-1)})/p^{j_1}}$) times $p^{(he_1-h-e_1+1)} = p^{(h-1)(e_1-1)}$ which is the contribution of the identity matrix **I**. The exponent y of $f^{y}_{p^{j_1}T}$ is

$$\begin{aligned} y &= \frac{p^h - 1}{T} \cdot \frac{p^{e_1} - p^{(e_1-1)}}{p^{j_1}} \cdot p^{(h-1)(e_1-1)} \\ &= (p^h - 1)p^{(e_1-1)}(p - 1)p^{(h-1)(e_1-1)}/p^{j_1}T \\ &= (p^h - 1)(p - 1)p^{h(e_1-1)}/p^{j_1}T \\ &\geq p^{h(e_1-1)}(p^h - 1)/p^{j_1}T = (p^{he_1} - p^{h(e_1-1)})/p^{j_1}T \end{aligned}$$

Thus enough cycles have been added and the realization exists. ▌

The present development has been abstract and some concrete examples may prove helpful.

EXAMPLE (OF THEOREM (5.10). Let $F = \mathbb{Z}_2$ and

$$\mathbf{A} = \begin{bmatrix} 0 & 1 & 0 & 0 & 0 & 0 \\ 0 & 0 & 1 & 0 & 0 & 0 \\ 0 & 0 & 0 & 1 & 0 & 0 \\ 0 & 0 & 0 & 0 & 1 & 0 \\ 0 & 0 & 0 & 0 & 0 & 1 \\ 1 & 1 & 1 & 0 & 1 & 0 \end{bmatrix}$$

$\mathbf{A} = \mathbf{C}_{f(x)}$ where $f(x) = x^6 + x^4 + x^2 + x + 1$. Consulting a table [16], or simple computation, shows that the exponent of $f(x)$ is 21 and the cycle structure (from Corollary 2 to Theorem 5.9) is $f_1 f_{21}^3$. Since $21 = 3 \cdot 7$, we again consult tables to find that there exists a polynomial $p_1(x) = x^2 + x + 1$, which has exponent 3, and a polynomial $p_2(x) = x^3 + x^2 + 1$, which has exponent 7. Take $t = 2$ and we have a decomposition

$$\mathbf{A}' = \left[\begin{array}{cc|ccc|cc} 0 & 1 & & & & & \\ 1 & 1 & & \mathbf{0} & & & \mathbf{0} \\ \hline & & 0 & 1 & 0 & & \\ \mathbf{0} & & 0 & 0 & 1 & & \mathbf{0} \\ & & 1 & 0 & 1 & & \\ \hline & & & & & 1 & 0 \\ \mathbf{0} & & & \mathbf{0} & & 0 & 1 \end{array}\right]$$

The cycle structure of $\mathbf{A}'$ is

$$C' = (f_1 f_3) \times (f_1 f_7) \times (f_1^4) = f_1^4 f_3^4 f_7^4 f_{21}^4$$

Thus every cycle of C is included in the cycle structure of C'.

EXAMPLE (OF THEOREM 5.11). Let $F = \mathbb{Z}_2$ and $f(x) = (1 + x + x^2)^6$ where $\mathbf{A} = \mathbf{C}_{f(x)}$ is a 12×12 matrix. Then $h = 2$, $e = 6$ and the exponent of $1 + x + x^2$ is 3. One computes (Theorem 5.9) that the cycle structure of $f(x)$ is

$$f_1 f_3 f_6^2 f_{12}^{20} f_{24}^{160}$$

For a decomposition, we take $\mathbf{A}_1 = C_{f_1(x)}$ where $f_1(x) = x^2 + x + 1$, $\mathbf{A}_2 = \mathbf{C}_{f_2(x)}$ where $f_2 = (x - 1)^6$ and we use an identity matrix of size $t = (e - 1)(h - 1) = 5$. Thus the cycle structure C' of $\mathbf{A}' = \mathbf{A}_1 \oplus \mathbf{A}_2 \oplus \mathbf{I}$ is

$$C' = (f_1 f_3) \times (f_1^2 f_2 f_4^3 f_8^6) \times f^{32} = f_1^{64} f_2^{32} f_3^{64} f_4^{96} f_6^{32} f_8^{192} f_{12}^{96} f_{24}^{192}$$

which contains C. Note that multiplying just the first two terms together does not provide enough cycles of length 24. Also taking $t = 4$ would not provide enough such cycles.

PROBLEMS

1. Let $\mathbf{A}_1$ and $\mathbf{A}_2$ be square matrices (LSM's with $\mathbf{B} = \mathbf{0}$). Show that if $\mathbf{A}' = \mathbf{A}_1 \oplus \mathbf{A}_2$, then $G_{\mathbf{A}'}$ is a normal subgroup of $G_{\mathbf{A}_1} \times G_{\mathbf{A}_2}$.

2. Prove that the definition of exponent is valid, i.e., for each polynomial $p(x)$ such that $x \nmid p(x)$ there exists a number k so that $p(x) \mid x^k - 1$ if F is finite.

3. Prove Proposition 5.1.

4. Prove Theorem 5.9 and its corollaries.

4. Parallel Decomposition (Case 5)

The most difficult case to be discussed is Case 5. The argument is long and involves many new concepts and ideas. Our development begins with a lemma concerning state assignments.

LEMMA 5.5. Let $M = \langle F, n, k, \mathbf{A}, \mathbf{B} \rangle$ be a finite LSM with $\mathbf{A}$ nonsingular and indecomposable. Let $M' = M_1 ⦶ M_2$ be a nontrivial linear parallel decomposition of M under the state assignment φ. If $W = \operatorname{col} \mathbf{L}_n$ and $W' = \operatorname{col} \mathbf{L}'_{n'}$, then φ satisfies the following conditions:

1. For each $q \in F_n$, $\varphi \mathbf{A} q = \mathbf{A}' \varphi q$.
2. φ is a linear map of W onto W'.
3. φ is one-to-one.
4. For each $q \in F_n$, $w \in W$,

$$\varphi(q + w) = \varphi q + \varphi w$$

Proof. (1), (2), and (3) have been stated before. We must prove (4). Since F is finite and $\mathbf{A}$ is indecomposable and nonsingular, there is a positive integer j so that $\mathbf{A}^j = \mathbf{I}$. (In fact, $j = \exp \mathbf{A}$.) There is a least number i_1 so that rank $\mathbf{L}_{i_1} =$ rank $\mathbf{L}_{i_1+1}$. It is clear that $j > i_1$. [Otherwise $\mathbf{A}^j\mathbf{B} = \mathbf{B}$ and all columns of $\mathbf{A}^r\mathbf{B}$, $r \geq j$ depend on earlier ones and i_1 is not minimal.]

Choose $q \in F_n$ and $w \in W$. Define $w' = \varphi w$. There exists $x \in F_k^j$ so that $w = \delta(\mathbf{0}, x)$ and $w' = \delta'(\mathbf{0}, x)$ because of the way W is formed and the properties of φ. Therefore

$$\delta(q, x) = \delta(q, \mathbf{0}^j) + \delta(\mathbf{0}, x) = \mathbf{A}^j q + w$$

and

$$\delta'(\varphi q, x) = \delta'(\varphi q, \mathbf{0}^j) + \delta'(\mathbf{0}, x) = (\mathbf{A}')^j \varphi q + w'$$

Since φ is an assignment

$$\varphi\delta(q, x) = \varphi(\mathbf{A}^j q + w) = (\mathbf{A}')^j \varphi q + w' = \delta'(\varphi q, x)$$

Now, note that $\mathbf{A}^j q = q$ implies $(\mathbf{A}')^j \varphi q = \varphi q$ because φ is one-to-one. Together, our results give that

$$\varphi(q + w) = \varphi(\mathbf{A}^j q + w) = (\mathbf{A}')^j \varphi q + w' = \varphi q + \varphi w \quad \blacksquare$$

It is possible to prove the preceding lemma in the infinite case but the argument becomes substantially more complicated.

The next result is simple, and it is used frequently without mention.

LEMMA 5.6. Let M_i and M_i^* be state-isomorphic sequential machines for $i = 1, 2$. M_2 state realizes M_1 if and only if M_2^* state realizes M_1^*. (Moreover, if there is a realization, then M_2 state realizes M_1^* and also M_2^* state realizes M_1.)

Our next result helps to classify the invariant subspaces of indecomposable matrices.

LEMMA 5.7. Let $\mathbf{A}$ be an indecomposable matrix. If W_1 and W_2 are $\mathbf{A}$-invariant subspaces, then $W_1 \subseteq W_2$ or $W_2 \subseteq W_1$.

Proof. Since $\mathbf{A}$ is indecomposable, $\varphi_{\mathbf{A}} = m_{\mathbf{A}} = [p(x)]^e$ where $p(x)$ is irreducible. Let $p_i(x)$ be the minimum function of W_i for $i = 1, 2$. Clearly $p_i(x) \mid m_{\mathbf{A}}(x)$ for $i = 1, 2$. [For if $m_{\mathbf{A}}$ annihilates the whole space, it annihilates W_i. Thus $m_{\mathbf{A}}(x)$ is in the ideal generated by $p_i(x)$.] Thus $p_1(x) = [p(x)]^{e_1}$ and $p_2(x) = [p(x)]^{e_2}$ and we assume $e_1 > e_2$. If $w \in W_2$, then $[p(\mathbf{A})]^{e_2} w = \mathbf{0}$ so that $[p(\mathbf{A})]^{e_1 - e_2}[p(\mathbf{A})]^{e_2} w = \mathbf{0}$. Thus $w \in W_1$ and $W_2 \subseteq W_1$. $\blacksquare$

The next lemma puts indecomposable matrices into a "normal form."

LEMMA 5.8. Let $\mathbf{A}$ be an indecomposable matrix where $\varphi_{\mathbf{A}} = m_{\mathbf{A}} = [p(x)]^e$ with $e > 1$. If $\mathbf{A}$ is similar to

$$\mathbf{A}' = \begin{pmatrix} \mathbf{Q} & \mathbf{Z}_0 \\ \mathbf{0} & \mathbf{Z}_1 \end{pmatrix}$$

then $\mathbf{Q}$ is indecomposable. Moreover $\varphi_{\mathbf{Q}} = m_{\mathbf{Q}} = [p(x)]^{e_1}$ with $1 \leq e_1 < e$.

Proof. If $\mathbf{Q}$ is decomposable, there is a nonsingular matrix $\mathbf{T}$ so that

$$\mathbf{TQT}^{-1} = \mathbf{Q}_1 \oplus \mathbf{Q}_2$$

where $\mathbf{Q}_1$ is an $r \times r$ matrix and $\mathbf{Q}_2$ is an $s \times s$ matrix. Then

$$\begin{pmatrix} \mathbf{T} & \mathbf{0} \\ \mathbf{0} & \mathbf{I} \end{pmatrix} \begin{pmatrix} \mathbf{Q} & \mathbf{Z}_0 \\ \mathbf{0} & \mathbf{Z}_1 \end{pmatrix} \begin{pmatrix} \mathbf{T}^{-1} & \mathbf{0} \\ \mathbf{0} & \mathbf{I} \end{pmatrix} = \begin{pmatrix} \mathbf{TQT}^{-1} & \mathbf{TZ}_0 \\ \mathbf{0} & \mathbf{Z}_1 \end{pmatrix}$$

Thus $\mathbf{A}$ is similar to

$$\mathbf{A}^* = \begin{pmatrix} \mathbf{Q}_1 & \mathbf{0} & \mathbf{P}_0 \\ \mathbf{0} & \mathbf{Q}_2 & \mathbf{P}_1 \\ \mathbf{0} & \mathbf{0} & \mathbf{Z}_1 \end{pmatrix}$$

and we will argue that this is impossible. Note that $\mathbf{Q}_1 \neq \mathbf{0}$ and $\mathbf{Q}_2 \neq \mathbf{0}$ since otherwise, rank $\mathbf{A}^* <$ rank $\mathbf{A}$.

Let

$$W_1 = \left\{ \begin{pmatrix} q \\ \mathbf{0} \end{pmatrix} \middle| \, q \in F_r \right\} \qquad \text{and} \qquad W_2 = \left\{ \begin{pmatrix} \mathbf{0} \\ q \\ \mathbf{0} \end{pmatrix} \middle| \, q \in F_s \right\}$$

It is easy to see that W_1 and W_2 are both $\mathbf{A}^*$-invariant subspaces (compute $\mathbf{A}^* W_i$) but this contradicts the previous lemma applied to $\mathbf{A}^*$. ▮

The previous proof also yields the following result which is convenient to note here.

PROPOSITION 5.2. Let $\mathbf{A} = \begin{pmatrix} \mathbf{Q} & \mathbf{Z}_0 \\ \mathbf{0} & \mathbf{Z}_1 \end{pmatrix}$ be an indecomposable matrix where $\varphi_{\mathbf{A}} = m_{\mathbf{A}} = [p(x)]^e$ with $e > 1$ and $\deg p(x) = h$.

If W is an invariant subspace then dim $W = he_1$ and $m_{\mathbf{Q}} = [p(x)]^{e_1}$.

Proof. Let $\mathbf{Q}$ be $m \times m$. Clearly $\left\{\begin{bmatrix} q \\ \mathbf{0} \end{bmatrix} \middle| q \in F_m\right\}$ is $\mathbf{A}$-invariant. By Lemma 5.8, $\varphi_{\mathbf{Q}} = m_{\mathbf{Q}} = [p(x)]^{e_1}$ where deg $\varphi_{\mathbf{Q}} = m$ and so $m = he_1$. ▮

CONVENTION. In the sequel, we will often write w instead of $\begin{bmatrix} w \\ \mathbf{0} \end{bmatrix}$ when we deal with an invariant subspace W of F_n.

In what follows, we may assume that the given LSM M is not controllable (i.e., strongly connected) (cf. Corollary to Theorem 5.6.). Furthermore, we can assume that $\mathbf{Z}_0 \neq \mathbf{0}$ since $\mathbf{A}$ is indecomposable.

Suppose that $M' = \langle F, n', k, \mathbf{A}', \mathbf{B}' \rangle$ is an LSM which state realizes $M = \langle F, n, k, \mathbf{A}, \mathbf{B} \rangle$ and F is finite. Furthermore, suppose the realization is a nontrivial linear parallel realization so that $\mathbf{A}' = \mathbf{A}_1 \oplus \mathbf{A}_2$. It is necessary to classify all such realizations M'.

LEMMA 5.9. Let $M = \langle F, n, k, \mathbf{A}, \mathbf{B} \rangle$ be a finite LSM. Assume $\mathbf{A}$ is indecomposable, $m_{\mathbf{A}} = \varphi_{\mathbf{A}} = [p(x)]^e$ where $p(x)$ is irreducible of degree h. Let $W = \text{col } \mathbf{L}_n$ have dimension he_0. If M' is a nontrivial linear parallel state realization of M, we may assume $M' = M_1 ⦶ \cdots ⦶ M_m ⦶ M''$ where for each i, $1 \leq i \leq m$, $M_i = \langle \mathbf{A}_i, \mathbf{B}_i \rangle$, $\mathbf{B}_i \neq \mathbf{0}$, $\mathbf{A}_i$ indecomposable, $m_{\mathbf{A}_i} = \varphi_{\mathbf{A}_i} = [p(x)]^{e_i}$, $e_i < e$. Moreover $\mathbf{A}_i = \begin{bmatrix} \mathbf{A}_{i1} & \mathbf{A}_{i2} \\ \mathbf{0} & \mathbf{A}_{i_3} \end{bmatrix}$ with $\mathbf{A}_{i1}$ indecomposable and $m_{\mathbf{A}_{i1}} = [p(x)]^{e_i^*}$ and $e_i^* \leq e_0$. Finally $e_i^* = e_0$, and $M'' = \langle \mathbf{A}'', \mathbf{B}'' \rangle$ and $\mathbf{B}'' = \mathbf{0}$, where $M'' = M_1' ⦶ \cdots ⦶ M_r'$ with $M_i' = \langle \mathbf{A}_i', \mathbf{0} \rangle$ and size $\mathbf{A}_i' <$ size $\mathbf{A}$ for $i = 1, \ldots, r$.

Proof. Suppose $M' = \langle F, n', k, \mathbf{A}', \mathbf{B}' \rangle$ is a nontrivial linear parallel state realization of M and $\mathbf{A}' = \mathbf{A}_1 \oplus \cdots \oplus \mathbf{A}_m \oplus \cdots \oplus \mathbf{A}_r$ where each $\mathbf{A}_i$ is indecomposable. Let

$$\mathbf{B}' = \begin{bmatrix} \mathbf{B}_1 \\ \cdot \\ \cdot \\ \cdot \\ \mathbf{B}_m \\ \mathbf{0} \\ \cdot \\ \cdot \\ \cdot \\ \mathbf{0} \end{bmatrix}$$

where no $\mathbf{B}_i = 0$ for $1 \leq i \leq m$. This can always be done.

Since $\dim W = he_0$, $\mathbf{A} = \begin{bmatrix} \mathbf{Q} & \mathbf{Z}_0 \\ \mathbf{0} & \mathbf{Z}_1 \end{bmatrix}$ where $\mathbf{Q}$ is indecomposable, $m_{\mathbf{Q}} = \varphi_{\mathbf{Q}} = [p(x)]^{e_0}$, $e_0 < e$ and $\mathbf{B} = \begin{bmatrix} \mathbf{B}^* \\ \mathbf{0} \end{bmatrix}$. Let $M^* = \langle F, he_0, k, \mathbf{A}^*, \mathbf{B}^* \rangle$ where $\mathbf{A}^* = \mathbf{Q}$. This is the $\mathbf{0}$-submachine of M. We do the same for each $M_i = \langle \mathbf{A}_i, \mathbf{B}_i \rangle$ and by a similarity transformation,

$$\mathbf{A}_i = \begin{bmatrix} \mathbf{A}_{i1} & \mathbf{A}_{i2} \\ \mathbf{0} & \mathbf{A}_{i3} \end{bmatrix}, \qquad \mathbf{B}_i = \begin{bmatrix} \mathbf{B}_{i1} \\ \mathbf{0} \end{bmatrix}$$

$\mathbf{A}_{i1}$ is indecomposable for each i, $1 \leq i \leq m$ but no $\mathbf{B}_{i1} = \mathbf{0}$ since no $\mathbf{B}_i = \mathbf{0}$. Let $M_i^* = \langle \mathbf{A}_i^*, \mathbf{B}_i^* \rangle = \langle \mathbf{A}_{i1}, \mathbf{B}_{i1} \rangle$ and define $M'^* = M_1^* \oplus \cdots \oplus M_m^*$ and $\mathbf{A}'^* = \mathbf{A}_1^* \oplus \cdots \oplus \mathbf{A}_m^*$. Each M_i^* is strongly connected. There is a one-to-one linear assignment from M^* into M'^*; hence there is a matrix $\mathbf{T}$ of rank he_0 (the size of $\mathbf{Q} = \dim W$) such that $\mathbf{TQ} = \mathbf{A}'^*\mathbf{T}$. By the proof of Theorem 5.6 in the appendix, $\mathbf{A}'^*$ must contain a block $\mathbf{A}_t^*$ with $m_{\mathbf{A}_t^*} = \varphi_{\mathbf{A}_t^*} = [p(x)]^{e_t^*}$ and $e_t^* \geq e_0$. By renumbering if necessary, take $e_1^* \geq e_0$.

Claim. If $m_{\mathbf{A}_i^*} = \varphi_{\mathbf{A}_i^*} = [q_i(x)]^{e_i^*}$ then $q_i(x) = p(x)$.

Proof of Claim. Suppose $q_i(x) \neq p(x)$ and let $w_i \neq \mathbf{0}$ be a state in M_i^*. There must exist $\{w_j \mid 1 \leq j \leq m, j \neq i\}$ such that

$$w' = \begin{bmatrix} w_1 \\ \cdot \\ \cdot \\ \cdot \\ w_m \end{bmatrix} = \varphi w$$

for some $w \in F_{he_0} = W^*$. [Otherwise M_1^* would be a zero machine.] If $w \in F_{he_0}$ its minimal annihilating polynomial m_w divides $[p(x)]^{e_0}$. If $\varphi w = w'$, then $m_{w'} = m_w$ by the linearity of φ on W. But $m_{w'} = \langle m_{w_1}, \ldots, m_{w_m} \rangle$. It is clear that $m_{w_i} = [q_i(x)]^t$ for some t so $q_i(x) \mid m_{w_i}$. Thus $q_i(x) \mid m_{w'}$, but $q_i(x) \nmid m_w = [p(x)]^{e_0}$ since $(p(x), q_i(x)) = 1$. This contradiction establishes the claim.

Next, we claim that $e_i^* \leq e_0$ for each $1 \leq i \leq m$. (The convention is that $e_1^* \geq e_0$.) If this were not true, then for some j, $e_j^* > e_0$. Then M_j^*, which is strongly connected, would have $p^{he_j^*} > p^{he_0}$ states. Thus the number of states reachable from the $\mathbf{0}$ state in M'^* exceeds the number of states reachable from $\mathbf{0}$ in M_i^* which would contradict that φ is one-to-one from W *onto* W'. Thus $e_1^* = e_0$.

It follows from the first claim that $m_{\mathbf{A}_i} = \varphi_{\mathbf{A}i} = [p(x)]^{e_i}$ with $e_i < e$ for all i, $1 \leq i \leq m$ ($e_i \geq e$ for some i would lead to a trivial realization).

To complete the proof, one takes all the machines with $\mathbf{B}_i = \mathbf{0}$ together to give M''. Each piece must satisfy the requirement stated if we want a nontrivial realization. ▮

Corollary. (a) $\dim W = \dim W_1 = \dim \varphi W$.
(b) If

$$\varphi w_1 = \begin{bmatrix} w_3 \\ \mathbf{0} \\ w_3' \\ \cdot \\ \cdot \\ \cdot \end{bmatrix}$$

and

$$\varphi w_2 = \begin{bmatrix} w_4 \\ \mathbf{0} \\ w_4' \\ \cdot \\ \cdot \\ \cdot \end{bmatrix} \quad \text{for} \quad w_1, w_2 \in W \quad \text{and} \quad w_1 \neq w_2$$

then $w_3 \neq w_4$.

Proof. dim W = dim φW is trivial. dim W_1 = size $\mathbf{A}_{11}$ (by definition of $\mathbf{A}_{11}$) and $\mathbf{A}_{11}$ is similar to $\mathbf{Q}$. Also size $\mathbf{Q}$ = dim W so dim W_1 = dim W.

To prove (b),

$$\varphi(\mathbf{A}^j\mathbf{B}a) = \begin{bmatrix} \mathbf{A}_1^j\mathbf{B}_1 a \\ \cdot \\ \cdot \\ \cdot \\ \mathbf{A}_m^j\mathbf{B}_m a \\ \mathbf{0} \end{bmatrix}$$

for each j, $a \in \Sigma = F_k$. But this set spans W and $\{\mathbf{A}_1^j\mathbf{B}_1 a\}$ spans W_1. By (a), dim W = dim W_1 = dim φW so that given any $w_1 \in W_1$, there exist $w_2, \ldots, w_m \in W_2, \ldots, W_m$ respectively so that

$$\varphi w = \begin{bmatrix} w_1 \\ \mathbf{0} \\ w_2 \\ \mathbf{0} \\ \cdot \\ \cdot \\ \cdot \\ w_m \\ \mathbf{0} \end{bmatrix} \quad \text{for some } w$$

Thus by a cardinality argument, the result follows. ∎

We will need to return to M to study the cycle structure of the state space. First, a new concept is required.

DEFINITION. Let $\mathbf{A} = \begin{bmatrix} \mathbf{Q} & \mathbf{Z}_0 \\ \mathbf{0} & \mathbf{Z}_1 \end{bmatrix}$ be indecomposable non-singular with $\varphi_{\mathbf{A}} = m_{\mathbf{A}} = [p(x)]^e, e > 1$, and $\mathbf{Q}$ indecomposable. Let $\begin{bmatrix} q_1 \\ q_2 \end{bmatrix}$ be given. q_2 is said to have *pseudo period* T (abbreviated *psp*) if T is the least positive integer i so that $\mathbf{Z}_1^i q_2 = q_2$.

We summarize some of the basic properties of pseudo periods and periods.*

PROPOSITION 5.3. Let $\mathbf{A}$ be as in the previous definition.

(a) In general, psp $q_2 \neq$ per $\begin{bmatrix} \mathbf{0} \\ q_2 \end{bmatrix}$.

(b) psp $q_2 \mid$ per $\begin{bmatrix} \mathbf{0} \\ q_2 \end{bmatrix}$.

(c) Let T_0 be the *basic period* ($=$ exp $p(x)$, cf. Theorem 5.9). For $q \neq \mathbf{0}$, $T_0 \mid$ per q.

(d) Let T_1 and T_2 be periods of two states. Then $T_1 \mid T_2$ or $T_2 \mid T_1$.

(e) For each state $\begin{bmatrix} q_1 \\ q_2 \end{bmatrix}$, $T_0 \mid$ psp q_2.

Proof. (a) and (b) are trivial. (c) follows from Theorem 5.9 since the periods are of the form $p^i T_0$. (d) follows from this remark also since $T_1 = p^i T_0$ and $T_2 = p^j T_0$. To prove (e), note that $\varphi_{\mathbf{Q}} = m_{\mathbf{Q}} = [p(x)]^{e_1}$ since $\mathbf{Q}$ is indecomposable. Moreover, $\varphi_{\mathbf{A}} = \varphi_{\mathbf{Q}} \varphi_{\mathbf{Z}_1}$ so that $\varphi_{\mathbf{Z}_1} = [p(x)]^{e_2}$. Thus the pseudo periods are seen to be of the form $p^i T_0$. ▮

* The *period* of any state q (abbreviated *per* q) is the least positive integer i such that $\mathbf{A}^i q = q$. The periods are the cycle lengths of Theorem 5.9.

Proposition 5.4. Let any square matrix $\mathbf{P} = \begin{pmatrix} \mathbf{P}_1 & \mathbf{P}_2 \\ \mathbf{0} & \mathbf{P}_3 \end{pmatrix}$ be given with $\mathbf{P}_1$, $\mathbf{P}_3$ square, and Z be the invariant subspace of dimension equal to the size of $\mathbf{P}_1$. Write $q = \begin{pmatrix} z \\ q_1 \end{pmatrix}$

(a) Let $i = \text{psp } q_1$, then $\mathbf{P}^j q = q + z_1$ for some $z_1 \in Z$ if and only if $j = ki$.

(b) The number of different states $q + z_1$ for some $z_1 \neq \mathbf{0}$ which are equal to $\mathbf{P}^j q$ for some j is (per q/psp q_1) $- 1$.

Proof. (a) Let $i = \text{psp } q_1$.

Then
$$\mathbf{P}^i q = \begin{pmatrix} z_0 \\ \mathbf{P}_3^i q_1 \end{pmatrix} = \begin{pmatrix} z_0 \\ q_1 \end{pmatrix}$$

since psp $(q_1) = i$.
Thus
$$\mathbf{P}^{ki} q = \begin{pmatrix} z_0' \\ \mathbf{P}_3^{ki} q_1 \end{pmatrix} = \begin{pmatrix} z_0' \\ q_1 \end{pmatrix}$$

Conversely, let $\mathbf{P}^j q = q + z_1$. Let $j = ki + i_1$, $0 \leq i_1 < i$ for some k.
$$\mathbf{P}^j q = \begin{pmatrix} z_j \\ \mathbf{P}_3^j q_1 \end{pmatrix}$$

Hence $\mathbf{P}_3^j q_1 = q_1$. Hence j is a multiple of i and $i_1 = 0$. (Otherwise $\mathbf{P}_3^{i_1} q_1 = q_1$ with $i_1 < i$ which cannot be since $i =$ psp q_1.)

(b) By (a) for each multiple j of i, $\mathbf{P}^j q \in q + Z$. When $j =$ per q then $\mathbf{P}^j q = q$. Hence the number is what we stated. (Note that if $j_1 < j_2 <$ per q then $\mathbf{P}^{j_1} q = \mathbf{P}^{j_2} q$ is impossible for then $\mathbf{P}^{j_2 - j_1} q = \mathbf{0}$ hence per $q \mid j_2 - j_1, j_2 - j_1 <$ per q.) Also note that if we do not require $z_1 \neq 0$ in the statement of (b), the result is per q/psp q_1. ∎

Next we must consider coset decompositions. We will deal with the subspaces W of F_n and W' of $F_{n'}$. A coset of W in F_n

which contains $\begin{bmatrix} \mathbf{0} \\ q \end{bmatrix}$ will be of the form

$$\left\{ \begin{bmatrix} w \\ q \end{bmatrix} \middle| \, w \in W \right\}$$

The form is similar for W'. More precisely, using Lemma 5.9 a coset of W' in $F_{n'}$ and containing

$$\begin{bmatrix} \mathbf{0} \\ q_1 \\ \mathbf{0} \\ \cdot \\ \cdot \\ \cdot \\ q_m \\ q'' \end{bmatrix} \quad \text{is} \quad \left\{ \begin{bmatrix} w_1 \\ q_1 \\ \cdot \\ \cdot \\ \cdot \\ w_m \\ q_m \\ q'' \end{bmatrix} \middle| \begin{bmatrix} w_1 \\ \mathbf{0} \\ \cdot \\ \cdot \\ \cdot \\ w_m \\ \mathbf{0} \\ \mathbf{0} \end{bmatrix} \in W \right\}$$

It may be appropriate to recall that not all possible combinations appear in W'; all possible w_i's do but $w_2, \ldots, w_m$ are uniquely determined when w_1 is given (corollary to Lemma 5.9).

At this point it is convenient to introduce a more refined canonical form for **A**. It will help proving general results about indecomposable matrices, producing less sophisticated proofs than a purely algebraic form. We shall need it again later.

Let **A** be indecomposable, $m_{\mathbf{A}} = \varphi_{\mathbf{A}} = [p(x)]^e$, $e > 1$. Then **A** is similar to

$$\mathbf{A}^* = \begin{bmatrix} \mathbf{RJ} & \mathbf{0} & & & \\ & \cdots & & & \\ & & \cdot\cdot & & \\ & & & \cdot\mathbf{RJ} & \\ & & & & \cdot\mathbf{R} \end{bmatrix}$$

with e blocks. Recall that $\mathbf{A}^*$ is the hypercompanion matrix of $[p(x)]^e$. (See Chapter 0, Section 5.) **R** is an $h \times h$ companion matrix of $p(x)$ (degree $p(x) = h$) and **J** is an $h \times h$ matrix which is 0 except for its lower left-hand element which is 1. By using a similarity transformation, we may assume that an LSM is described as $M = \langle F, n, k, \mathbf{A}^*, \mathbf{B}^* \rangle$ where $\mathbf{A}^*$ is the hyper-companion matrix of $\mathbf{A}$ and $\mathbf{B}^* = \begin{bmatrix} \mathbf{B}_0 \\ \mathbf{0} \end{bmatrix}$ where $\mathbf{B}_0$ has its size equal to the dimension of W.

DEFINITION. Let M be a finite LSM of the type in Case 5. We shall call the *maximum period* (abbreviated max-per) the largest period (or cycle length) in the cycle structure of M.

LEMMA 5.10. Given an indecomposable matrix $\mathbf{A}$, and an $\mathbf{A}$-invariant subspace (not the whole space) Z which induces a decomposition of the space into cosets; if y is not in Z then per $y \geq$ maximum period in Z.

Proof. Let $\varphi_{\mathbf{A}} = m_{\mathbf{A}} = [p(x)]^e$ where $p(x)$ is irreducible. Then $Z = \{r \mid [p(\mathbf{A})]^{e_0} r = \mathbf{0}\}$ since the annihilating polynomial of Z is $[p(x)]^{e_0}$ for some $e_0 < e$ (for it divides $\varphi_{\mathbf{A}}$). Any state $r \notin Z$ satisfies $[p(\mathbf{A})]^{e_1} r = 0$ for some $e_1 > e_0$ [for $e_1 \leq e_0$ would imply $r \in Z$]. Thus per $r = \exp [p(x)]^{e_1} \geq \exp [p(x)]^{e_0}$ by Theorem 5.9. But the max-per of Z is equal to $\exp [p(x)]^{e_0}$. ∎

LEMMA 5.11. With the same hypothesis as in Lemma 5.10, any two states in a coset of Z, distinct from Z, have the same period. Hence there is a coset of Z, not Z, where all the states have maximum period.

Proof. Let $\varphi_{\mathbf{A}} = m_{\mathbf{A}} = [p(x)]^e$. $Z = Z_0 = \{r \mid [p(\mathbf{A})]^{e_0} r = \mathbf{0}\}$ for some positive integer $e_0 < e$. Define for each $i > 0$ such that $e_0 + i \leq e$, $Z_i = \{x \mid [p(\mathbf{A})]^{e_0+i} x = \mathbf{0}\}$. Define $X_i = Z_i - Z_{i-1}$ for each i.

CLAIM. Every state in X_i has the same period.

This is clear for any state q in X_i is such that the minimum annihilating polynomial of q is $[p(\mathbf{A})]^{e_0+i}$ (for otherwise

$$[p(\mathbf{A})]^{e_0+i-1} q = 0$$

hence $q \in Z_{i-1}$). Therefore, every state in X_i has the same period equal to $\exp [p(\mathbf{A})]^{e_0+i}$.

Now it suffices to show that if $q \in X_i$ for some i (hence $q \notin Z$), then $q + Z \subseteq Z_i - Z_{i-1}$. If not $(q + Z) \cap Z_{i-1} \neq \emptyset$ i.e., there are $z \in Z$, $z_{i-1} \in Z_{i-1}$ such that $q + z = z_{i-1}$. But $Z \subseteq Z_{i-1}$. Hence $z \in Z_{i-1}$. Therefore, $q \in Z_{i-1}$ which is a contradiction. We have proved that every state in $q + Z$ has the same period, for any $q \notin Z$.

To show that there is $q + Z$ for some q where all states have max-per, we only need to note that since Z is not the whole space, there is $q \notin Z$ which has max-per (by Lemma 5.10 we know that per $q \geq$ max-per in Z for any $q \in Z$). Then any state in $q + Z$, by the first part of the lemma, has max-per. ∎

Note that this lemma could have been proven using the hypercompanion form.

LEMMA 5.12. With the same hypotheses as in Lemma 5.10, if there is $q \notin Z$ such that $\delta(q, \mathbf{0}^i) = q + z_1$ with $z_1 \neq \mathbf{0}$ for some i, then for all $q' \in q + Z$, $\delta(q', \mathbf{0}^i) = q' + z_1'$ with $z_1' \neq \mathbf{0}$.

Proof. Because of the invariance property,

$$\mathbf{A} = \left(\begin{array}{c|c} \mathbf{T}_0 & \mathbf{T}_1 \\ \hline \mathbf{0} & \mathbf{T}_2 \end{array}\right), \qquad \mathbf{T}_0 \text{ and } \mathbf{T}_2 \text{ square}$$

and

$$Z = \left\{ \left. \begin{pmatrix} z \\ \mathbf{0} \end{pmatrix} \right| z \in F_r, r < n \right\}$$

Let $q = \begin{pmatrix} z \\ t \end{pmatrix}$ where $t \neq \mathbf{0}$ (i.e., $q \notin Z$). Let i be the least integer s such that $\mathbf{A}^s q = q + z_1$ for some $z_1 \in Z$, $z_1 \neq \mathbf{0}$; let q' be in the same coset as q, i.e., $q' = q + z'$ for some $z' \in Z$. Then $\mathbf{A}^i q' = \mathbf{A}^i(q + z') = \mathbf{A}^i q + \mathbf{A}^i z'$ or $\mathbf{A}^i q' = q + z_1 + \mathbf{A}^i z' = q' + z_1'$ [$z_1' = z_1 + \mathbf{A}^i z' - z' \in Z$ since Z is an $\mathbf{A}$-invariant subspace].

If $z_1' = \mathbf{0}$ then per $q' \mid i$ since $\mathbf{A}^i q' = q'$. Then per $q' <$ per q since per $q > i$ (for i was the least integer such that under zero inputs q reaches $q + z_1$). This is a contradiction to Lemma 5.10. Hence $z_1' \neq \mathbf{0}$. q' was arbitrary, thus the result is proved. ∎

Now we prove another useful theorem.

THEOREM 5.12. Let $M = \langle F, n, k, \mathbf{A}, \mathbf{B} \rangle$ be a finite LSM which is not strongly connected. Assume that $\mathbf{A}$, $\mathbf{B}$ satisfy the conditions of Case 5. Let $W = \text{col } \mathbf{L}_n$ be of dimension he_0. There exists a coset (containing $\begin{bmatrix} \mathbf{0} \\ q \end{bmatrix}$, $q \neq \mathbf{0}$), $\left\{ \begin{bmatrix} w \\ q \end{bmatrix} \middle| \, w \in W \right\}$ where each state q_1 has maximum period and satisfies $\delta(q_1, \mathbf{0}^i) = q_1 + z_1$ for some $i > 0$ and $z_1 \neq \mathbf{0}$.*

Proof. By Lemmas 5.12 and 5.11 it is enough to show that there is $q \notin W$ such that q has maximum period and q reaches another state in the coset under zero-inputs. So if $q = \begin{bmatrix} w \\ t \end{bmatrix}$ it is enough to show (by Proposition 5.4(b)) that psp $t <$ per $q =$ max-per.

Let

$$\mathbf{A} = \begin{bmatrix} \mathbf{RJ} & & & & & & & & & \\ & \ddots & & & & & & & & \\ & & \mathbf{RJ} & & & & & & & \\ & & & \mathbf{RJ} & & & & & & \\ & & & & \ddots & & & & & \\ & & & & & \mathbf{RJ} & & & & \\ & & & & & & \mathbf{RJ} & & & \\ & & & & & & & \ddots & & \\ & & & & & & & & & \mathbf{R} \end{bmatrix}$$

* In other words, every state in the coset is on a cycle of length greater than one and which contains states from other cosets together with states from the same coset.

and

$$q = \begin{bmatrix} w \\ t_1 \\ \mathbf{0} \end{bmatrix} \qquad \text{where } w \in W = F_{he_0}$$

and $\mathbf{0} \neq t_1 \in F_r$ for some r satisfying $e' - e_0 \leq r < e'$ where e' is the least integer j such that $\exp[p(x)]^j = \exp[p(x)]^e$. Then $\operatorname{per} q = \exp[p(x)]^{e_0+r} \geq \exp[p(x)]^{e'}$ by Theorem 5.9. Therefore $\operatorname{per} q = \text{max-per}$. Also psp $t_1 = \exp[p(x)]^r < \exp[p(x)]^{e'}$ since $r < e'$ and by definition of e'. Thus psp $t_1 <$ max-per and the theorem is proved. ▮

We now state the equivalent theorem in M'.

THEOREM 5.13. Let $M = \langle F, n, k, \mathbf{A}, \mathbf{B} \rangle$ be a finite LSM and **A, B** satisfy the conditions of Theorem 5.12. Let

$$M' = \left[\bigoplus_{i=1}^{m} M_i \right] \oplus M''$$

be a nontrivial linear parallel state realization of M of the form given in Lemma 5.9. Let $W = \operatorname{col} \mathbf{L}_n$ and $W' = \operatorname{col} \mathbf{L}'_{n'}$. Then there is at least one coset in M' different from W' in which each state q' has maximum period and satisfies $\delta'(q', \mathbf{0}^i) = q' + w'$ for some $i > 0$ and $w' \in W'$, $\mathbf{0} \neq w'$.

Proof. This is a mere restatement of Theorem 5.12 applied to M', using the fact that there is a state assignment φ which is one-to-one and maps cosets onto cosets (Lemma 5.5). ▮

We are now going to develop necessary conditions for parallel state-realizations. Three theorems giving increasingly restrictive conditions will be needed.

THEOREM 5.14. Let $M = \langle F, n, k, \mathbf{A}, \mathbf{B} \rangle$ be a finite LSM where **A, B** satisfy Case 5. If

$$M' = \left[\bigoplus_{i=1}^{m} M_i \right] \oplus M''$$

is a nontrivial linear parallel state realization of M, then there exists an integer $e' < e$ such that $\exp[p(x)]^{e'} = \exp[p(x)]^e$ where $m_{\mathbf{A}} = \varphi_{\mathbf{A}} = [p(x)]^e$.

Proof. By Lemma 5.9 each $\mathbf{A}_i$ is indecomposable and $m_{\mathbf{A}_i} = \varphi_{\mathbf{A}_i} = [p(x)]^{e_i}$ with $e_i < e$. W_i is an invariant subspace of dimension he_i', $e_i' \leq e_i$ and $\deg p(x) = h$. W is of dimension he_0; $e_1' = e_0$, i.e.,

$$\mathbf{A}_1 = \begin{bmatrix} \mathbf{A}_{11} & \mathbf{A}_{12} \\ \mathbf{0} & \mathbf{A}_{13} \end{bmatrix}$$

$\mathbf{A}_{11}$ similar to $\mathbf{Q}$, i.e. $\mathbf{A} = \begin{bmatrix} \mathbf{Q} & \mathbf{Z}_0 \\ \mathbf{0} & \mathbf{Z}_1 \end{bmatrix}$ with $\mathbf{Q}$ indecomposable.

$$W' = \left\{ \begin{bmatrix} w_1 \\ \mathbf{0} \\ w_2 \\ \cdot \\ \cdot \\ \cdot \\ w_m \\ \mathbf{0} \\ \mathbf{0} \end{bmatrix} \middle| \; w_1 \in F_{he_0}, w_2, \ldots, w_n \text{ are determined by } w_1 \text{ uniquely.} \right\}$$

For the sake of simplicity we assume $m = 2$; i.e., $M' = M_1 \circledcirc M_2 \circledcirc M''$. By Theorem 5.13 there is a state

$$q = \begin{bmatrix} w_1 \\ q_1 \\ w_2 \\ q_2 \\ q'' \end{bmatrix}$$

which has max-per and for which there is $t > 0$ and a state

$$w' = \begin{bmatrix} w_1' \\ \mathbf{0} \\ w_2' \\ \mathbf{0} \\ \mathbf{0} \end{bmatrix} \in W'$$

such that $\delta'(q, \mathbf{0}^t) = q + w'$ and $w' \neq \mathbf{0}$, $q \notin W'$. Note that:

$$\text{per}\begin{bmatrix} w_1 \\ q_1 \\ w_2 \\ q_2 \\ q'' \end{bmatrix} = \langle \text{per}\begin{bmatrix} w_1 \\ q_1 \\ \mathbf{0} \\ \mathbf{0} \\ \mathbf{0} \end{bmatrix}, \text{per}\begin{bmatrix} \mathbf{0} \\ \mathbf{0} \\ w_2 \\ q_2 \\ \mathbf{0} \end{bmatrix}, \text{per}\begin{bmatrix} \mathbf{0} \\ \mathbf{0} \\ \mathbf{0} \\ \mathbf{0} \\ q'' \end{bmatrix} \rangle = \text{per}\, q.$$

Let $t_1 = \begin{bmatrix} w_1 \\ q_1 \end{bmatrix}$, $t_2 = \begin{bmatrix} w_2 \\ q_2 \end{bmatrix}$, and $t_3 = q''$.

Let T_0 be the basic period in M $(= \exp p(x))$. per q = max-per $= p^j T_0$ for some j by Theorem 5.9 and the choice of q. We noted that $\varphi_{\mathbf{A}_i} = [p(x)]^{e_i}$, hence the basic period for each M_i, $i = 1, 2$ is also T_0. Then it should be clear that

$$\text{per}\begin{bmatrix} w_1 \\ q_1 \\ \mathbf{0} \\ \mathbf{0} \\ \mathbf{0} \end{bmatrix} = p^{j_1} T_0$$

for some positive integer j_1. Similarly in M_2, i.e., per $t_2 = p^{j_2} T_0$ for some j_2. Note that $j_i \leq j$ since $j_i > j (i = 1$ or $i = 2)$ would imply per $t_i >$ per q = max-per. Thus

$$p^j T_0 = \langle p^{j_1} T_0, p^{j_2} T_0, \text{per}\begin{bmatrix} \mathbf{0} \\ \mathbf{0} \\ \mathbf{0} \\ \mathbf{0} \\ q'' \end{bmatrix} \rangle \qquad (*)$$

Assume that $j > j_1$. Since $(p, T_0) = 1$ by Corollary 1 to Theorem 5.9 and by (∗),

$$\text{per}\begin{bmatrix}\mathbf{0}\\ \mathbf{0}\\ \mathbf{0}\\ \mathbf{0}\\ q''\end{bmatrix} = p^j T \qquad \text{for some } T \mid T_0$$

Next we are going to ask how many states of its coset does q reach, i.e., what are the different values of r such that $\mathbf{A}'^r q = q + w'$ for some $w' \in W'$?

Unfortunately the concept of pseudo period does not conveniently generalize because not every state of the form

$$\begin{bmatrix}w_1\\ \mathbf{0}\\ w_2\\ \mathbf{0}\\ \mathbf{0}\end{bmatrix}$$

is in W'. Let s_1 be the least i such that

$$\begin{bmatrix}\mathbf{A}_1^i t_1\\ \mathbf{A}''^i t_3\end{bmatrix} = \begin{bmatrix}t_1\\ t_3\end{bmatrix} + \begin{bmatrix}w_0'\\ \mathbf{0}\end{bmatrix}$$

for some $w_0' \in W_1$; i.e., i is the least integer such that

$$\begin{bmatrix}\mathbf{A}_{13}^i q_1\\ \mathbf{A}'' q''\end{bmatrix} = \begin{bmatrix}q_1\\ q''\end{bmatrix}$$

$\left[\text{Recall that } \mathbf{A}_1 = \begin{bmatrix}\mathbf{A}_{11} & \mathbf{A}_{12}\\ \mathbf{0} & \mathbf{A}_{13}\end{bmatrix}.\right]$ Equivalently $s_1 = \text{psp}\begin{bmatrix}q_1\\ q''\end{bmatrix}$.

It follows that $\begin{bmatrix}\mathbf{A}_1^i t_1\\ \mathbf{A}''^i t_3\end{bmatrix} = \begin{bmatrix}t_1\\ t_3\end{bmatrix} + \begin{bmatrix}w_1\\ \mathbf{0}\\ \mathbf{0}\end{bmatrix}$ for some $w_1 \in W_1$

if and only if i is a multiple of s_1 (Proposition 5.3(a)). Now let r_1 be the least i such that $\mathbf{A}'^i q = q + w'$ for some

$$w' = \begin{bmatrix} w_1' \\ \mathbf{0} \\ w_2' \\ \mathbf{0} \\ \mathbf{0} \end{bmatrix} \in W' \qquad (w' \neq \mathbf{0} \text{ by choice of } q)$$

or such that

$$\begin{bmatrix} \mathbf{A}_1^i t_1 \\ \mathbf{A}_2^i t_2 \\ \mathbf{A}''^i t_3 \end{bmatrix} = \begin{bmatrix} t_1 \\ t_2 \\ t_3 \end{bmatrix} + \begin{bmatrix} w_1' \\ \mathbf{0} \\ w_2' \\ \mathbf{0} \\ \mathbf{0} \end{bmatrix}$$

In particular

$$\begin{bmatrix} \mathbf{A}_1^{r_1} t_1 \\ \mathbf{A}''^{r_1} t_3 \end{bmatrix} = \begin{bmatrix} t_1 \\ t_3 \end{bmatrix} + \begin{bmatrix} w_1' \\ \mathbf{0} \\ \mathbf{0} \end{bmatrix}$$

hence by the above remark $s_1 \mid r_1$. Finally note that q reaches $\rho = (\text{per } q)/r_1$ states belonging to its coset under zero-inputs. (Proposition 5.4(b).) ρ is an integer and $\rho > 1$ by choice of q ($\rho = 1$ if and only if q reaches only itself). There are now two cases.

Case 1. If $q_1 \neq 0$ then

$$s_1 = \text{psp} \begin{bmatrix} q_1 \\ q'' \end{bmatrix} = \langle \text{psp} \begin{bmatrix} q_1 \\ 0 \end{bmatrix}, \quad \text{per} \begin{bmatrix} \mathbf{0} \\ \mathbf{0} \\ \mathbf{0} \\ \mathbf{0} \\ q'' \end{bmatrix} \rangle$$

$\text{psp}\begin{bmatrix} q_1 \\ \mathbf{0} \end{bmatrix} = p^{i_1}T_0$ for some $i_1 \leq j$ since $\text{psp}\begin{bmatrix} q_1 \\ \mathbf{0} \end{bmatrix}$ is the least m such that $\mathbf{A}_{13}^m q_1 = q_1$ and $\varphi_{\mathbf{A}_{13}} = [p(x)]^{d_1}$ since $\varphi_{\mathbf{A}_{13}} \mid \varphi_{\mathbf{A}_1} = [p(x)]^{e_1}$. The result follows from Theorem 5.9. Moreover $i_1 \leq j$ since p^jT_0 is max-per. Hence $\text{psp}\begin{bmatrix} q_1 \\ q'' \end{bmatrix} = \langle p^{i_1}T_0, p^jT \rangle$ where $T \mid T_0$. Since $(p, T_0) = 1$ and $j \geq i_1$ then $\text{psp}\begin{bmatrix} q_1 \\ q'' \end{bmatrix} = s_1 = p^jT_0 = \text{max-per}$. It follows that $r_1 = s_1$ for $r_1 \leq \text{max-per} = s_1$ and $s_1 \mid r_1$. Hence q reaches p^jT_0/p^jT_0 states of its coset under zero-inputs, i.e., only itself, which contradicts the choice of q. Therefore Case 1 cannot hold.

Case 2. $q_1 = \mathbf{0}$. Then $s_1 = \langle 1, p^jT \rangle = p^jT$ since

$$\text{psp}\begin{bmatrix} q_1 \\ \mathbf{0} \end{bmatrix} = \text{psp}\begin{bmatrix} \mathbf{0} \\ \mathbf{0} \end{bmatrix} = 1$$

We compute $p^jT_0/r_1 = \rho$. Since $r_1 = k_1s_1$ for some k_1 (see the remarks above Case 1), $\rho = p^jT_0/k_1s_1 = T_0/Tk_1$. We claim that $(p, \rho) = 1$. This follows from $(p, T_0) = 1$, $Tk_1 \mid T_0$ (for $\rho = T_0/Tk_1$ is an integer). Using the state assignment φ, q is $\varphi\begin{bmatrix} w_0 \\ t \end{bmatrix}$ where $\begin{bmatrix} w_0 \\ t \end{bmatrix}$ has the same properties as $\varphi\begin{bmatrix} w_0 \\ t \end{bmatrix} = q$, i.e., max-per, etc. It is clear that $\begin{bmatrix} w_0 \\ t \end{bmatrix}$ can reach under zero-inputs exactly $\rho' = \text{per}\begin{bmatrix} w_0 \\ t \end{bmatrix} \Big/ \text{psp}\ t$ states of its coset, i.e., $\rho' = p^jT_0/p^iT_0$ for some $i < j$ ($\text{psp}\ t = p^iT_0$ by Proposition 5.3(c) and $i < j$ since $\begin{bmatrix} w_0 \\ \mathbf{0} \end{bmatrix}$ must reach a state different from itself and in its coset). $\rho' = p^{j-1} > 1$. We know that φ preserves transitions so that $\begin{bmatrix} w_0 \\ t \end{bmatrix}$ and $\varphi\begin{bmatrix} w_0 \\ t \end{bmatrix}$ reach the same number of states in their respective cosets, i.e., $\rho = \rho'$. But $(p, \rho') \neq 1$ and $(p, \rho) = 1$. This contradicts $\rho = \rho'$. Therefore Case 2 does not hold.

Therefore it is not possible for j_1 and j_2 to be less than j. Thus

$$\text{per}\begin{bmatrix} w_1 \\ q_1 \\ w_2 \\ q_2 \\ \mathbf{0} \end{bmatrix} = \text{max-per}$$

This period is

$$\langle \text{per}\begin{bmatrix} w_1 \\ q_1 \end{bmatrix}, \ \text{per}\begin{bmatrix} w_2 \\ q_2 \end{bmatrix} \rangle = \max \{\text{per}\begin{bmatrix} w_1 \\ q_1 \end{bmatrix}, \ \text{per}\begin{bmatrix} w_2 \\ q_2 \end{bmatrix}\}$$

since $\varphi_{\mathbf{A}_1} = [p(x)]^{e_i}$ implies $\text{per}\begin{bmatrix} w_i \\ q_i \end{bmatrix} = p^{j_i}T_0$, $i = 1$ and 2. These periods divide the exponents of $[p(x)]^{e_i}$, so $\exp[p(x)]^{e_1} = \exp[p(x)]^{e} = \text{max-per}$ or $\exp[p(x)]^{e_2} = \exp[p(x)]^{e}$. Let $e' = e_1 < e$ or $e_2 < e$, according to which case holds. By convention if e_1 satisfies the requirement we let $e' = e_1$. Thus $e > e' \geq e_1$ always holds. It is now a trivial matter to carry out an induction on m for $m > 2$.† ∎

THEOREM 5.15. Let $M = \langle F, n, k, \mathbf{A}, \mathbf{B}\rangle$ be a finite LSM in which $\mathbf{A}$ satisfies the conditions of the previous theorem. Let $W = \text{col}\, \mathbf{L}_n$ and let it be of dimension he_0 where $h = \deg p(x)$ and $\mathbf{A} = \begin{bmatrix} \mathbf{Q} & \mathbf{Z}_0 \\ \mathbf{0} & \mathbf{Z}_1 \end{bmatrix}$, $W = \left\{\begin{bmatrix} w \\ \mathbf{0} \end{bmatrix}\right\}$ (hence $m_{\mathbf{Q}} = \varphi_{\mathbf{Q}} = [p(x)]^{e_0}$). If $M' = \left[\bigoplus_{i=1}^{m} M_i\right] \oplus M''$ is a linear parallel state realization of M, then there is an integer e' such that $e^* \leq e' < e$, $e_0 < e'$ where

$$e^* = \min_{0 \leq i \leq e} \{i \mid \exp[p(x)]^i = \exp[p(x)]^e\}.$$

† Note that the proof for $m = 1$ is simpler but its extension to $m > 1$ is not quite straightforward since the notion of pseudo period does not extend to $m > 1$.

Proof. Recall that $\mathbf{A}_1 = \begin{bmatrix} \mathbf{A}_{11} & \mathbf{A}_{12} \\ \mathbf{0} & \mathbf{A}_{13} \end{bmatrix}$ where $\mathbf{A}_{11}$ is similar to $\mathbf{Q}$, i.e., size $\mathbf{A}_{11} = he_0$. Thus size $\mathbf{A}_1 = he_1$ ($m_{\mathbf{A}_1} = \varphi_{\mathbf{A}_1} = [p(x)]^{e_1}$) and $he_1 \geq he_0$. Recall that e' was defined in the proof of Theorem 5.14 to be such that if $\varphi_{\mathbf{A}_i} = m_{\mathbf{A}_i} = [p(x)]^{e_i}$, $i = 1, \ldots, m$, then $\exp [p(x)]^{e'} = \max_{i=1,\ldots,m} \{\exp [p(x)]^{e_i}\}$; also it was shown that $e^* \leq e' < e$. It suffices to show that $e_0 < e'$. We may suppose that $e_0 \geq e^*$ since if $e_0 < e^*$, then $e_0 < e^* \leq e'$ implies that $e_0 < e'$ and we would be done. For simplicity let $m = 2$.

Since $e_1 \geq e_0$, $\exp [p(x)]^{e_1} \geq \exp [p(x)]^{e_0} = \exp [p(x)]^{e'} =$ max-per. Thus e' by our convention can be chosen to be e_1. Suppose for the sake of contradiction that $e' \leq e_0$. Combining with the fact that $e' = e_1 \geq e_0$, we get $e_1 = e' = e_0$ and $\mathbf{A}_1 = \mathbf{A}_{11}$. Let $\begin{bmatrix} w_0 \\ q \end{bmatrix}$, $q \neq \mathbf{0}$, satisfy Theorem 5.12 and

$$\begin{bmatrix} w_1 \\ w_2 \\ q \\ q'' \end{bmatrix} = \varphi \begin{bmatrix} w_0 \\ q \end{bmatrix}$$

satisfy Theorem 5.13, i.e., they both have maximum period and reach under zero-inputs other states belonging to their respective cosets. q_1 disappeared in

$$\begin{bmatrix} w_1 \\ w_2 \\ q_2 \\ q'' \end{bmatrix} \qquad \text{since } \mathbf{A}_1 = \mathbf{A}_{11}$$

φ maps the coset $\begin{bmatrix} w \\ q \end{bmatrix}$ onto

$$\left\{ \begin{bmatrix} w_1 \\ w_2 \\ q_2 \\ q'' \end{bmatrix} + \begin{bmatrix} w_1' \\ w_2' \\ \mathbf{0} \\ \mathbf{0} \end{bmatrix} \middle| \begin{bmatrix} w_1' \\ w_2' \\ \mathbf{0} \\ \mathbf{0} \end{bmatrix} \in W' \right\}$$

Let w_0' be such that

$$\varphi\begin{bmatrix} w_0' \\ q \end{bmatrix} = \begin{bmatrix} \mathbf{0} \\ w_2' \\ q_2 \\ q'' \end{bmatrix}$$

w_0' exists by the onto property and the corollary to Lemma 5.9.

By choice of $\begin{bmatrix} w_0 \\ q \end{bmatrix}$ there is i so that

$$\delta\left[\begin{bmatrix} w_0 \\ q \end{bmatrix}, \mathbf{0}^i\right] = \begin{bmatrix} w_0 \\ q \end{bmatrix} + \begin{bmatrix} w_3 \\ \mathbf{0} \end{bmatrix}$$

for $\mathbf{0} \neq w_3 \in W$. By Lemma 5.12 it follows that

$$\delta\left[\begin{bmatrix} w_0' \\ q \end{bmatrix}, \mathbf{0}^i\right] = \begin{bmatrix} w_0' \\ q \end{bmatrix} + \begin{bmatrix} w_4 \\ \mathbf{0} \end{bmatrix}$$

and $\mathbf{0} \neq w_4 \in W$. By the linearity of φ inside cosets

$$\delta'\left[\varphi\begin{bmatrix} w_0' \\ q \end{bmatrix}, \mathbf{0}^i\right] = \varphi\begin{bmatrix} w_0' \\ q \end{bmatrix} + \varphi\begin{bmatrix} w_4 \\ \mathbf{0} \end{bmatrix}$$

Hence

$$\mathbf{A}'^i\begin{bmatrix} \mathbf{0} \\ w_2' \\ q_2 \\ q'' \end{bmatrix} = \begin{bmatrix} \mathbf{0} \\ w_2' \\ q_2 \\ q'' \end{bmatrix} + \begin{bmatrix} w_5 \\ w_6 \\ \mathbf{0} \\ \mathbf{0} \end{bmatrix}$$

$$= \begin{bmatrix} \mathbf{0} \\ \mathbf{A}_2^i\begin{bmatrix} w_2' \\ q_2 \end{bmatrix} \\ \mathbf{A}''^i q'' \end{bmatrix} \quad \text{with} \quad \begin{bmatrix} w_5 \\ w_6 \\ \mathbf{0} \\ \mathbf{0} \end{bmatrix} \in W'$$

Then $w_5 = \mathbf{0}$. But

$$\varphi\begin{bmatrix} w_4 \\ \mathbf{0} \end{bmatrix} = \begin{bmatrix} \mathbf{0} \\ w_6 \\ \mathbf{0} \\ \mathbf{0} \end{bmatrix}$$

which by the Corollary to Lemma 5.9(b) and by linearity of φ (namely $\varphi(\mathbf{0}) = \mathbf{0}$) implies that $w_6 = \mathbf{0}$ and $w_4 = \mathbf{0}$ which is a contradiction. Therefore $e' = e_0$ cannot hold. Since $e' \geq e_0$ it follows $e' > e_0$. Now a trivial induction on $m > 2$ will finish the proof. We omit it. ∎

In order to obtain the strongest necessary condition we shall derive a last result. Here it will be helpful to use again the hypercompanion form for the **A** matrix. We first summarize some properties of matrices having that general form.

PROPOSITION 5.5. Let

$$\mathbf{T} = \begin{bmatrix} \mathbf{T}_1 & \mathbf{T}_2 & \cdots & & \mathbf{T}_m \\ & \mathbf{T}_1 & \mathbf{T}_2 & \cdots & \mathbf{T}_{m-1} \\ & & \ddots & \ddots & \\ & & & \ddots & \vdots \\ \mathbf{0} & & & \ddots & \mathbf{T}_2 \\ & & & & \mathbf{T}_1 \end{bmatrix}$$

where each $\mathbf{T}_i$ is a $t \times t$ matrix. Then the following properties hold.

(1)

$$\mathbf{T}^i = \begin{bmatrix} \mathbf{T}_1^i & \mathbf{T}_2' & \cdots & \mathbf{T}_m' \\ & \mathbf{T}_1^i & \cdots & \mathbf{T}_{m-1}' \\ & & \ddots & \vdots \\ \mathbf{0} & & & \mathbf{T}_1^i \end{bmatrix}$$

where for each $2 \leq k \leq m$, $\mathbf{T}_k'$ is a function of only the $\mathbf{T}_j$'s for $1 \leq j \leq k$.

(2) Let m be the number of distinct blocks in **T**. Let $\mathbf{T}_j$ be the

first nonzero matrix, i.e., $\mathbf{T}_1 = \cdots = \mathbf{T}_{j-1} = \mathbf{0}$, and $\mathbf{T}_j \neq \mathbf{0}$. Then rank $\mathbf{T} = (m - j + 1)$ rank $\mathbf{T}_j$.

This result is very important.

THEOREM 5.16. Let $M = \langle F, n, k, \mathbf{A}, \mathbf{B} \rangle$ be a finite LSM which satisfies the conditions of the previous theorem. If $M' = \left(\overset{m}{\underset{i=1}{\textcircled{\scriptsize{||}}}} M_i \right) \textcircled{\scriptsize{||}} M''$ is a linear parallel state realization of M, then $e - e_0 \geq e^*$ where e_0, e^*, e are defined in Theorem 5.15.

Proof. For the sake of simplicity we shall assume $m = 2$.† Then recall that $\mathbf{A}' = \mathbf{A}_1 \oplus \mathbf{A}_2 \oplus \mathbf{A}''$ and

$$\mathbf{A}_1 = \begin{bmatrix} \mathbf{A}_{11} & \mathbf{A}_{12} \\ \mathbf{0} & \mathbf{A}_{13} \end{bmatrix}$$

with size $\mathbf{A}_{11} = he_0$ = dimension W and size of $\mathbf{A}_1 = he_1$, size of $\mathbf{A}_2 = he_2$; e' defined earlier ($e' \geq e_1$) satisfies $e_0 < e'$ and $e^* \leq e' < e$. $\mathbf{A}_1$ is indecomposable and $\varphi_{\mathbf{A}_1} = m_{\mathbf{A}_1} = [p(x)]^{e_1}$. Hence passing to the hypercompanion matrix of $\mathbf{A}$ we can identify a submatrix $\mathbf{A}_1$ of $\mathbf{A}$. The picture is

$$\mathbf{A} = \left[\begin{array}{ccc|ccc|ccc}
\mathbf{RJ} & & & & & & & & \\
& \mathbf{R} & & & \mathbf{0} & & & \mathbf{0} & \\
& & \ddots \; \mathbf{R} & \mathbf{J} & & & & & \\
\hline
& & & \mathbf{RJ} & & & & & \\
& \mathbf{0} & & & \ddots & & & \mathbf{0} & \\
& & & & & \mathbf{R} & \mathbf{J} & & \\
\hline
& & & & & & \mathbf{RJ} & & \\
& \mathbf{0} & & & \mathbf{0} & & & \ddots & \mathbf{J} \\
& & & & & & & & \mathbf{R}
\end{array}\right] = \left[\begin{array}{c|c}
\mathbf{A}_1 & \mathbf{0} \\ \cline{2-2}
 & \mathbf{P}_2 \\ \hline
\mathbf{0} & \mathbf{P}_1
\end{array}\right]$$

† Here again the proof for $m = 1$ does not extend directly to $m > 1$.

and

$$\mathbf{A}_1 = \left(\begin{array}{c|c} \mathbf{Q} & \mathbf{M}_0 \\ \hline \mathbf{0} & \mathbf{M}_3 \end{array}\right)$$

where $\mathbf{A}_1$ is $he_1 \times he_1$ and $\mathbf{Q}$ is $he_0 \times he_0$. If $e_0 = e_1$ then $\mathbf{A}_1 = \mathbf{Q}$. $\mathbf{P}_1$ is nonnull since $e > e' \geq e_1$.

Also write $\mathbf{A} = \begin{pmatrix} \mathbf{F}_1 & \mathbf{F}_2 \\ \mathbf{0} & \mathbf{F}_3 \end{pmatrix}$ where $\mathbf{F}_3$ is a square matrix of size $h(e^* - 1)$. Now we compute $\mathbf{A}^r$ and $\mathbf{A}_1^r$ using Proposition 5.5 and letting $r = p^{j-1}T_0$. Since $\mathbf{R}^r = \mathbf{I}$ ($\mathbf{I}$ is $h \times h$) because r is a multiple of the exponent of $p(x)$ which is T_0, we have

$$\mathbf{A}^r = \left(\begin{array}{cccc|cccc} \mathbf{I} & \mathbf{J}_1 & \mathbf{J}_2 & & \cdots & & & \mathbf{J}_{e-1} \\ \mathbf{0} & \mathbf{I} & & & & & & \\ & & & \mathbf{I} & \mathbf{J}_1 & \cdots & & \mathbf{J}_{e*-1} \\ \hline & & & & \mathbf{I} & \mathbf{J}_1 & & \mathbf{J}_{e*-2} \\ & \mathbf{0} & & & & & & \mathbf{I} \end{array}\right) = \begin{pmatrix} \mathbf{F}_1^r & \mathbf{F}_2' \\ \mathbf{0} & \mathbf{F}_3^r \end{pmatrix}$$

Claim. $\mathbf{F}_3^r = \mathbf{I}$ (of size $h(e^* - 1)$) and $\mathbf{J}_{e*-1} \neq \mathbf{0}$. To prove the claim note that $m_{\mathbf{F}_3} = \varphi_{\mathbf{F}_3} = [p(x)]^{e^*-1}$ by the hypercompanion form. Moreover the exponent of $[p(x)]^{e^*-1}$ is less than the exponent of $[p(x)]^{e^*}$ which is p^jT_0 by the definition of e^*. More precisely the exponent of $[p(x)]^{e^*-1}$ is $p^{j-1}T_0$. Therefore $\mathbf{F}_3^r = \mathbf{I}$. Therefore $\mathbf{J}_1 = \cdots \mathbf{J}_{e*-2} = \mathbf{0}$ by observing the form of $\mathbf{F}_3^r$. Note that $\mathbf{J}_{e*-1} \neq \mathbf{0}$ because the matrix

$$\mathbf{S} = \left(\begin{array}{c|cc} \mathbf{R} & \mathbf{J} & \mathbf{0} \\ \hline \mathbf{0} & \mathbf{F}_3 & \end{array}\right)$$

has minimum polynomial $[p(x)]^{e^*}$ and period p^jT_0. If $J_{e*-1} = \mathbf{0}$, then $\mathbf{S}^r = \left(\begin{array}{c|c} \mathbf{I} & \mathbf{0} \\ \hline \mathbf{0} & \mathbf{I} \end{array}\right) = \mathbf{I}$ so that this contradicts that the period is p^jT_0. The claim has been verified.

Thus we have shown that

$$\mathbf{A}^r - \mathbf{I} = \begin{bmatrix} \mathbf{0} & \cdots & \mathbf{J}_{e*-1} & \cdots\cdots & & \mathbf{J}_{e-1} \\ \mathbf{0} & \cdots & \mathbf{0} & \mathbf{J}_{e*-1} & \cdots & \mathbf{J}_{e-2} \\ & & \cdot & & & \\ & & \mathbf{0} & \cdot & \cdot & \\ & & & & \cdot & \\ & & & & \cdot & \mathbf{J}_{e*-1} \\ & & & & & \mathbf{0} \end{bmatrix}$$

By (2) of Proposition 5.5, rank $(\mathbf{A}^r - \mathbf{I}) = (e - 1 - (e^* - 1) + 1)$ rank $\mathbf{J}_{e*-1} = (e - e^* + 1)$ rank $\mathbf{J}_{e*-1}$. In an analogous fashion we compute $\mathbf{A}_1{}^r$ where $\mathbf{A}_1$ has size he_1 and $e_1 < e$. This yields

$$\mathbf{A}_1 = \begin{bmatrix} \mathbf{R} & \mathbf{J} & & & \\ & \cdot & & & \\ & & \cdot & & \\ & & & \cdot & \mathbf{J} \\ & & & & \cdot \\ & & & & \mathbf{R} \end{bmatrix}$$

of size he_1. We obtain

$$\mathbf{A}_1^r = \begin{bmatrix} \mathbf{I} & \mathbf{J}_1 & \cdots & \mathbf{J}_{e_1-1} \\ & \cdot & & \\ & & \cdot & \\ & & & \cdot \ \ \mathbf{J}_1 \\ & & & \mathbf{I} \end{bmatrix}$$

with the same $\mathbf{J}_i$ as in $\mathbf{A}^r$ by Proposition 5.5(a), but now

$$\text{rank } (\mathbf{A}_1^r - \mathbf{I}) = \begin{cases} (e_1 - 1 - (e^* - 1) + 1) \text{ rank } \mathbf{J}_{e*-1} \text{ if} \\ e_1 \geq e^*. \\ 0 \text{ otherwise since } e_1 < e^* \text{ implies } \mathbf{A}_1^r = \mathbf{I}. \end{cases}$$

(The last observation means that $e_1 < e^*$ implies $\varphi_{\mathbf{A}_1} = m_{\mathbf{A}_1} = [p(x)]^{e_1}$ whose exponent is less than or equal to exp $[p(x)]^{e^*-1}$

by Theorem 5.9 and hence is at most $p^{j-1}T_0 = r$.) Hence

$$\text{rank } (\mathbf{A}_1^r - \mathbf{I}) = \begin{cases} (e_1 - e^* + 1) \text{ rank } \mathbf{J}_{e^*-1} \text{ if } e_1 \geq e^* \\ 0 \text{ if } e_1 < e^* \end{cases}$$

Recalling now that we wrote

$$\mathbf{A} = \begin{bmatrix} \mathbf{Q} & \mathbf{M}_0 & \mathbf{0} \\ \mathbf{0} & \mathbf{M}_3 & \mathbf{P}_2 \\ \mathbf{0} & \mathbf{0} & \mathbf{P}_1 \end{bmatrix}$$

then we write a state q of M as

$$q = \begin{bmatrix} w_1 \\ q_1 \\ q_2 \end{bmatrix}$$

$\mathbf{A}' = \mathbf{A}_1 \oplus \mathbf{A}_2 \oplus \mathbf{A}''$ and we write

$$q' = \begin{bmatrix} w_1' \\ q_1' \\ w_2' \\ q_2' \\ q'' \end{bmatrix}$$

where $\dim \begin{bmatrix} w_1' \\ q_1' \end{bmatrix} = he_1$, $\dim \begin{bmatrix} w_2' \\ q_2' \end{bmatrix} = he_2$, $\dim (q'') = \text{size } \mathbf{A}''$.

For the sake of contradiction, suppose the theorem false, i.e., $e - e_0 < e^*$. Then if $q = \begin{bmatrix} w \\ q_1 \\ q_2 \end{bmatrix}$, $\dim \begin{bmatrix} q_1 \\ q_2 \end{bmatrix} = h(e - e_0) < he^*$ or equivalently no $\begin{bmatrix} w \\ q_1 \\ q_2 \end{bmatrix}$ is such that $\text{psp} \begin{bmatrix} q_1 \\ q_2 \end{bmatrix} = \text{max-per} = p^j T_0$ (by definition of e^*).

CLAIM. $(\mathbf{A}^r - \mathbf{I})\begin{bmatrix} w \\ q_1 \\ q_2 \end{bmatrix} \neq \mathbf{0}$ if and only if per $\begin{bmatrix} w \\ q_1 \\ q_2 \end{bmatrix} =$ max-per. The claim is clear since the only period which does not divide r is $p^j T_0$ ($r = p^{j-1}T_0$ and every period is $p^i T_0$, $i = 0, \ldots, j$).

Choose $\begin{bmatrix} w_0 \\ q_1 \\ q_2 \end{bmatrix}$ of maximum period. Then $\mathbf{A}^r \begin{bmatrix} w_0 \\ q_1 \\ q_2 \end{bmatrix} = \begin{bmatrix} w_1 \\ q_1 \\ q_2 \end{bmatrix}$ because psp $\begin{bmatrix} q_1 \\ q_2 \end{bmatrix} <$ max-per by the above, and then using Proposition 5.3. Hence

$$(\mathbf{A}^r - \mathbf{I})\begin{bmatrix} w_0 \\ q_1 \\ q_2 \end{bmatrix} = \begin{bmatrix} w_2 \\ \mathbf{0} \\ \mathbf{0} \end{bmatrix} \qquad (*)$$

where $w_2 = w_1 - w_0$. Since the assignment φ is linear inside cosets by Lemma 5.5, letting

$$\varphi \begin{bmatrix} w_0 \\ q_1 \\ q_2 \end{bmatrix} = \begin{bmatrix} w_1' \\ q_1' \\ w_2' \\ q_2' \\ q'' \end{bmatrix}$$

we have that

$$\varphi \mathbf{A}^r \begin{bmatrix} w_0 \\ q_1 \\ q_2 \end{bmatrix} = \varphi \left[\begin{bmatrix} w_0 \\ q_1 \\ q_2 \end{bmatrix} + \begin{bmatrix} w_2 \\ \mathbf{0} \\ \mathbf{0} \end{bmatrix} \right] = \varphi \begin{bmatrix} w_0 \\ q_1 \\ q_2 \end{bmatrix} + \varphi \begin{bmatrix} w_2 \\ \mathbf{0} \\ \mathbf{0} \end{bmatrix}$$

$$= \begin{bmatrix} w_1' \\ q_1' \\ w_2' \\ q_2' \\ q'' \end{bmatrix} + \varphi \begin{bmatrix} w_2 \\ \mathbf{0} \\ \mathbf{0} \end{bmatrix} = (\mathbf{A}')^r \begin{bmatrix} w_1' \\ q_1' \\ w_2' \\ q_2' \\ q'' \end{bmatrix}$$

This equation is equivalent to the following statement: Given $\begin{bmatrix} w_0 \\ q_1 \\ q_2 \end{bmatrix}$, there is

$$\begin{bmatrix} w_1' \\ q_1' \\ w_2' \\ q_2' \\ q'' \end{bmatrix} \quad \text{such that} \quad ((\mathbf{A}')^r - \mathbf{I})\begin{bmatrix} w_1' \\ q_1' \\ w_2' \\ q_2' \\ q'' \end{bmatrix} = \varphi((\mathbf{A}^r - \mathbf{I})\begin{bmatrix} w_0 \\ q_1 \\ q_2 \end{bmatrix})$$

The proof will be completed by showing that this is not possible for all $\begin{bmatrix} w_0 \\ q_1 \\ q_2 \end{bmatrix}$.

$\dim \{(\mathbf{A}^r - \mathbf{I})q \mid q \text{ is in } M\} = t = (e - e^* + 1) \text{ rank } J_{e*-1}$ by the above. But $V = \{(\mathbf{A}^r - \mathbf{I})q \mid q$ is in M and q has max-per$\} = \{(\mathbf{A}^r - \mathbf{I})q \mid q \text{ is in } M\}$ because if q does not have max-per, $(\mathbf{A}^r - \mathbf{I})q = \mathbf{0}$. Therefore $\dim V = t$ and $V \subseteq W$ from (*). But $V \subseteq W$ implies $\varphi V \subseteq W'$. Thus $\varphi V = \{((\mathbf{A}')^r - \mathbf{I})q' \mid q' = \varphi q$, q has max-per in $M\}$. Thus

$$\varphi V = \left\{ \begin{pmatrix} (\mathbf{A}_1^r - \mathbf{I})\begin{bmatrix} w_1' \\ q_1' \end{bmatrix} \\ (\mathbf{A}_2^r - \mathbf{I})\begin{bmatrix} w_2' \\ q_2' \end{bmatrix} \\ ((\mathbf{A}'')^r - \mathbf{I})q'' \end{pmatrix} \middle| \begin{bmatrix} w_1' \\ q_1' \\ w_2' \\ q_2' \\ q'' \end{bmatrix} = \varphi \begin{bmatrix} w_0 \\ q_1 \\ q_2 \end{bmatrix}, \begin{bmatrix} w_0 \\ q_1 \\ q_2 \end{bmatrix} \text{ has max-per} \right\}$$

$$\varphi V \subseteq \varphi W = \left\{ \begin{bmatrix} w_1' \\ \mathbf{0} \\ w_2' \\ \mathbf{0} \\ \mathbf{0} \end{bmatrix} \in W' \right\}$$

In particular

$$\left\{ (\mathbf{A}_1^r - \mathbf{I}) \begin{bmatrix} w_1' \\ q_1' \end{bmatrix} \right\} \subseteq \left\{ \begin{bmatrix} w_1' \\ \mathbf{0} \end{bmatrix} \right\}$$

implies that cardinality of $\varphi V \leq$ cardinality V' where

$$V' = \left\{ (\mathbf{A}_1^r - \mathbf{I}) \begin{bmatrix} w_1' \\ q_1' \end{bmatrix} \middle| \text{ there is } \begin{bmatrix} w_2' \\ q_2' \\ q'' \end{bmatrix} \text{ so that } \begin{bmatrix} w_1' \\ q_1' \\ w_2' \\ q_2' \\ q'' \end{bmatrix} \right.$$

$$\left. = \varphi \begin{bmatrix} w_0 \\ q_1 \\ q_2 \end{bmatrix}, \begin{bmatrix} w_0 \\ q_1 \\ q_2 \end{bmatrix} \text{ has max-per} \right\}$$

because given $\begin{bmatrix} w_1' \\ \mathbf{0} \end{bmatrix} \in W_1$ there is a *unique* (by Corollary to Lemma 5.9) state

$$\begin{bmatrix} w_1' \\ \mathbf{0} \\ w_2' \\ \mathbf{0} \\ \mathbf{0} \end{bmatrix} \in W' = \varphi(W)$$

But cardinality $V' \leq$ cardinality V'' where

$$V'' = \left\{ (\mathbf{A}_1^r - \mathbf{I}) \begin{bmatrix} w_1' \\ q_1' \end{bmatrix} \middle| \text{ all } \begin{bmatrix} w_1' \\ q_1' \end{bmatrix} \right\}$$

We know that cardinality $V'' = p^{t'}$ where $t' = 0$ or $t' = (e_1 - e^* + 1)$ rank J_{e*-1}. In any case cardinality $V'' <$ cardinality $V = p^t$ since dim $V = t > t'$. Hence cardinality $\varphi V \leq$ cardinality $V' <$ cardinality V which implies that φ is not one-to-one and contradicts that φ was an assignment. Therefore $e - e_0 < e^*$ cannot hold, and $e - e_0 \geq e^*$. Again a trivial induction extends to $m > 2$. ▮

Our results can now be combined to give a sufficient condition for linear parallel decomposition. Finally, Case 5 is completed.

THEOREM 5.17. Let $M = \langle F, n, k, \mathbf{A}, \mathbf{B} \rangle$ be a finite LSM which is not strongly connected. Assume $\mathbf{B} \neq \mathbf{0}$, $m_{\mathbf{A}} = \varphi_{\mathbf{A}} = [p(x)]^e$, $e > 1$, and $p(x)$ is irreducible of degree h. Let $W = \text{col } \mathbf{L}_n$ be of dimension he_0 where $e_0 < e$ and define $e^* = \min \{v \mid \exp [p(x)]^v = \exp [p(x)]^e\}$. If there is e' such that $e > e' > e_0$, $e' \geq e^*$ and if $e - e_0 \geq e^*$, then there exists $M' = M_1 \oplus M_2$ which is a linear parallel state realization of M.

Proof. We may assume that

$$\mathbf{A} = \begin{bmatrix} \mathbf{R} & \mathbf{J} & & & & \\ & \mathbf{R} & \mathbf{J} & & & \\ & & \cdot & & & \\ & & & \cdot & & \\ & & & & \mathbf{R} & \mathbf{J} \\ & & & & & \mathbf{R} \end{bmatrix}$$

with e blocks, $\mathbf{R}$ is a companion matrix of $p(x)$, $\mathbf{J}$ is an $h \times h$ matrix with one 1 in the lower left entry, and $\mathbf{B} = \begin{bmatrix} \mathbf{B}_0 \\ \mathbf{0} \end{bmatrix}$ with $\mathbf{B}_0$ is $he_0 \times k$. We shall exhibit $M_1 = \langle F, h(e-1), k, \mathbf{A}_1, \mathbf{B}_1 \rangle$ and $M_2 = \langle F, h(e - e_0), k, \mathbf{A}_2, \mathbf{B}_2 \rangle$

$$\mathbf{A}_1 = \begin{bmatrix} \mathbf{R} & \mathbf{J} & & & & & \\ & \mathbf{R} & \mathbf{J} & & & & \\ & & \cdot & & & & \\ & & & \cdot & & & \\ & & & & \cdot & & \\ & & & & & \mathbf{R} & \mathbf{J} \\ & & & & & & \mathbf{R} \end{bmatrix} \quad \text{of dimension } h(e-1)$$

$\mathbf{A}_2$ is of the same form but has dimension $h(e - e_0)$, $\mathbf{B}_1 = \begin{bmatrix} \mathbf{B}_0 \\ \mathbf{0} \end{bmatrix}$ has $h(e-1)$ rows while $\mathbf{B}_2 = \mathbf{0}$ has $h(e - e_0)$ rows.

We can partition $\mathbf{A}$ as follows. Let $\mathbf{Q}$ be a diagonal block of size he_0, $\mathbf{A}_1$ a diagonal block of size $h(e-1)$ and $\mathbf{M}_0 = \mathbf{A}_2$ a diagonal block of size $h(e - e_0)$ for which we count from the lower right hand corner. Thus

$$\mathbf{A} = \begin{bmatrix} \mathbf{Q} & \mathbf{R}_1 & \mathbf{P}_{11} \\ \mathbf{0} & \mathbf{R}_2 & \mathbf{P}_{12} \\ \mathbf{0} & & \mathbf{P}_2 \end{bmatrix},$$

$$\mathbf{A}_1 = \begin{bmatrix} \mathbf{Q} & \mathbf{R}_1 \\ \mathbf{0} & \mathbf{R}_2 \end{bmatrix} \quad \text{and} \quad \mathbf{A}_2 = \begin{bmatrix} \mathbf{R}_2 & \mathbf{P}_{12} \\ \mathbf{0} & \mathbf{P}_2 \end{bmatrix}$$

Let $\mathbf{A}' = \mathbf{A}_1 \oplus \mathbf{A}_2$ and $\mathbf{B}' = \begin{bmatrix} \mathbf{B}_1 \\ \mathbf{B}_2 \end{bmatrix}$. Thus a state $q \in Q$ is written $\begin{bmatrix} w \\ q_1 \\ q_2 \end{bmatrix}$ while a state q' in Q' is written

$$\begin{bmatrix} w'_1 \\ q'_1 \\ q'_2 \\ q'_3 \end{bmatrix}$$

We claim that for any $\begin{bmatrix} w \\ q_1 \\ q_2 \end{bmatrix}$ with $q_2 \neq \mathbf{0}$,

1. per $\begin{bmatrix} w \\ q_1 \\ q_2 \end{bmatrix}$ = max-per.

2. psp $\begin{bmatrix} q_1 \\ q_2 \end{bmatrix}$ = max-per.

3. No state $\begin{bmatrix} w \\ q_1 \\ q_2 \end{bmatrix}$ $q_2 \neq \mathbf{0}$ can reach under $\mathbf{0}$ any state in its coset, other than itself.

Proof of Claim. (1) If $q_2 \neq \mathbf{0}$, per $\begin{bmatrix} w \\ q_1 \\ q_2 \end{bmatrix} \geq$ max-per in $\left\{\begin{bmatrix} w \\ q_1 \\ \mathbf{0} \end{bmatrix}\right\}$. Since $\left\{\begin{bmatrix} w \\ q_1 \\ \mathbf{0} \end{bmatrix}\right\}$ is an $\mathbf{A}'$-invariant subspace to which

$\begin{bmatrix} w \\ q_1 \\ q_2 \end{bmatrix}$, $q_2 \neq \mathbf{0}$ does not belong, Lemma 5.10 applies. Therefore

$$\text{per}\begin{bmatrix} w \\ q_1 \\ q_2 \end{bmatrix} \geq \text{max-per}\left\{\begin{bmatrix} w \\ q_1 \\ \mathbf{0} \end{bmatrix}\right\} = \exp\,[p(x)]^{e-1}$$

since size of $\mathbf{A}_1 = h(e-1)$; but by assumption there is e' so that $e^* \leq e' < e$; therefore $\exp\,[p(x)]^{e^*} \leq \exp\,[p(x)]^{e-1} \leq \exp\,[p(x)]^{e}$ (Theorem 5.9) which by definition of e^* gives $\exp\,[p(x)]^{e-1} = $ max per. Therefore per $\begin{bmatrix} w \\ q_1 \\ q_2 \end{bmatrix} =$ max per for all $q_2 \neq \mathbf{0}$ and all w_1, q_1.

(2) Note that $\mathbf{A}_2$ is indecomposable.

$$\varphi_{\mathbf{A}_2} = m_{\mathbf{A}_2} = [p(x)]^{e-e_0}$$

Also note that $\begin{bmatrix} q_1 \\ \mathbf{0} \end{bmatrix}$ is $\mathbf{A}_2$-invariant of dimension equal to size $\mathbf{R}_2 = h(e - e_0 - 1)$. Since by assumption $e - e_0 \geq e^*$, $e - e_0 - 1 \geq e^* - 1$. If $e - e_0 - 1 \geq e^*$ then for any $q_2 \neq \mathbf{0}$, any q_1, psp $\begin{bmatrix} q_1 \\ q_2 \end{bmatrix} \geq$ max-per in $\begin{bmatrix} q_1 \\ \mathbf{0} \end{bmatrix} =$ max-per. If $e - e_0 - 1 = e^* - 1$, by definition of e^* we have psp $\begin{bmatrix} q_1 \\ q_2 \end{bmatrix} >$ max-per in $\begin{bmatrix} q_1 \\ \mathbf{0} \end{bmatrix}$ for all $q_2 \neq \mathbf{0}$, all q_1; but max-per in $\begin{bmatrix} q_1 \\ \mathbf{0} \end{bmatrix} = \exp\,[p(x)]^{e^*-1} = p^{j-1}T_0$; hence psp $\begin{bmatrix} q_1 \\ q_2 \end{bmatrix} = p^jT_0 =$ max-per.

(3) follows from (1), (2), and Proposition 5.3.

We can now define the mapping φ. For any w, q_1, let

$$\varphi\begin{bmatrix} w \\ q_1 \\ \mathbf{0} \end{bmatrix} = \begin{bmatrix} w \\ q_1 \\ \mathbf{0} \end{bmatrix}$$

Fix $\begin{bmatrix} w_0 \\ q_1 \\ q_2 \end{bmatrix}$ with $q_2 \neq \mathbf{0}$. Let

$$\varphi\begin{bmatrix} w_0 \\ q_1 \\ q_2 \end{bmatrix} = \begin{bmatrix} w_0' \\ q_1' \\ q_1 \\ q_2 \end{bmatrix} \quad \text{for any } w_0', q_1'$$

Let

$$\varphi\left[\mathbf{A}^i\begin{bmatrix} w_0 \\ q_1 \\ q_2 \end{bmatrix} + \begin{bmatrix} w \\ \mathbf{0} \\ \mathbf{0} \end{bmatrix}\right] = (\mathbf{A}')^i\begin{bmatrix} w_0' \\ q_1' \\ q_1 \\ q_2 \end{bmatrix} + \begin{bmatrix} w \\ \mathbf{0} \\ \mathbf{0} \\ \mathbf{0} \end{bmatrix}$$

for all i and $w \in W$. Thus we have assigned states to the cosets of the orbit of a fixed state. If there is an unassigned state in M, fix it using a state* in M' which has not been used and repeat the process until all states in M have been encoded.

To complete the proof, we must show that φ is a state assignment. It is clear that

1. φ is linear on W (it is the "identity")
2. $\varphi(\mathbf{A}q + \mathbf{B}a) = \mathbf{A}'\varphi q + \mathbf{B}'a$ by the definition of φ and the fact that $\mathbf{B}a \in W$.

It only remains to prove that φ is one-to-one. Suppose

$$\varphi\begin{bmatrix} w_1 \\ q_1 \\ q_2 \end{bmatrix} = \varphi\begin{bmatrix} w_2 \\ q_3 \\ q_4 \end{bmatrix}$$

---

* It is always possible to find such a state since F is finite and M' is bigger than M since $e - e_0 \geq e^*$ and $e^* > 1$ (this should be clear), so that $e - e_0 + e - 1 > 1 + e - 1 = e$.

with $q_2 \neq \mathbf{0}$ and $q_4 \neq \mathbf{0}$. [If $q_2 = \mathbf{0}$ or $q_4 = \mathbf{0}$ then the above equality is impossible.] Thus

$$\varphi\begin{bmatrix} w_1 \\ q_1 \\ q_2 \end{bmatrix} = \begin{bmatrix} w_1' \\ q_1' \\ q_1 \\ q_2 \end{bmatrix} = \begin{bmatrix} w_2' \\ q_3' \\ q_3 \\ q_4 \end{bmatrix} = \varphi\begin{bmatrix} w_2 \\ q_3 \\ q_4 \end{bmatrix}$$

implies $\begin{bmatrix} q_1 \\ q_2 \end{bmatrix} = \begin{bmatrix} q_3 \\ q_4 \end{bmatrix}$ and hence

$$\begin{bmatrix} w_2 \\ q_1 \\ q_2 \end{bmatrix} \in \left\{ \mathbf{A}^i \begin{bmatrix} w_1 \\ q_1 \\ q_2 \end{bmatrix} + \begin{bmatrix} w \\ \mathbf{0} \\ \mathbf{0} \end{bmatrix} \middle| \, i \geq 0, w \in W \right\}$$

Therefore $\mathbf{A}^i \begin{bmatrix} w_1 \\ q_1 \\ q_2 \end{bmatrix} = \begin{bmatrix} w_3 \\ q_1 \\ q_2 \end{bmatrix}$ for some w_3 and i; but psp $\begin{bmatrix} q_1 \\ q_2 \end{bmatrix}$ = max-per from (2) in the above claim. Therefore, either $i = 0$ or $i = p^j T_0$. Now, if $w_1 = w_2$ then we are done. Suppose $w_1 \neq w_2$ and then $w \neq \mathbf{0}$. We have

$$\varphi\begin{bmatrix} w_2 \\ q_1 \\ q_2 \end{bmatrix} = \varphi\left[\begin{bmatrix} w_1 \\ q_1 \\ q_2 \end{bmatrix} + \begin{bmatrix} w \\ \mathbf{0} \\ \mathbf{0} \end{bmatrix}\right] = \varphi\begin{bmatrix} w_1 \\ q_1 \\ q_2 \end{bmatrix} + \varphi\begin{bmatrix} w \\ \mathbf{0} \\ \mathbf{0} \end{bmatrix}$$

by the construction of φ. Continuing,

$$\varphi\begin{bmatrix} w_2 \\ q_1 \\ q_2 \end{bmatrix} = \varphi\begin{bmatrix} w_1 \\ q_1 \\ q_2 \end{bmatrix} + \begin{bmatrix} w \\ \mathbf{0} \\ \mathbf{0} \\ \mathbf{0} \end{bmatrix} \neq \varphi\begin{bmatrix} w_1 \\ q_1 \\ q_2 \end{bmatrix}$$

since φ is the "identity" on W and $w \neq \mathbf{0}$. Thus $w_1 = w_2$ and φ is one-to-one. ▮

PROBLEM

In Theorem 5.17, it is assumed that M is not strongly connected. Where is this assumption used in the proof?

5. The Main Theorem on Parallel Decompositions

It is now possible to summarize our results on linear parallel decompositions.

THEOREM 5.18. Let $M = \langle F, n, k, \mathbf{A}, \mathbf{B} \rangle$ be a finite LSM. M has a nontrivial linear parallel state realization if and only if one of the following holds

(1) $\mathbf{A}$ is decomposable.

(2) $\mathbf{A}$ is indecomposable [i.e., $m_{\mathbf{A}} = \varphi_{\mathbf{A}} = [p(x)]^e$, $p(x)$ irreducible of degree h], $\mathbf{A}$ is non-nilpotent, M is not strongly connected, and

(a) $\mathbf{B} = \mathbf{0}$ and $e > 1$,

or

(b) $\mathbf{B} = \mathbf{0}$, $e = 1$, and if T is the exponent of $p(x)$, there exist $r > 1$, $T_1, \ldots, T_r$, $T_i = \exp p_i(x)$ where the $p_i(x)$ are irreducible polynomials and $T = \langle T_1, \ldots, T_r \rangle$ with $\deg p_i(x) < h$ for each $1 \leq i \leq r$,

or

(c) $\mathbf{B} \neq \mathbf{0}$, and if col $\mathbf{L}_n = W$ with dim $W = he_0$, then there is $e' \geq 1$ such that $e > e' > e_0$ and $e' \geq e^* = \min \{\nu \mid \exp [p(x)]^\nu = \exp \{p(x)]^e\}$, and $e - e_0 \geq e^*$.

Proof. The result follows from Theorems 5.2, 5.7, 5.8, 5.10, 5.11, 5.15, and 5.17. ∎

It is of interest to note that finiteness is used extensively in parts of this development. We suspect that one can prove a similar result for an infinite LSM.

OPEN PROBLEM. Give necessary and sufficient conditions for an infinite LSM to have a linear parallel state realization.

6. Serial Realizations

It will be comparatively simple to characterize linear serial decompositions. Some sufficient conditions have already been obtained (Theorem 5.2). Thus, it only remains for us to consider the case in which **A** is indecomposable.

THEOREM 5.19. Let $M = \langle F, n, k, \mathbf{A}, \mathbf{B} \rangle$ be a finite LSM with **A** indecomposable $[m_{\mathbf{A}}(x) = \varphi_{\mathbf{A}}(x) = [p(x)]^e$ and $p(x)$ irreducible]. If $e > 1$, then there is a nontrivial linear serial decomposition of M by $M' = M_2 \ominus M_1$ and moreover the state assignment φ is linear.

Proof. If such a decomposition exists, then the forms of $\mathbf{A}'$ and $\mathbf{B}'$ are as follows:

$$\mathbf{A}' = \begin{bmatrix} \mathbf{A}_1 & \mathbf{0} \\ \mathbf{B}_2\mathbf{C}_1 & \mathbf{A}_2 \end{bmatrix} \qquad \mathbf{B}' = \begin{bmatrix} \mathbf{B}_1 \\ \mathbf{B}_2\mathbf{D}_1 \end{bmatrix}$$

Since **A** is indecomposable and $e > 1$, there exist nontrivial **A** invariant subspaces and by choosing the right basis **A** is similar to $\mathbf{A}^*$ where

$$\mathbf{A}^* = \begin{bmatrix} \mathbf{A}_0 & \mathbf{0} \\ \mathbf{P}_0 & \mathbf{P}_1 \end{bmatrix} = \mathbf{T}^{-1}\mathbf{A}\mathbf{T}$$

where **T** is nonsingular.† Now let $\mathbf{B}^* = \mathbf{T}^{-1}\mathbf{B}$. Then M is similar to $M^* = \langle F, n, k, \mathbf{A}^*, \mathbf{B}^* \rangle$. Write $\mathbf{B}^* = \begin{bmatrix} \mathbf{B}_1^* \\ \mathbf{B}_2^* \end{bmatrix}$ and take $M' = M^*$. $M' = M^*$ will be the desired realization if

† This form is not unique.

there always exist solutions to the following equations.

$$\mathbf{A}_1 = \mathbf{A}_0 \tag{1}$$
$$\mathbf{B}_2\mathbf{C}_1 = \mathbf{P}_0 \tag{2}$$
$$\mathbf{A}_2 = \mathbf{P}_1 \tag{3}$$
$$\mathbf{B}_1 = \mathbf{B}_1^* \tag{4}$$
$$\mathbf{B}_2\mathbf{D}_1 = \mathbf{B}_2^* \tag{5}$$

where the unknowns are $\mathbf{A}_1$, $\mathbf{B}_1$, $\mathbf{C}_1$, $\mathbf{D}_1$, $\mathbf{A}_2$, $\mathbf{B}_2$. The method of proof is to show that nontrivial solutions always exist. (1), (3), and (4) always have solutions. We must now find a nontrivial solution of

$$\left.\begin{aligned}\mathbf{B}_2\mathbf{C}_1 &= \mathbf{P}_0\\ \mathbf{B}_2\mathbf{D}_1 &= \mathbf{B}_2^*\end{aligned}\right. \tag{$*$}$$

for $\mathbf{B}_2$, $\mathbf{C}_1$, $\mathbf{D}_1$. The essential observation is that the output dimension of M_1 (= input dimension of M_2) is not fixed. Let $M_1 = \langle F, n_1, k_1, l_1, \mathbf{A}_1, \mathbf{B}_1, \mathbf{C}_1, \mathbf{D}_1\rangle$ and $M_2 = \langle F, n_2, l_1, \mathbf{A}_2, \mathbf{B}_2\rangle$.

Since l_1 is arbitrary we can choose $l_1 = n_2$. Thus $\mathbf{B}_2$ becomes $n_2 \times n_2$ and $\mathbf{B}_2$ is a square matrix. Now a possible solution of $(*)$ is

$$\begin{aligned}\mathbf{B}_2 &= \mathbf{I} \qquad (n_2 \times n_2 \text{ matrix})\\ \mathbf{C}_1 &= \mathbf{P}_0\\ \mathbf{D}_1 &= \mathbf{B}_2^*\end{aligned}$$

Since the steps described can always be carried out, a solution and hence a realization always exists. ▌

The previous development did not include the case where $e = 1$.

THEOREM 5.20. Let $M = \langle F, n, k, \mathbf{A}, \mathbf{B}\rangle$ be a finite LSM. Suppose that $m_{\mathbf{A}}(x) = \varphi_{\mathbf{A}}(x) = p(x)$ where $p(x)$ is irreducible and that $\mathbf{B} \neq \mathbf{0}$. Then M has no nontrivial linear serial decomposition.

Proof. Note that since $\mathbf{B} \neq \mathbf{0}$ and $p(x) = m_{\mathbf{A}}(x)$ then M is strongly connected. [By Lemma 5.2, M has no nontrivial $\mathbf{A}$ invariant subspaces. Since $\dim W \geq 1$ (because $\mathbf{B} \neq \mathbf{0}$), we have that $W = F_n$.]

Assume that there is such a decomposition and φ is the state assignment. By Theorem 5.5, φ is linear on W. So write $\varphi q = \mathbf{T}q$ where $\mathbf{T}$ has rank n. We know that

$$\mathbf{A}'\mathbf{T} = \mathbf{T}\mathbf{A}$$

Since $\mathbf{T}$ is an $n' \times n$ matrix of rank n (φ is one-to-one), we use the proof of Theorem 5.6 in the Appendix and we know that the elementary divisors of $\mathbf{A}$ must be elementary divisors of $\mathbf{A}'$. Since $p(x)$ is irreducible, it follows that $p(x) \mid \varphi_{\mathbf{A}'}$. $\mathbf{A}'$ may be taken to be of the form

$$\mathbf{A}' = \begin{bmatrix} \mathbf{A}_1 & \mathbf{0} \\ \mathbf{A}_2 & \mathbf{A}_3 \end{bmatrix}$$

Since $\varphi_{\mathbf{A}'} = \varphi_{\mathbf{A}_1} \cdot \varphi_{\mathbf{A}_3}$ and $p(x)$ is irreducible, we know that $p(x) \mid \varphi_{\mathbf{A}_1}$ or $p(x) \mid \varphi_{\mathbf{A}_3}$. But this means that the size of $\mathbf{A}_1$ (or $\mathbf{A}_3$) is greater than the size of $\mathbf{A}$ which would be a trivial realization and is ruled out. ▮

There is only one case which has not yet been treated. This is where $\mathbf{B} = \mathbf{0}$ and $e = 1$.

THEOREM 5.21. Let $M = \langle F, n, k_1, \mathbf{A}, \mathbf{B} \rangle$ be a finite LSM with $m_{\mathbf{A}} = \varphi_{\mathbf{A}} = p(x)$, $p(x)$ is irreducible, and suppose $\mathbf{B} = \mathbf{0}$. There is a linear serial state realization of M if and only if there is a nontrivial linear parallel state realization.

Proof. Suppose $M' = \langle F, n', k, \mathbf{A}', \mathbf{B}' \rangle$ is a nontrivial linear serial state realization of M.

Suppose that $\mathbf{A}'$ is indecomposable. Then

$$\mathbf{A}' = \begin{bmatrix} \mathbf{A}_1 & \mathbf{0} \\ \mathbf{A}_2 & \mathbf{A}_3 \end{bmatrix}$$

and $\varphi_{\mathbf{A}'} = \varphi_{\mathbf{A}_1}\varphi_{\mathbf{A}_3} = [p'(x)]^{e_1}[p'(x)]^{e_2} = m_{\mathbf{A}'} = [p'(x)]^{e'}$. The periods induced by $\mathbf{A}'$ are of the form p^iT' where $(p, T') = 1$. But $\mathbf{A}$ induces a base period T and so it is necessary that $T = T'$. But, this implies that deg $p(x) =$ deg $p'(x)$. [For $T = \exp m_{\mathbf{A}} = T' = \exp m_{\mathbf{A}'}$. Let $h =$ deg $p(x)$ and $h' =$ deg $p'(x)$. From field theory [34], $T \mid p^h - 1$ and $T' \mid p^{h'} - 1$ where h and h' are the least such numbers. Therefore $h = h'$.] But this is a trivial decomposition since the size $\mathbf{A}_1 \geq$ size $\mathbf{A}$ or size $\mathbf{A}_3 \geq$ size $\mathbf{A}$.

Suppose that $\mathbf{A}'$ is decomposable, i.e., $\mathbf{A}' = \mathbf{A}_1 \oplus \mathbf{A}_2$. This reduces to the parallel case and the proof of the "only if" part is complete. The other direction is immediate. ▮

7. The Main Theorem on Serial Decompositions

The serial case is now summarized by the following result.

THEOREM 5.22. Let $M = \langle F, n, k, \mathbf{A}, \mathbf{B}\rangle$ be a finite LSM. M has a nontrivial linear serial state realization if and only if one of the following hold.

(1) $\mathbf{A}$ is decomposable.

(2) $\mathbf{A}$ is indecomposable, $m_{\mathbf{A}} = \varphi_{\mathbf{A}} = [p(x)]^e$ where $p(x)$ is irreducible of degree h and either

(a) $e > 1$

or

(b) $e = 1$, $\mathbf{B} = 0$ and if $T = \exp p(x)$, there exist $r > 1$, $T_1, \ldots, T_r$, $T_i = \exp p_i(x)$ where the $p_i(x)$ are irreducible polynomials, and

$$T = \langle T_1, \ldots, T_r\rangle$$

and

$$\deg p_i(x) < h \qquad \text{for all } i, \qquad 1 \leq i \leq r.$$

Because of Theorem 5.21, the serial case was reduced to the parallel case. Thus, Theorem 5.22 is only valid in the finite case. This leaves the following problem.

OPEN PROBLEM. Give necessary and sufficient conditions for an infinite LSM to have a linear serial state realization.

8. Epilogue on Linear Decompositions

In this section, we shall briefly sketch how the theory developed here extends to the cases in which outputs are considered. These cases, including the effects of state splitting, are given in [12, 13].

DEFINITION. Let $M_i = \langle Q_i, \Sigma_i, \Delta_i, \delta_i, \lambda_i \rangle$, $i = 1, 2$, be sequential machines. M_2 is said to *realize* M_1 if there exist three mappings α, β, φ such that

(i) α maps Σ_1 into Σ_2
(ii) β maps Δ_2 into Δ_1
(iii) φ maps Q_1 into Q_2
(iv) for each $(q, a) \in Q_1 \times \Sigma_1$

$$\varphi\delta_1(q, a) = \delta_2(\varphi q, \alpha a)$$

(v) for each $(q, a) \in Q_1 \times \Sigma_1$

$$\lambda_1(q, a) = \beta\lambda_2(\varphi q, \alpha a)$$

Note that this definition is *not* the same as the one given in Chapter 4. The distinction is crucial.

As we are dealing with LSM's, i.e., devices which are modelled by linear networks, the following convention is reasonable.

CONVENTION. α and β are restricted to be linear maps.

From this convention, we have the following result.

PROPOSITION 5.6. A sequential machine has a linear realization with α and β linear if and only if it has a linear realization with both α and β the identity maps.

We can now state the two main results on such decompositions.

THEOREM 5.23. Let* $M = \langle F, n, k, l, \mathbf{A}, \mathbf{B}, \mathbf{C}, \mathbf{D} \rangle$ be a finite LSM with $\mathbf{C} \neq \mathbf{0}$. M has a nontrivial linear parallel realization if and only if one of the following holds:

(i) $\mathbf{A}$ is decomposable
(ii) $\mathbf{A}$ is indecomposable and M is not minimal

Turning to serial realizations, the pertinent result is the following.

THEOREM 5.24. Let M be an LSM over an arbitrary field F. M has a nontrivial linear serial realization if and only if it is not the case that $\varphi_{\mathbf{A}} = m_{\mathbf{A}} = p(x)$ where $p(x)$ is irreducible over F.

We conclude with the following research problem.

OPEN PROBLEM. Let M be an LSM with state dimension n. Give necessary and sufficient conditions for M to have a "series-parallel" decomposition into LSM's M_i (with state dimension n_i) and where $n_i < n$ for each i.

---

* If $\mathbf{C} = \mathbf{0}$ then this case is covered by Theorem 5.18.

APPENDIX

A Proof of Theorem 5.6

We now embark on a proof of Theorem 5.6. A number of results from matrix and field theory will be stated without proof.

LEMMA A.1. Let **A** be an $n \times n$ indecomposable matrix over F where $m_{\mathbf{A}} = \varphi_{\mathbf{A}} = [p(x)]^e$; $p(x)$ is irreducible over F. There is no nontrivial* solution to the equation $\mathbf{A}'\mathbf{T} = \mathbf{TA}$ for some $n' \times n'$ matrix $\mathbf{A}' = \mathbf{A}_1 \oplus \cdots \oplus \mathbf{A}_r$, each $\mathbf{A}_i$ indecomposable and some $n' \times n$ matrix **T** with rank $\mathbf{T} = n$.

Proof. Suppose there is such a solution **T** and $\mathbf{A}'$. We recall the work of Gantmacher [15] on the solution of the matrix equation $\mathbf{TA} = \mathbf{BT}$ where **A** and **B** are square. Let

$$(x - \lambda_1)^{e_1}, \ldots (x - \lambda_s)^{e_s}$$

be the elementary divisors for **A** and $(x - \varphi_1)^{i_1}, \ldots (x - \varphi_t)^{i_t}$ be those for **B** over a common extension field F'. Then a solution **T** is equivalent to $\tilde{\mathbf{T}}$ of size $n' \times n$ where

$$\tilde{\mathbf{T}} = \begin{bmatrix} \tilde{\mathbf{T}}_{11} & & \tilde{\mathbf{T}}_{1s} \\ \cdot & & \\ \cdot & & \\ \cdot & & \\ \tilde{\mathbf{T}}_{t1} & \cdots & \tilde{\mathbf{T}}_{ts} \end{bmatrix}$$

and each $\tilde{\mathbf{T}}_{jk}$ is of size $i_j \times e_k$ and $\tilde{\mathbf{T}}_{jk} = \mathbf{0}$ if $\lambda_k \neq \varphi_j$.

$$\tilde{\mathbf{T}}_{jk} = \begin{bmatrix} a & b & \cdots & \\ & a & \ddots & \\ & & \ddots & b \\ \mathbf{0} & & & a \end{bmatrix}$$

* Nontrivial means a solution in which no block $\mathbf{A}_i$ is as large as **A**.

if $\lambda_k = \varphi_j$ and $e_k < i_j$

$$\tilde{\mathbf{T}}_{jk} = \begin{bmatrix} \mathbf{0} & a & b & \cdots & \\ & \mathbf{0} & a & \ddots & \\ & & \ddots & \ddots & \\ & & & \ddots & b \\ & \mathbf{0} & & & a \end{bmatrix}$$

if $\lambda_k = \varphi_j$ and $e_k > i_j$.

The nonzero entries are in F'. Since $\mathbf{T}$ (in our problem) must have rank n, neither $\mathbf{T}$ nor $\tilde{\mathbf{T}}$ can have any all zero columns. Thus, for each m, $\lambda_m = \varphi_j$ for some j and moreover $e_m \leq i_j$. Then the set of elementary divisors of $\mathbf{A}'$ includes the set of elementary divisors of $\mathbf{A}$. It is known that if $\mathbf{A}' = \mathbf{A}_1 \oplus \cdots \oplus \mathbf{A}_r$, then the set of elementary divisors of $\mathbf{A}'$ is the union of the set of elementary divisors of each $\mathbf{A}_i$. Now we compute the elementary divisors of $\mathbf{A}$. They are all the polynomials $(x - \lambda_i)^e$ such that $\prod_{i=1}^{s} (x - \lambda_i) = p(x)$.

Let $q(x)$ be any polynomial in $F[x]$. If there is some $i \leq s$ so that λ_i is a root of $q(x)$, then $p(x) \mid q(x)$. [For then $(x - \lambda_i) \mid q(x)$ and $(x - \lambda_i) \mid p(x)$, hence $(x - \lambda_i) \mid d(x)$, their greatest common divisor which is not trivial. Since $d(x)$ must be in $F[x]$ and is not trivial, $d(x) = p(x)$ and $p(x) \mid q(x)$.] Hence if $(x - \lambda_i)^{e'}$ with $e' \geq e$ is to be an elementary divisor of $\mathbf{A}_j$ for some j, we must have $[p(x)]^{e'} \mid q(x)$ where we take $q(x) = m_{\mathbf{A}_j} = \varphi_{\mathbf{A}_j}$. Therefore the size of $\mathbf{A}_j$ exceeds that of $\mathbf{A}$ which would be a contradiction of the existence of a nontrivial solution. ▮

We now turn to the proof of Theorem 5.6.

THEOREM 5.6. If an LSM $M = \langle F, n, k, \mathbf{A}, \mathbf{B} \rangle$ has a nontrivial parallel linear decomposition and if $\mathbf{A}$ is indecomposable, then the state assignment φ is not linear.

Proof. Suppose there is a linear assignment φ of M into $M' = \langle F, n', k, \mathbf{A}', \mathbf{B}' \rangle$. Then φ can be represented as an $n' \times n$ matrix $\mathbf{T}$. Since φ is one-to-one, $\mathbf{T}$ has rank n. Clearly $\mathbf{A}'\mathbf{T} = \mathbf{T}\mathbf{A}$ since φ is an assignment [and $\varphi\delta(q, \mathbf{0}) = \delta'(\varphi q, \mathbf{0})$]. The result now follows from the fact that $\mathbf{A}' = \mathbf{A}_1 \oplus \mathbf{A}_2$ and Lemma A.1. ∎

References

1. Arbib, M. A., A common framework for automata theory and control theory. *J. SIAM Control*, Ser. A, **3**, 206–222 (1965).
2. Berlekamp, E. R., "*Algebraic Coding Theory*." McGraw-Hill, New York, 1968.
3. Brzozowski, J. A., Regular expressions for linear sequential circuits. *IEEE Trans.*, **EC–14**, 148–156 (1965).
4. Cohn, M., Properties of linear machines. *J. Assoc. Comp. Mach.*, **11**, 296–301 (1964).
5. Cohn, M., Controllability in linear sequential networks. *IRE Trans.*, **CT–9**, 74–78 (1962).
6. Cohn, M. and Even, S., Identification and minimization of linear machines. *IEEE Trans.*, **EC–14**, 367–376 (1965).
7. Cook, S. A., Solvability problems for computable fields. (in preparation).
8. Davis, W. A. and Brzozowski, J. A., On the linearity of sequential machines. *IEEE Trans.*, **EC–15**, 21–29 (1966).
9. Deuel, D. R., Time-varying linear sequential machines. Doctoral dissertation, University of California at Berkeley, 1967.
10. Dickson, L. E., "*Linear Groups*." Dover Press, New York, 1958.
11. Elspas, B., The theory of autonomous linear sequential networks. *IRE Trans.*, **CT–6**, 45–60 (1959).
12. Gallaire, H. and Harrison, M. A., Decomposition of linear sequential machines. *Math. Systems Theory*, Vol. **3** (1969).
13. Gallaire, H., Decomposition of linear sequential machines–II. *Math. Systems Theory* (to appear).
14. Gallaire, H., Gray, J. N., Harrison, M. A., and Herman, G. T., Infinite Linear Sequential Machines. *Journal of Computer and System Sciences*, **2**, 381–419 (1968).
15. Gantmacher, F. R., "*The Theory of Matrices*." Vols. I and II, Chelsea, New York, 1959.
16. Gill, A., "*Linear Sequential Circuits*." McGraw-Hill, New York, 1966.
17. Gill, A., "*Introduction to the Theory of Finite State Machines*." McGraw-Hill, New York, 1962.
18. Gill, A., The minimization of linear sequential circuits. *IEEE Trans.*, **CT–12**, 292–294 (1965).

19. Ginzburg, A., "*Algebraic Theory of Automata*." Academic Press, New York, 1968.
20. Golomb, S. W. (ed.), "*Digital Communication with Space Applications*." Prentice-Hall, Englewood Cliffs, N.J., 1964.
21. Gray, J. N. and Harrison, M. A., The theory of sequential relations. *Information and Control*, **9**, 435–468 (1966).
22. Harrison, M. A., "*Introduction to Switching and Automata Theory*." McGraw-Hill, New York, 1965.
23. Harrison, M. A., On the classification of boolean functions by the general linear and affine groups. *J. SIAM*, **12**, 285–299 (1964).
24. Hartmanis, J. and Stearns, R. E., "*Algebraic Structure Theory of Sequential Machines*." Prentice-Hall, Englewood Cliffs, N.J., 1966.
25. Jacobson, N., "*Lectures in Abstract Algebra*." Vol. I, 1951; Vol. II, 1953; Vol. III, 1964. Van Nostrand, Princeton.
26. Kalman, R. E., Canonical structure of linear dynamical systems. *Proc. Natl. Acad. Sci. U.S.A*, **48**, 596–600 (1962).
27. Kalman, R. E., A mathematical description of linear dynamical systems. *J. SIAM Control* Ser. A, **1**, 152–192 (1963).
28. Kautz, W. H. (ed), "*Linear Sequential Switching Circuits—Selected Technical Papers*." Holden-Day San Francisco, 1965.
29. Krohn, K. B. and Rhodes, J. L., Algebraic theory of Machines. I. *Trans. Amer. Math. Soc.*, **116**, 450–464 (1965).
30. Lang, S., "*Algebra*." Addison-Wesley, Reading, Mass., 1965.
31. Nerode, A., Linear automaton transformations. *Proc. Amer. Math. Soc.*, **9**, 541–544 (1958).
32. Rabin, M. O., Computable algebra, general theory and theory of computable fields. *Trans. Amer. Math. Soc.*, **87**, 341–360 (1960).
33. Slepian, D., Some further theory of group codes. *Bell System Tech. J.*, **39**, 1219–1252 (1960).
34. Srinivasan, C. V., State diagram of linear sequential machines. *J. Franklin Inst.*, **273**, No. 5, 383–418 (1962).
35. Stern, T. E. and Friedland, B., The linear modular sequential circuit generalized. *IRE Trans.*, **CT–8**, 79–80 (1961).
36. Thrall, R. M. and Tornheim, L., "*Vector Spaces and Matrices*." Wiley, New York, 1957.
37. van der Waerden, B. L., "*Modern Algebra*." Vols. I and II, Ungar Press, New York, 1949.
38. Yau, S. S. and Wang, K. C., Linearity of sequential machines. *IEEE Trans.*, **EC–15**, 337–354 (1966).
39. Zadeh, L. A. and Desoer, C. A., "*Linear System Theory*." McGraw-Hill, New York, 1963.

Index

A

Acceptance of tapes, 36
Accessibility problem, 106–112
Adjoint, 12
Analyzable machine, 75
Arbib, Michael A., 203
Assignment
  linear, 143, 145, 156, 193, 200, 201
  state, 41, 142, 143, 156, 190
Autonomous network, 60

B

Basic period, 151, 163, 196
Berlekamp, Elwyn R., 203
Brzozowski, Janusz A., 203

C

Canonical form
  matrix
    classical, 28–30, 113, 140
    rational, 20–28, 30, 74, 110, 113
    Smith, 3–7, 21–23, 28
Cayley, Arthur, 12
Cayley–Hamilton Theorem, 12
Characteristic polynomial, 12, 14, 144
Classical canonical form, 28–30, 113, 140
Cohn, Martin, 203
Companion matrix, 13, 14, 22, 61, 66, 110, 152, 165
Complex numbers, 1, 98, 133, 137
Computable field, 60, 72, 97–104, 106, 110, 112
Concatenation, 31, 32
Connected machine, 84, 89
Controllable machine, 80–83, 85, 89, 159
Controllable state, 85–89
Cook, Stephen A., 99, 203
Coset, 140, 141, 164, 167–169, 172–174
Cross operation, 150, 151, 155
Cycle structure, 149, 163
Cyclic group, 147
Cyclic linear transformation, 18, 19, 89
Cyclic space, 17

D

Davis, Wayne A., 203
DeBruijn, Nicolaas G., 40
Decision problems, 97–113

Decomposition of LSM's, 85–90, 139–201
Decomposition
  parallel, 43–45
    linear, 139–193, 195, 196, 198, 200
    nontrivial, 43, 44
  serial, 46–48
    linear, 139, 193–198
Definite condition, 54, 55, 78
Desoer, Charles A., 204
Deuel, Donald R., 203
Diagnosability condition, 54, 56, 75, 76, 80, 118
Dickson, Leonard E., 203
Direct sum of matrices, 16, 19, 144, 150
Direct sum of subspaces, 14
Domain of a relation, 103

E

Elementary divisors, 29, 30, 195, 199, 200
Elspas, Bernard, 203
Equality problem for computable fields, 99
Equivalence problem of LSM's, 99–101
Equivalence
  of sequential machines, 34, 38, 65, 91, 94–97
  of states, 36, 68
Even, Shimon, 203
Exponent, 148, 151, 152, 154, 166, 168, 169, 175, 180, 186, 192, 196
Extendability, 103

F

Feedback free condition, 54, 55, 77, 78, 80
Field, 1, 133–137
  algebraically closed, 30
  complex, 1, 98, 133, 137
  computable, 60, 72, 97–104, 106, 110, 112
  extension, 98, 133–137, 147, 199
    finite, 133–137
    infinite, 133, 137
  finite, 98, 147
  rational, 1, 98, 137
  real, 1, 98, 133, 137
Final states, 35
Finite automaton, 35, 36
Finite memory condition, 54–57, 75, 77, 79, 94, 95
Finiteness problem for computable fields, 98
Free monoid, 32
Friedland, Bernard, 204
Function
  of an LSM, 93
  length preserving, 33

G

Gallaire, Hervé, 203
Gantmacher, Felix R., 199, 203
Gill, Arthur, 203
Ginzburg, Abraham, 204
Golomb, Solomon W., 204
Gray, James N., 203
Group, 51, 147, 148
  cyclic, 147
  symmetric, 53
Group machine, 53, 147

H

Hamilton, William R., 12
Harrison, Craig A., v
Harrison, Evalee, 206
Harrison, Michael A., 203, 204

Hartmanis, Juris, 204
Herman, Gabor T., 203
Homomorphic image
  of monoids, 51
  of sequential machines, 37
Homomorphism
  of monoids, 49, 116, 117, 119
  of sequential machines, 37
Hypercompanion matrix, 28, 29, 165, 179

I

Ideal, 12
Indecomposable matrix, 144–147, 152, 157, 192, 193, 196, 199, 200
Indexing
  admissible, 98
  definition of, 98
Initial state, 35
Integers, 1
Invariant factor, 4, 18, 21, 23, 28
Invariant subspace, 15, 17
Isomorphic sequential machines, 37, 38
Isomorphism
  of LSM's, 96
  of sequential machines, 37, 41, 65
  state, 51, 52, 141, 157

J

Jacobson, Nathan, 204
Join, 42

K

Kalman, Rudolph, E., 204
Kautz, William H., 204
Kleene, Stephen C., 32
Kleene closure operation, 32
Krohn, Kenneth B., 204

L

Lagrange, Joseph Louis, 147
Lagrange's Theorem, 147
Lang, Serge, 204
Lattice, 42
Left value of matrix polynomial, 10
Length preserving function, 33
Linear assignment, 143, 145, 156, 193, 200, 201
Linear realization, 115, 116, 118, 119–121, 133, 139–143, 197, 198
Linear realization, finite, 121–131
Linear sequential machine
  definition of, 60
  time varying, 63, 64
LSM, definition of, 60
LSM's, decomposition of, 85–90, 139–201
Linear transformation, cyclic, 18, 19, 89

M

Matrices
  direct sum of, 16, 19, 144, 150
  equivalence of, 4, 199
  similar, 8, 12, 21–23, 29
Matrix
  adjoint, 12
  companion, 13, 14, 22, 61, 66, 110, 152, 165
  exponent of, 148, 166
  hypercompanion, 28, 29, 165, 179
  indecomposable, 144, 147, 152, 157, 192, 193, 196, 199, 200
  invariant factors of, 4, 18, 21, 23, 28

Matrix *continued*
nilpotent, 13, 77, 146
degree of, 13
rank of, 22, 129, 195, 199
rational canonical form of, 20-28, 30, 74, 110, 113
transpose of, 134
unimodular, 4
Matrix polynomials, 8–11
degree of, 8
left value, 10
order of, 8
regular, 8, 9
right quotient, 9
right remainders, 9
right value, 10
Max-per, 166, 168–171, 174, 175
Mealy, George H., 32, 75
Mealy machine, 32, 75
Minimal polynomial, 12, 14, 16, 17, 62, 144
Minimal sequential machines, 37–39, 43, 89
Minimality of LSM's, 65–75, 91–93, 96, 118
Minimization of sequential machines, 36–40
Monoid, 50–53
free, 32
of an LSM, 93, 147
of a sequential machine, 50, 52, 120
Moore, Edward F., 32, 75, 125
Moore machine, 32, 75, 125

N

Natural numbers, 1
Nerode, Anil, 204
Nilpotent matrix, 13, 77, 146
Normal subgroup, 147
Null space, 15, 69
Null word, 32

O

Observability, 76
Open Problems, 74, 93, 106, 112, 127, 132, 137, 193, 197, 198
Order of matrix polynomial, 8
Output function, 32

P

Parallel connection, 43, 140
Parallel decomposition, 43–45
linear, 139–193, 195, 196, 198, 200
nontrivial, 43, 44
Period, 163, 164, 166, 167, 171, 173, 175, 196
basic, 151, 163, 196
maximum, 166, 168–171, 174, 175
Polyá, George, 40
Polynomial
characteristic, 12, 14, 144
division
left, 9
right, 9
exponent of, 148, 151, 152, 164, 166, 168, 169, 175, 180, 186, 192, 196
matrix (*See* Matrix polynomials)
minimal, 12, 14, 16, 17, 62, 144
minimum annihilating, 166
monic, 5
primary, 151
Predicate, 90
Principal ideal domain, 12
Product of sets, 32
Pseudo period, 163, 164, 172, 174, 175

Q

Quotient, right, 9
Quotient machine, 42
Quotient machine without output, 42

R

Rabin, Michael O., 98, 204
Range of a relation, 103
Rank
  of an equivalence relation, 47
  of a matrix, 22, 129, 195, 199
Rational canonical form, 20–28, 30, 74, 110, 113
Rational numbers, 1, 98, 137
Real numbers, 1, 98, 133, 137
Realization, 48, 49, 115–120, 133–137
  linear, 115, 116, 118–121, 133, 139–143, 197, 198
  finite, 121–133
  second definition, 197
  state, 41, 51, 53, 139, 157
  without state splitting, 49, 116
Recursive function, 97, 98
Recursive set, 98, 102
Reduced sequential machines, 37
Regular expression, 93
Regular matrix polynomial, 8, 9
Regular set, 36, 102
Relation
  domain of, 103
  input-output, 34, 35
    of LSM's, 91–93
  range of, 103
  sequential, 91, 103
  which preserves output, 42
Relational equivalence, 34, 91, 94–97, 99–101
Relations, join of, 42
Remainder, right, 9
Rhodes, John L., 204
Right congruence relation, nontrivial, 42, 44
Right congruence relations, 36, 37, 42, 44, 139, 141
Right quotient, 9
  of matrix polynomial, 9
Right remainder of matrix polynomial, 9
Right value of matrix polynomial, 10
Row space, 67

S

Sequential function, 35, 53
  finite, 53
Sequential machine
  analyzable, 75
  connected, 84, 89
  controllable, 80–83, 85, 89, 159
  countable, 46
  definition of, 32
  input-output relation of, 34
  Mealy model, 32
  minimal, 37–39, 43, 89
  Moore model, 32
  quotient, 42
  reduced, 37
  set of functions of, 34
  strongly connected, 35, 80, 83, 85, 143, 145, 159
Sequential machines
  equivalence of, 34, 38, 65, 91, 94–97
  isomorphic, 37, 38
Sequential relation, 35
Serial connection, 46, 140–142
Serial decomposition, 46–48
  linear, 139, 193–198
  nontrivial, 46

Shift register, 62, 66, 74, 75, 80
Similarity, 8, 12, 21–23, 29
  of LSM's, 65, 66, 73, 74, 106
Slepian, David, 204
Smith, Henry J. S., 3–7, 21–23, 28
Smith canonical form, 3–7, 21–23, 28
Srinivasan, C. V., 204
Star operation, 32
State assignment, 41, 142, 143, 156, 190
State diagram, 34
State isomorphism, 51, 52, 141, 157
State realization, 41, 51, 53, 139, 157
State splitting 115, 116, 118, 119, 128
States, equivalence of, 36, 68
Stearns, Richard E., 204
Stern, Thomas E., 204
Strongly connected sequential machine, 35, 80, 83, 85, 143, 145, 159
Subfield, 133
Submachine, 49, 52
Subspace, primary, 20
Subspace property, 90
Substitution property, 42
Superfield, 133
Sylvester, James J., 129
Sylvester's inequality, 129
Symmetric group, 53

T

Thrall, Robert M., 204
Time-varying LSM, 63, 64
Tornheim, Leonard, 204
Transduction expression, 93
Transition function, 32
Transpose of a matrix, 134
Turing, Alan M., 97
Turing machine, 97

U

Unimodular matrix, 4
Unobservable state, 85–89

V

van der Waerden, Bartel L., 204

W

Wang, Kung-chi, 204
Word, 31
  null, 32
  length of, 32

Y

Yau, Stephen S., 204

Z

Zadeh, Lotfi A., 204
Zero submachine, 84, 85, 142, 160